Grizzly Bear Mountain

Grizzly Bear Mountain

by Jack Boudreau

Caitlin Press Inc.
Prince George, BC

Published by
Caitlin Press Inc.
Box 2387 Station B
Prince George BC V2N 2S6

Book design by Eye Design Inc.
Cover by Roger Handling, Terra Firma Graphics
Photos supplied from author's personal collection.
Editorial assistance from Elizabeth Jones, A-Z Wordsmith

Canadian Cataloguing in Publication Data

Boudreau, Jack, 1933–
  Grizzly mountain

  Includes index
  ISBN 0-920576-81-8

  1. Boudreau, Jack, 1933- 2. Grizzly bear 3.Nature photography.
I. Title
QL737.C27B68 2000   599.784   C00-910024-5

Caitlin Press acknowledges the financial support of Canada Council for the
Arts for our publishing program. Similarly we acknowledge the support of
the Arts Council of British Columbia.

Printed in Canada

*To all the pioneers who
faced the wilderness before me,
to those who roamed the mountains
before me I dedicate this book.
When I realize the enormity of the
challenges you faced, I feel humbled.
The mountains still echo to the sounds
of your axes, and some of the trees
you blazed to mark your trails
are still standing.*

*Sometimes when I sit upon
a mountain peak and reminisce,
I realize that there is but a shadow
of the immense wilderness you roamed.
Then I appreciate all the more the
many sacrifices that were the
foundation of our heritage.*

ACKNOWLEDGEMENTS

First, I wish to thank the *Prince George Citizen* for their permission to include reprints. Specific credits are given in order.

Also, I must thank the Prince George Public Library for their endless assistance.

To the individuals who helped and inspired me: many thanks to Melanie Cummins, Maxine and Peter Koppe, Lana and Don Redden, Elarry Evasin, Roy Mulvahill. Greg Saugstad, Maurice Schultz, Bob Harkins, Luis Siguenza and Steve Marynovitch. To my daughter Kim, a special thank you for your encouragement and inspiration. To my son Kelly, it was your no-nonsense warning that if 'I didn't write this you were going to' that spurred me to action—thanks much.

Finally, I wish to acknowledge the people who shared so many wilderness adventures with me: my brothers—Joe and Clarence, Vic Litnosky, Virgil Brandner, Lindy Chambers, Gunther Peemoeler, Bob Agrey, Bob Gobbi, Lou Siguenza, Herb Metzmeier, Marlin Priebe, and Bill Benedict, who climbed so many mountains with me. To all the other woodsmen who shared wilderness adventures with me—thanks for the memories. Now pull a log up beside the campfire, grab the billy can, and pour yourself a cup of coffee mixed with campfire ashes; sit back and enjoy.

CONTENTS

Introduction 1

1 Childhood 7

2 Young Adventurers 18

3 Grizzlies 31

4 Along the Railroad 60

5 Big Grizzlies 110

6 Mountain Safety 139

7 Wilderness Humor 159

8 Forestry 186

9 Mountain Memories 213

INTRODUCTION

"At length, thoroughly worn out and exhausted, I reached the summit, but after a short rest soon felt freshened up again. We now proceeded along a narrow ridge of snow, a yawning abyss studded with sharp-pointed rocks on one side, and a gentle slope just sufficient to prevent the possibility of stopping one's self in the event of a slip, on the other. Truly, this was as nasty look-ing a place as I had as yet set eyes on, and I defy anyone to stand on that narrow slipping ridge without feeling a shudder pass through them. Assuredly the grizzly bears had chosen a grizzly retreat."

J. Turner Turner,
*Three Years Hunting and Trapping
in America and the Great Northwest*

These were the thoughts of J. Turner Turner 113 years ago as his Indian guides led him through the ridges to the moun-tain they had appropriately named: Grizzly Bear Mountain

ONE HUNDRED AND SIXTEEN YEARS AGO, AN ADVENTUROUS SOUL named J. Turner Turner left England with his wife. After spend-ing a couple years hunting in the USA, they came to British Columbia in 1886. Along with a friend named Fred, they spent a few years hunting and trapping in BC. In the fall of 1887 they left Fort George [Prince George] along with some Indian guides and paddled their canoes up the Fraser River, past the Goose River (Salmon River), and then past the Caribou River (Willow River). They con-tinued on to the Grand Canyon where they hunted for a few days. Then they went another 25 miles upriver where they built a shanty and then spent that winter trapping. This was right in the area of Penny, where I was born and raised.

They suffered through an extremely tough winter that started when they neglected to put enough pitch in the cabin roof. This resulted in every thing in the cabin getting mildew from the endless rains that fell. In a last ditch effort to stop the leaks, they got clay from the riverbank and plastered it all over the roof. No sooner did they get finished, then the rains came again and washed it all through the roof poles into the cabin. Only in late winter did they finally cut up some tents they had brought along. Placed over the roof, this served to keep most of the weather out.

As I had never heard of lynx attacking anything as large as a caribou, I was most interested in how Turner described Fred walking his trapline one day when he came upon a caribou lying on the snow. A close look showed that it had two serious injuries on its back. Fred then spotted a lynx and then a second lynx lying in wait nearby. The sign showed him that these two lynx had ambushed the caribou, severely injuring it, and were just biding their time waiting for it to die. Fred returned to their cabin and got his rifle, then shot the caribou and brought some much-needed meat back to the cabin. They later managed to bag a lynx on the remains. Surprisingly, to me at

Known as Grizzly Bear Mountain to the Indians, it was later renamed Red Mountain.

least, Mr. Turner tells of finding several different places where lynx had followed caribou and attempted to ambush them.

Several times the Indians returned from Fort George that winter, bringing bacon, mail, and many other badly-needed supplies. It seems apparent that without the assistance of these Indians, the Turners would have perished.

Because of this man's desire to get a grizzly bear, the Indians guides took him on a whirlwind hike back into the mountains to a place that always had an abundance of grizzlies. For that reason, they admitted it was a place they seldom visited. In one spot they had to crawl across an ice ridge with a steep canyon on one side and a deep near-vertical drop on the other.

Many times as a youngster I followed in their footsteps across the dangerous ice ridge, and made my way to this mountain that the grizzlies have always frequented in great numbers. For 54 years I have first hunted and then watched these great beasts in this area, and I have to say that the Indians got it right when they called it Grizzly Bear Mountain.

Now called Red Mountain because of the iron oxide stained rock that stands out so vividly on its southeasterly peak, this mountain has been one of my favorite haunts throughout the years.

A Life in Context

BORN INTO A BIG FAMILY IN THE TINY, ISOLATED COMMUNITY OF Penny, BC, I guess it was only natural that I would get interested in the forests and mountains. My dad was a never-ending source of stories about the wild and he certainly passed that trait on to his sons. His stories of adventure on the trapline would keep me riveted in my seat for hours, and I believe it was the basis for the life I chose to follow.

From the time we were just lads, my two brothers and I spent an endless amount of time in the forest. With slingshots we hunted grouse and wild rabbits which were readily devoured at the kitchen table. We often fished the trout-laden stream, sometimes camping out beneath the stars, and this always seemed like a wonderful adventure to me. By the time I was 15 years old I had made several trips into the high mountains and had already fought against several forest fires. At the age of 16, I had my first rifle and that's when my mountain adventures really began.

It was a vast wilderness area that we roamed. So much so, that the first 20 years that I traveled the mountains with friends, only once did we ever meet anyone else there. For many years there were no trails, so packing large, heavy packs through the dense undergrowth was only for true nature lovers.

Because we were always running around the woods, the Forest Service regularly kcocked at our door, wanting us to fight wildfires for them. I didn't mind this a bit, though, as it gave me an excuse to be in the woods and get paid for it.

Throughout the 54 years that I have visited the alpine, I have seen a very large number of grizzly bears. Obviously, there is no way to know how many, because of duplication. During these years we have had many interesting adventures with these animals and have had a close look at their incredible personalities. After all these years and all my adventures, I can honestly say that I have as much or more respect for these great bears as I had way back then.

Among the emotions I have experienced in regards to grizzly bears: respect, intense interest, fear, terror, humour, surprise, loneliness, sorrow, admiration, and just about any other feeling you can imagine.

The first 28 years that I wandered and hunted the mountains, I tried my best to hunt these bears. Frequently the old boars made absolute fools out of us up there. We learned that it is one thing to see a big boar on an adjacent mountain, but it is another thing to try to sneak up on him. Often the natural curvature of the mountain will prevent one from seeing them until they are very close. This puts everything in the bears' favour, because it means that any noise a person makes is a warning to the bears, and even if they don't leave the area, they may move into cover until they are certain what's about. Also, any sudden gust of wind that takes one's scent to them can guarantee that the hunt is over. A careful stalk of an hour can get a hunter near the spot where the bear was, but the hunter may find that this fast-moving creature has shifted and is now half a mile away on another ridge.

About 26 years ago I gave up hunting these animals and concentrated on watching and photographing them. Then I noticed a strange thing: the sense of loss that I had felt when I left the mountains after shooting grizzlies was gone. No more did I have the feeling that something great and mysterious was gone from the area. Now I spend days there watching and studying them. On most trips we leave the area without their even knowing we were there, and I just can't possibly imagine how it can ever get any better than that.

I ask the reader to try to understand that it was a huge wilderness area that we hunted. The number of animals we took didn't amount to much and had little or no effect on bear populations. The real control on bear numbers was the long winters that resulted in den deaths—sometimes to the point where we could scarcely find any bears after an especially long winter.

Some years the snow came to stay on the mountains as early as September 1st and stayed there until July. This allowed for less than two months summer around timberline. This not only caused a great number of den deaths, directly, but also the early frosts had a negative effect on their food supply—berries, roots, bulbs, mice, etc. If the frosts were early and heavy, then the ground froze hard and the bears could not dig, and so were denied a major portion of their food supply, such as roots, bulbs, etc. With the longer summers of the last decade, the bears appear much fatter prior to den time. Also, one of their favorite foods—mice, have experienced a population explosion around the timberline.

After these long winters with their resulting den deaths, it was almost impossible to get close to the few bears that were left. They would run at the slightest sound in the forest, and the most we could hope for was to see their back ends disappearing through the trees. This is a far cry from what we find today. With the easy winters of the last many years, the bears, especially grizzly bears, have grown to unprecedented numbers and have become very aggressive. Surely this explains why we have seen and photographed so many grizzlies chasing other grizzlies in the last six years—something I never saw in the previous 48 years combined.

Since the main focus of this book is on mountains and grizzlies, I have not limited myself to the area of Grizzly Bear Mountain; many other lakes and mountains are included.

I hope the reader will enjoy and appreciate the results of the endless hours we spent studying these great bears. There were times when I watched families of grizzlies from early morning until dusk. Throughout that period they were in sight most of the time except for a few hours around midday when they bedded down in a thicket. Because of the endless hours that my friends and I have spent viewing, I have so many great memories of these magnificent animals that I wish to share with others.

It has been said that we are the sum total of our experiences, and it is experiences that have formed the views I have about bears. Many may disagree with my assumptions, and rightfully so if their experiences and observations have led them to other conclusions. I can only say that I have done my best to be open and admit my many errors. The many people that shared these trips with me can attest to that.

It will be noticed that I often refer to trees that are lying down in the forest, as downtrees. Down-timber sounds too stiff and doesn't lend itself well to a single tree—such as "I walked along a down-timber." Also, deadfall is often a misnomer that should only apply to snags, because many trees are still green when they fall or are blown down.

As I am from the old school, I still think in yards as opposed to metres. Anyone not familiar with the yard measurement can easily convert them to metres by adding one-tenth.

Finally, it is my sincere wish that many of the mistakes we made will be noted by others. If because of this book, one accident or unnecessary confrontation with sow grizzlies and cubs can be avoided, then my candidness will have been worthwhile.

Enjoy.

Jack Boudreau

1

CHILDHOOD

I

T WAS TOUGH BEING A YOUNG LAD IN THE '30S. THERE WERE SO many things that didn't seem to make sense. Santa Claus for instance. I spent many fruitless hours trying to figure out how he got into the house. Mom said he came down the chimney, but our chimney ended in two six-inch stove pipes and each had a damper right through the center, which reduced it to three inches. Even allowing that Santa was a slippery cuss and could wiggle his way through, how did he get the presents through? The doors were always locked so he couldn't come in that way. Yet the presents were always there in the morning so there was no disputing the fact that he did it.

After fighting a losing battle with Santa, I got the chance to redeem myself when I was six years old. It happened the day we were told to go outside and watch for the stork because it was going to bring us a baby brother or sister. Out the door we went, my two older brothers, Joe and Clarence, and me, where we positioned ourselves in three different locations. There were three vantage points where we could observe both doors, all the windows, and—lest he pull a Santa Claus trick on us—the chimney. There was just no way that bird was going to get in without us seeing it.

After a couple of hours of constant attention, we were told to come in the house because we had a baby sister. Dumbfounded, we went in and sure enough, there she was. Not only did that bird get in carrying June, but it got back out again without us seeing it. Understandably we spent some time accusing each other of sleeping on the job.

As if figuring out all these problems wasn't enough, we also had a major problem out in the yard where Clarence had been having a running battle with one of our roosters over who was in charge around there. One day they squared off and flew right at it. At least the rooster did. He flew into Clarence and knocked him down, then went to work on him. By the time mom came to the rescue, Clarence was decidedly the loser. Mom bandaged up his wounds, which were really nothing compared to the wound to his pride. The tough part was the realization that we were no longer able to play out in the yard without looking over our shoulder to see if that bird was attacking. Worse yet, was the ribbing Clarence would get at school if the other little angels found out that he had been clobbered by a chicken.

Obviously this situation was unacceptable, so we went into a huddle and formed our battle plan. We bided our time until mom was busy cooking. Then we went to work on what was to be education day on the farm. So help me, that rooster should have stayed in bed. Because if there is one thing on this earth that is for certain, it's that the rooster that is a match for two young lads with clubs has never been hatched. He showed fight for the first minute or two, then tried to get away when he realized he was outgunned. We were not about to let him escape, though, so we batted that poor bird all over the yard and didn't quit until it was lying on its side in the little stream that ran through our property.

Realizing what we had done, we ran and hid, knowing full well what we were in for when mom found out that we had killed the old red rooster. But to our surprise, we found the rooster back with the chickens a short time later. How he survived that severe beating is nothing short of a miracle. We didn't kill him, but we sure achieved our objective of establishing the pecking order out in the yard. After that we just had to come out the front door of the house and that rooster headed for cover.

There are so many childhood memories—such as the day Clarence and I were up to no good when mom told us that we had better stop it or dad was going to raise the roof when he got home. Since dad was working in a logging camp, we couldn't ask him, so we went upstairs and tried to figure out for ourselves how he was going to do it. We inspected the inside of the ceiling and it seemed to be fastened all the way around. We studied it for a time and finally concluded that if dad could raise it by himself, then the two of us working together should be able to raise it as well. A tall dresser stood against one wall, so we climbed on top of it, put our backs against the ceiling and pushed up with all our strength. Then we felt something starting to move. Trouble was, it wasn't the ceiling. Instead, the dresser tipped out from the wall and we dropped in behind it, then the dresser came back and pinned us against the wall. Once again it was mom to the rescue. After moving the dresser out, she asked, "How did you crazy kids get back in there?" Our all too obvious answer: "We were trying to raise the roof." Not only did mom get a kick out of this, but when dad came home and she told him, he really cracked up.

Many times as children we heard terrifying stories of animals attacking people. There were ghosts, spooks, monsters, and bogeymen. There were stories of cougars jumping on people, and I believe this was done to keep us children at home. They didn't want us wandering away and getting lost in the endless forests that stretched in all directions. After listening to these stories, I sometimes considered it a miracle that some people were still alive on the earth.

When we three boys went fishing, we had a terrible time walking the narrow trails. We had heard that cougars would hide in a tree and then jump on the last person, thereby picking them off one at a time. Because of this, the last two people in line would walk side by side. It was really tough walking those narrow trails side by side, but we managed.

My two brothers and I slept together in a large bed, and we were pretty frightened of the dark. We would let the person who slept on the front of the bed have all the pillows and blankets so he could build a protective wall along the front of the bed. We figured it was better to be cold than dead. Our preferred way of getting into bed was by taking a flying leap through the air from a distance of about six feet, so that anything hiding under the bed could not grab our legs.

We didn't have power in our home, therefore a trip to the outhouse had to be done in the dark. This required enormous courage. When one of us had to pay a necessary visit at night, he was afraid to go alone, and since one of us couldn't stay in bed alone, this meant we moved about as a unit. One night we were lying in bed when

Clarence said, "C'mon you guys, I've got to go." As one, we headed to the bathroom, but when we got there, Joe took first dibs as he was the oldest. All the while Clarence was saying, "Hurry up, Joe, hurry up."

In due time, Joe said, "Okay, I'm done, you can go now."

Then a strange thing happened when Clarence responded with, "I don't have to go now."

The following morning all hell broke loose when mom found a present on the bathroom floor, and a few minutes later, a brown stain on the curtain by our bed. She questioned us at length and after finding that we knew nothing about it, said she was (pardon the pun) going to get to the bottom of it. She went downstairs and came back up with a measuring tape, then measured the distance from the brown spot to the floor. Next, she called us boys together and measured from the floor to you-know-where. Now mom did her best, but she was no Sherlock Holmes. Clarence had been running when he went by the curtain so had of necessity lifted it. Yet when mom did her calculations, she neglected to allow for the lift factor, therefore it fitted me exactly, not Clarence. The moral of the story? Well, I got a big time licking for lying, had to wash the brown spot out of the curtain, and last but not least, I had to clean up the present on the bathroom floor. Boy! That sure taught me a lesson.

My younger sister Margaret was the butt of many of our sick jokes, and I often wonder how she managed to survive. I recall the evening she took a flashlight and bravely made her way to our three-holed biffy by herself. I was very upset that she was trying to show up us boys, so I decided to teach her a lesson. I followed her outside and hid behind an old sleigh that leaned against the house, then waited for her return. A short time later, Marg came by right beside me on her way back into the house. I let out a mighty roar, which was quickly followed by a terrible scream and Marg in full flight toward the house. Unknown to me, Clarence had seen me leave the house, had followed me out and was hiding in the shadows. Just as I sat back for a good laugh, I heard a roar right beside me. Terror-stricken, believing that my roar had attracted a real bear, I headed for the house and almost passed Marg on the way in. I met mom at the door and yelled, "There's a bear, there's a bear." Mom didn't buy it though, instead she washed my mouth out with soap and then gave me a spanking for scaring Marg.

It didn't take me very long to learn that it wasn't a good idea to swear around mom. Her reaction was swift and unforgettable. She would say, "We'll wash that filth out of your mouth." Then she would grab the lyesoap and apply it liberally into my mouth. (Oh, God! How I learned to hate that lye soap!)

Somehow it didn't seem right that my mouth should be punished for what my mind was thinking—talk about killing the messenger.

On one occasion, Clarence and I went much too far when we played a cruel joke on Marg. We were talking in the kitchen, pretending we didn't know she was in the living room. At one point we said it was sure too bad about Marg, but because we were short of food for the winter, mom and dad had decided they would have to butcher and can her. Now Marg had seen the cows and hogs go down prior to their being canned, so she didn't want any part of it. Suddenly a horrible scream erupted from the living room and within seconds, mom arrived from where she had been working in the garden. She tried to comfort Marg, but to no avail. Marg was sure that mom was in on the plot and it took a good deal of time to convince her otherwise.

Marg was on the receiving end of so many cruel jokes that one day she decided to run away from home. She left our farm and was walking away up the valley when Clarence shouted in a loud voice, "Look at that bear coming down the valley. It's a monster!" Marg turned in her tracks and set a new land speed record coming back to the house. Apparently home didn't seem so bad after all.

One of our favorite pastimes was building weapons, and we boys were forever designing and building new ones. And just as generals would do, we were always looking for something to test them on. One day after we had built some handguns that shot arrows, we were testing them when Marg came by. As we had always called Marg 'Diggit bug', Clarence hollered out, "There's a Diggit bug".

Instantly mom responded with, "Kill it!"

Without further ado, Clarence lifted his handgun and shot Marg right in the neck at point blank range. I can still see Marg standing there screaming with an arrow sticking out of her neck. Fortunately the rubber bands that propelled these arrows had so little power that no real damage was done.

After hearing the story of David and Goliath, we three boys set to work and each built a sling. When we were done, we went to try them out. Clarence wound up his sling and let it go, intending to send the rock away from us. Instead, he let go at the wrong time and the rock came back and struck brother Joe in the face. Down he went, as if he had been struck by a train. Several times he fell down before he made his way to the house to get mom's assistance, while Clarence and I stood anxiously by, saying, "Is he going to die?" Joe survived, although he carried the scar of that wound throughout his life.

We didn't get discouraged, though, and kept on making new weapons, some of which are laughable as I look back. Our bows and arrows, for instance: I don't think one of our arrows ever hit a target. They were made from strips of cedar that were never straight and some of them came very close to performing as boomerangs. The safest place to be when they were fired was directly in front of them—no danger there.

There were many humorous incidents during the years of our childhood: such as the time that sister Isie talked mom into taking her to a dance because she had reached the ripe old age of 16. Mom agreed, and at the dance Isie met a fine specimen of the male gender who asked if he could take her home. All excited, Isie rushed over and asked mom if it would be all right and mom agreed. As the dance ended and everyone headed for home, Isie and her date walked along the trail toward home, while mom followed along right at their heels carrying a lantern. At the door of our house the young man quickly departed, never to return. What's that saying about being over-protective of your firstborn?

Then there was that summer when mom's garden was invaded by what she thought was a gopher. Determined to get the culprit which was continually stealing her peas, mom set a trap in the pea patch.

That same afternoon mom heard some wailing coming from the garden, so she checked the trap and there, caught by the hand, was sister Isie.

Another recollection was the time I heard mom hollering and ran outside just in time to see her run out of our feed shed doing a very unusual dance. She was waving her arms this way and that, all the while shouting, "Get out of there! Get out of there!" Thinking that us eight children had finally got to her, I ran toward her and arrived just in time to see a mouse jump off her head. After she calmed down a bit, she explained what had happened: she had gone into the shed to get some laying mash for our chickens, and had no sooner put the can into the mash, then a mouse ran up her arm and under her blouse. It had been running around on the bare skin of her back while she was doing that strange dance. A lot of scratch marks on her back showed that she had endured an interesting few minutes.

This was just one of several incidents that occurred with mice, which were so abundant on our farm. These open-topped barrels that we stored feed in were mouse traps, in that mice could easily get in, but could not climb out again. On one occasion we found nine mice in a barrel so we decided to try an experiment: we called our big tomcat which was an excellent mouser, and threw him into the barrel. Instantly the cat grabbed one mouse with a paw, then stared in confusion as the other mice ran all around it, including over its paws. In a blink, the cat leapt out of the barrel. Then, when we tried to put it back in, he got very upset and refused to cooperate. Great mouser that he was, our cat had never had to contend with more that one mouse at a time and he simply did not know how to deal with the situation. It actually looked frightened when it came out of the barrel.

It seems that when times are going great something always happens to spoil things, and one of the worst things I can recall happened when Clarence decided he was going to learn to play dad's fiddle. Oh! God! The horrible screechy noises that emanated from our home for a time! It's hard to remember precisely, but I think Joe and I finally bought him off with our ration of chocolate bars.

The problem I found most perplexing in my childhood was sex. I had seen the rooster jumping on the chickens and the bull jumping on the cows, so I asked dad why they were doing that, and he answered, "Oh! He's just showing them who's boss." That seemed to make sense so I didn't pursue it any further. But when tomcats would visit our mama cat they would keep us awake most of the night with their screams. At times like that, I used to think they were pretty stupid to stay up all night trying to find out who was the boss.

Shortly after I started school, two of the older boys took me aside and gave me the true version of sex, and I was amazed. I finally understood why the bull jumped on the cows and why we had been unable to spot the elusive stork. When these two boys finished explaining things to me, I was in a state of shock. They made it clear to me that a person had to be very careful when having sex. They explained that if anything startled the woman, her hip bones could slam together catching a guy's pecker in a vise-like grip. Only by taking them to the hospital could they be separated, and this meant the doctor had to cut off the guy's pecker. I made a vow then and there that hell would freeze over before they got mine.

After we got what we thought was the true version of sex, Clarence and I did some calculating and made a discovery: we realized that dad didn't get done with trapping beaver until May, and that when he got home, he sure must have been horny. I mean how else could it be that we were both born in February?

One thing that we children really looked forward to was our daily ration of figs. We were just crazy about them, but mom would only allow us two each. Clarence and I decided that this wasn't enough and made plans to up the ration a bit. Trouble was, mom kept a very close eye on the cupboard where the figs were stored. We finally came up with a foolproof plan, though, by waiting until mom had gone to bed. Then I would climb on Clarence's back and he would carry me down the stairs, making it sound like only one person. At the foot of the stairs, I would get off and tiptoe to the cupboard and grab a bunch of figs. Meanwhile, Clarence would get a drink of water at the sink. If it took more then 10 seconds, mom's voice would ring out, "Here now, it doesn't take that long to get a drink."

Quick as possible, I would jump on Clarence's back and he would carry me back upstairs. Mom never did figure that one out, although she would frequently say, "Where on earth are the figs going?"

One thing that used to please mom no end, was just how willing Clarence and I always were to go down in our cellar to get things for her: canned preserves, carrots, potatoes, beets, turnips, onions, and the many other goods that were kept down there. We always requested at least one thing from the cellar for practically every meal. While we were down in the cellar, we always managed to open a gallon of mom's dandelion wine, which ranked second to none. It was absolutely amazing how a couple good pulls on that jug would change a person's whole outlook on life. Mom never did figure that out—or did she? Was it just by coincidence that she stopped making wine?

There is something remarkable about how mothers only remember the good times when they reminisce. I recall the time mom was telling some visitors about what a good child I had been. She said that all she had to do was put me in behind a board on the living room floor and I would play all day without fussing. Unable to bear

The Boudreau homestead, 1950.

it, I replied, "C'mon, Mom, tell them the whole story; tell them that the board I was playing behind was all that was left of the living room."

My mother was such a hard worker. Yet she had an outlook on life that was so uplifting. It was a common occurrence to hear her singing early Sunday morning as she baked a dozen pies that were always gone by Sunday evening. Whenever anything seemed to go wrong, mom always had an answer. One of her favorite sayings was, "This is nothing compared to what we had to put up with back in Saskatchewan when I was a kid; sometimes we went months with nothing to live on but faith and slough water." Another was, "Raising a big family is just like being in heaven: all day and no night."

Dad, too, seemed to have infinite patience with us children, but if we worked at it long enough, we managed to get to him. When dad noticed we were stepping out of line, he would come out the door of our home whistling a tune, then head down to a willow patch by the little stream that ran through our property. Very carefully he would select out a nice long willow which he would then cut off and proceed to trim the limbs from. All this while he would be loudly whistling. By the time he got finished, there wasn't one of us in sight, which of course was his plan all the while.

One day dad caught Clarence and I both riding on one of the little calves at the same time. The poor creature's back was heavily bowed from our combined weight. Dad told us in no uncertain terms that we had better not do that again, and so we didn't, for a little while. A few days later, Clarence and I were riding said calf around the barn when dad suddenly burst into view right beside us. I couldn't believe it—there had been no whistling and yet he had a switch in his hand. We both jumped off the calf and headed for cover, but it was too late. Then I heard the whistling, but it wasn't from dad—it was from the switch. Boy! He got us some good shots that day.

Dad sure had a special way of getting a point across, and never was it put to better use than on 'the night of the alarm clock'. This took place because dad was an avid reader who would stay up in his room in the evenings devouring books. Quite often, an elderly neighbor gentleman used to visit us when he felt lonely, and often he and mom would play crib. One evening they were busy playing crib when dad came down the stairs with his alarm clock in hand. He walked up to this gentleman, wound the clock, and then set the alarm right beside his ear. Presto! Before you could count to ten, this chap had his coat on and had disappeared out the door.

As wise as we thought he was, I think dad made the understatement of the century when he defined us as 'little buggers', because he never even knew half of it. For instance, I don't think dad ever knew about the tricks we played on our cats and dogs; such as the wiener trick. We would peel the skin off a wiener in a strip about 18 inches long, making certain we left enough meat on it to interest the cat. Once the cat started eating, it made a total commitment, because it couldn't stop until it was done. We would bide our time for a few days until one end of the wiener skin showed itself. Then we would tie that end to a fence post and sic the dog on the cat. It was amazing how tough that wiener skin was, because that cat sometimes took two or three good runs before the entire length of skin came out.

That was the sort of entertainment we managed to provide for ourselves, and though there was no doubt our childhood was quite an adventure, the real adventures still lay ahead with our years of travel in the forests and mountains we learned to love so dearly.

2

YOUNG ADVENTURERS

EVEN AS YOUNG LADS WE ALWAYS HELPED PUT FOOD ON THE TABLE. This was made a whole lot easier when a local man named Halvor Mellos decided to go into the mink-raising business. As food for the mink, he purchased many rabbits. Well, it wasn't very long until he realized that this venture was a flop. The loud noise produced by the steam whistles of passing trains was more than the mink could bear, and so they killed their young. When Halvor gave up the mink venture, he turned all these rabbits loose. This resulted in the best hunting any young lads could ever hope for. There were rabbits everywhere.

If it wasn't the many rabbits we shot with our slingshots, it was the fish we always brought home from the trout-laden streams. To me, it was like heaven to wander through the forest and then camp out by these mountain streams. It was common to catch 30 or 40 fish each, then return the next weekend and do the same again. We would meet others along the streams, each person loaded down with fish. Some large Dolly Varden (bull trout) used to travel these streams to spawn; many were so large they looked out of place in the smaller streams. We often watched the mouths of the creeks in May and June to see schools of trout as they left the dirty river water and started up the streams.

I remember when a friend, Joe Michaylenko, pulled a huge fish part way out of a small stream. The fish got off his hook and Joe jumped into the shallow stream right on top of it. A frantic fight ensued with Joe doing his best to hold on. When the fish finally got away, Joe sat on the creek bank with tears in his eyes. As for myself, I just stood there staring in amazement, unable to believe a fish that big could be in that tiny stream.

Often we would walk for miles along the railroad tracks during May and early June, where we would find the fish bunched up at the downstream side of culverts. Many times it was impossible to let your line settle to the bottom before a fish was on it. One of the streams we often visited was called Guilford Creek, and in order to visit this creek we had to walk by Guilford Sawmills. I will never forget this spot, because on our way by we would stop to visit the Chinese cook, a one-eyed man named Lou. As soon as he noticed us hanging around outside, he would always invite us in for fresh pies. Many times the three or four of us would eat two pies from among the many that were present, while the cook would say, "Eat boys, help yourself." I thought he was absolutely the greatest.

Some memories bring back smiles, such as the time my two brothers and I, along with a friend, ran into a large animal in the woods. We couldn't see it, but it made a loud crash in the woods right beside us. Try to imagine four young lads climbing the same tree at the same time and you'll get a picture of the state of confusion that followed. We later checked and found that it had been a moose.

A lesson was well learned about moose the day a cow came by our home calling steadily for what must have been a missing calf. When she got quite a distance from us, we started calling, pretending we were its calf. Quick as a wink that cow turned and charged right back to our house, while we ran inside and hid. Mom gave us a talking to about the danger of animals with young, but she needn't have, as we had already got the message loud and clear.

Mom also told us how to deal with a charging bear. You simply waited until the last instant when it opened its mouth to bite, then you quickly stuck your arm down its throat, grabbed it by the bum and turned it inside out. This meant it was automatically running in the opposite direction. For a few years I actually believed it, and I used to try to picture what a bear looked like with the fur on the inside.

When I was about 10 years old, an odd thing happened that brought a lot of attention to our home. My brother Joe was searching our quarter section of land, trying to find our cows so he could drive them home for milking. As he walked along a swamp, he saw a dead animal lying there. He knew enough not to go close because there could have been a bear near it, so he came home and told the family about it. That's where it stood until several weeks later when he happened by there again and took a close look. He came home and told dad that these were the bones of a strange looking animal and he wanted dad to go look at them. Dad went to the carcass which was stripped of all flesh by this time. In fact, the skull and leg bones had been dragged away leaving only the spine and ribcage. Dad sure enough agreed that they looked strange, so he put them in a burlap bag, brought them home and stored them in a shed.

Just a short time later we were visited by a first-class woodsman and trapper. While we were eating lunch dad mentioned the bones, suggesting that perhaps this elderly trapper might be able to identify them. Without hesitation this gentleman said, "Oh! I'll know what they are all right."

Down to the shed we went, filled with expectation. We watched as he studied the skeleton for several minutes, after which he shook his head and conceded, "You know, Joe, I don't know what kind of an animal that was." And so the mystery deepened.

A few weeks later, an internationally known big game guide visited our home and dad again mentioned the bones. Again we were told, "Oh! I'll know what they are all right."

Back down to the shed we went, this time convinced that we would learn the answer. For several minutes this guide studied the bones and at last replied, "Joe! That's the bones of a huge grizzly bear."

Dad didn't believe it though, and at that point he was ready to send the bones away for positive identification, but it was not to be. Just a short time later someone left the shed door open and dogs proceeded to drag the bones all over creation.

The end of the story? No. About ten years later Clarence and I were following the railroad tracks looking for bears on train-killed moose. As we walked along, we came upon the complete skeleton of an animal whose bones had been picked clean by maggots. There before our eyes lay the mystery animal, and it was just an ordinary moose. Though these men had butchered many moose, they had obviously never seen the complete skeleton of one before. The bones that stick up to form the moose's hump had fooled them completely.

Another memory from my youth was the manner in which some people used to fish for salmon. Unlike modern-day fishermen, they were far too busy to have time for fishing with a rod and reel, so they used dynamite for bait. In all fairness, though, I must point out that this was before we found out that all the salmon belonged to people that lived on the coast. Anyway, these fellows would find a hole in the stream where several salmon were resting and then toss in a stick or two of dynamite. Immediately after the blast, they would stand in the shallows downstream from the hole and pick up the stunned salmon.

The only time I ever witnessed this operation occurred when a friend and I went upriver, supposedly to watch the salmon. Suddenly this chap pulled a package from his pack and exposed two sticks of dynamite. Before I fully realized what was happening, he lit the fuse and threw it downstream from the point where we were drifting in the riverboat. It had no sooner disappeared beneath the water when I shouted to him that we were going to drift right over top of it. Somewhat surprised, this guy grabbed the starting rope and frantical-ly began pulling it in an effort to start the outboard engine, but he

The Boudreau family, left to right: June, Margaret, Jack, Josie, Clarence, Evie, Joie and Isabelle.

only succeeded in flooding it. Helpless, I did the only thing I could think of and stuck my fingers in my ears, then hoped for the best. When the blast went, it stung the bottom of my feet and left them numb for several minutes. The only reason we survived at all was because there happened to be about six feet of water in that spot. Not only did we not get any salmon, we didn't even get a squawfish or sucker; we only succeeded in scaring the devil out of ourselves. This was my only experience with blasting fish and it was more than enough to last.

In an effort to make their own entertainment, my teenage sisters, Evie and Josie, decided to go mountain climbing. For company, they gathered up four teenage girlfriends to take along. The only reason mom allowed them to go was because they said an elderly man was going with them and taking a rifle along. Once they got out in the mountains and darkness approached, they got frightened and spent the night crammed inside of a hollow cedar tree. The next day, they carried on and walked right into a grouse with young. The grouse flew straight at them and scared the dickens out of them, and so our heroines moved on. A short time later, Evie fainted, and the others were in the process of building a stretcher when she came to. By this time they had endured enough adventure so they decided to return home. But there was a problem—no one knew which way to go. As there was no trail to follow, these girls wandered around in the forest for hours before finally finding their way home. When mom found out that these girls had been wandering around the mountains in grizzly country by themselves, she was shocked. And we wonder why mothers turn grey!

Of all our adventures, though, it was the grizzly bears that always elicited excitement. Just the thought of them being in the forests and mountains added a measure of interest to any trip.

One grizzly bear's visit to Penny sure caused a stir of excitement. This happened when my brother Joe was working with assistant ranger Gary Ward at the ranger station in 1957. As they worked, several women had a bridge game going in the house right beside them. At this same time, a grizzly chased a moose through the town and when it realized where it was, it turned to go back to the forest. As luck would have it, it ran through the yard where the two men were working. A big dog spotted the bear and immediately gave chase, but it was not for long. As soon as the bear saw the dog approaching, it turned and chased the dog back toward the men. Then, before you could blink, the dog was under the house and the women were up two bridge players.

My sister Josie had the experience of a lifetime back in the early '50s, when she went with her husband—Bud Proctor—on the 14-mile hike into Slim Lake. As they walked along about seven miles into their journey, Josie, who was in the lead, walked right into a grizzly bear. As it stood up right in front of them, they saw that it was feeding on a moose it had killed. Bud only had a single-shot 30-30 rifle which he didn't feel was adequate for a big bear. As well, he had no previous experience with grizzly bears. Perhaps this may have played a part in his voice acquiring a feminine tone as it sputtered, "Holy Jesus! A grizzly!" With that, Bud refused to shoot. Instead he hoisted Josie up into a tree and then began climbing it himself.

After a few minutes of sizing things up, the bear moved back into the trees and disappeared from view. A few minutes later, Josie and Bud came down the tree and made a circle around the carcass, then headed toward an old cabin a few miles away where they intended to stay the night. Just a short distance away from the moose carcass, they came upon the fresh tracks of a mother grizzly with a lone cub. Now this was far more than they could handle. They carried on to the cabin, making as much noise as possible, with Josie already convinced that they would not return home alive. When they reached the cabin, she wrote a message on the cabin door that stayed legible for many years, "Met grizzly bear on the trail. Don't know if we'll make it home. Goodbye all. Josie and Bud Proctor."

As I had dropped them off with a riverboat and was not expecting them back for three days, they were stranded and had to stay at this tiny cabin until then. On the third morning they decided to try returning home. They filled a pail with rocks and made a great deal of noise going through the forest. Then when they got near the moose carcass, they circled far around it to make sure they didn't tempt the bear again. I was waiting at the river with a boat when they came out and I can assure all that they were really shook up. Three days of terror and they never even got to the lake—let alone catch a fish.

This Slim Lake, so often referred to by me, was a true paradise in the 1940s and 1950s before logging roads reached the area. I have so many special memories of it and so many thanks to the trapper and guide of the area—Oliver Prather—for the liberal use of his cabin and boats.

There was the time that Clarence, Lindy Chambers, and I arrived at Oliver's cabin to find that a black bear had broken in. What a mess! There was debris scattered everywhere: the stove was turned upside down on the opposite side of the cabin; the kettle and many other items had been packed away into the woods; a trail of flour was visible along the bear's trail for a great distance, and there was not a bit of food left that was worth eating.

The sign plainly showed that the bear had torn halfway through the logs on the side of the cabin before it gave up and went to work

Left: Ernest Turner, who drowned in the Fraser River, with Oliver Prather at Slim Lake, 1950.

on the door. Oliver had spiked a crosscut saw across the door with the teeth pointing up, and somehow that bear had removed it without getting cut. The bear returned that evening and the next but we drove it off. The following night a heavy snowfall drove the bear to its den.

At Slim Lake it was common to see as many as eight moose at one time feeding on aquatic plants; moose that would often refuse to get out of our way when we tried to move the canoe along the waterway. One time Lindy Chambers and I were coming down the creek when the moose were in rut. Around us we could hear at least five moose grunting at the same time. Suddenly a bull exploded out of the brush straight at us and all hell broke loose. I started paddling with all my might, while Lindy grabbed for my rifle in the front of the canoe, almost upsetting it in the process. As I was paddling for dear life, I must have rocked the canoe a lot because Lindy fired all six bullets without hitting the charging moose. Startled by all the noise and confusion, the moose turned and passed by the rear of the canoe less than five feet from me. As it disappeared into the trees on the opposite bank, we both breathed a sigh of relief.

I don't know what caused the moose to attack; perhaps it was driven out by another bull. Maybe it heard the paddle striking the side of the canoe and took it as a challenge. Whatever the reason, it certainly got our hearts pumping double-time.

It was always a pleasure to visit the Slim area: loons forever calling, eagles diving for fish or else diving to steal fish from the ospreys that always patrolled the area. One of nature's finest achievements in my opinion, is the ability of eagles to drop with such breathtaking speed, then pull out at the last instant to avoid a collision with the ground or water.

Sometimes they screw up though, as testified to by an eagle that landed in a big cottonwood tree right in the community of Penny. For two days it sat in the tree without moving. Then Lindy Chambers and I walked to the tree to try to drive it away. We threw a few rocks at it but it wouldn't budge. Finally we brought out a set of binoculars and looked at it for a minute and noticed that the upper portion of its beak was broken off and just hanging by one side. It was obvious that this bird was starving to death, so we put it out of its misery. A closer look showed that it was blind in one eye. Then we got to wondering how its beak got broken. We finally agreed that its lack of binocular vision caused it to misjudge distance, and that it probably failed to pull out of a high-speed dive in time to avoid a collision with the ground.

Another memory of Slim Lake concerned a friend, Herb Metzmeier, who had arrived from Germany a few years earlier and fallen in love with the area. He and I had poled up the creek from Slim to Tumuch Lake to do some fishing, and as we paddled the canoe along, we spotted three moose standing in two feet of water. This was rutting season, and it instantly became apparent that these two bulls were fighting over a cow. Herb suggested that we paddle the canoe right between the two bulls, but I said that I had a better idea—that he let me off on shore and then he could go between the two moose by himself. Well he didn't go, but the lack of respect he had for moose was to undergo a dramatic change the following year.

Jack Boudreau with black bear shot in Penny in the spring of 1954.

This event took place after Herb had spent some time fishing in Slim Lake during the month of May. He brought the canoe into shore, pulled it out of the water, and proceeded to clean his catch of fish at the water's edge. As he worked on the fish, he noticed a movement beside him and whirled erect. There was a cow moose with a newborn calf on the opposite side of the canoe, and only a few feet away. Without hesitating, the moose jumped over the canoe, while Herb threw himself to the side. Then followed a race to the cabin with the moose breathing down his neck. As Herb dove in under the porch, the moose's front hooves landed right behind him and left an imprint that stayed visible for some time. Having spent time with Herb both before and after this episode, I think I'm in a position to say that he learned brand new respect for moose that day.

A year later, Herb and I again walked to Slim Lake. The next morning we went out and fished for a few hours, then returned to the cabin to have lunch. Herb had caught a three-pound trout which he left at the edge of the lake while we went in to eat lunch. After we finished eating, Herb went out to clean the fish which we were going to eat for our evening meal. Almost at once he began calling to me so I went out to investigate. He was standing at the lakeshore beckoning to me, so I walked to him and could scarcely believe my eyes. A mink had laid claim to his fish and had dragged it a few feet to where it was all tangled up in sedge. The mink refused to give it up, though, and stood upright right beside Herb and hissed at him. What unbelievable courage—this tiny animal calling the bluff of something a thousand times its size. After marveling at its audacity for several minutes, a compromise was struck when Herb gave it the head of the fish which it dragged away, occasionally turning to hiss at us.

On our third morning at the lake, I got up at daylight and took the canoe out on the lake to enjoy the peace and beauty. As I sat there listening to the loons and watching moose feeding, my attention was drawn to a commotion on the bank. A squirrel was putting up a steady chatter and all at once it came out on a limb and jumped to land with a splash in the lake. Behind it, I saw a marten run out. It looked at the squirrel as it dove into the water, then disappeared into the branches again. The squirrel was swimming straight toward me so I remained motionless as it climbed onto the canoe and shook itself off. Then it spotted me, and ran up to the front of the canoe where it put up a steady chatter.

After chattering back and forth with the squirrel for several minutes, I paddled back toward the cabin, calling out to Herb to come see what I had. After several minutes he came down the trail, tucking in his shirt and wiping the sleep from his eyes. "Do you see anything unusual on the canoe?" I asked.

He looked, then laughed and said, "How the devil did you do that?"

I let him guess for a minute and then told him. A minute later I brought the canoe into shore, and at once the squirrel jumped and headed back along the edge of the lake to where it had started from. I have to say I believe that squirrels swimming must be an unusual event because that was the only time in my life that I saw a squirrel in water.

Herb Metzmeier at Tumuch Lake Cabin, 1954.

A few years later, I told this story to an elderly trapper named Harry Weaver, who always had a comeback story, usually with humor added. He smiled and then responded with, "Sure, it's lots of fun for the marten, that is until it meets up with a flying squirrel—then it gets some of its own. Chased up a tree by the marten, the flying squirrel will glide to another tree, then when the marten goes down the tree and climbs the next tree, the squirrel glides again.

"Remember," He added, "if you're walking through the forest and you see a marten standing on a limb banging its head against a tree, then you can bet it has just had a session with a flying squirrel."

This same gentleman was also the first person to tell me that fishers kill porcupines right up in the trees. Just recently I learned that someone has discovered that the fishers chase them up a tree, then climb above them to attack. The porcupines cannot run forward down a tree, so they are forced to back down. Then the fisher comes at them from above and gets them by the throat, easily killing them.

Harry was called Beaver Man by some people because of his great knowledge of these animals and because of the many years he spent trapping problem beavers for different levels of government. Many years ago this man told me that beavers can stay underwater for at least 15 minutes. This too, has been established by other sources.

While I'm on the subject of unusual things that take place in nature, I want to repeat a story that I first heard from Prince George pioneer Ted Williams. It concerned an unusual animal that was captured in Prince George when he was a young man. In my research for *Crazy Man's Creek*, I stumbled on to it. This story was carried in the May 7, 1931 edition of the *Prince George Citizen*:

Trappers Fail to Fix New Type of Fur-bearer

"The origin and classification of the strange looking fur-bearer which was captured by A.G.Mann while clearing on his Pineview property two weeks ago, remains as much a mystery as ever. The animal had something of the appearance of a beaver, weighing between eight and ten pounds, but instead of the beaver tail it had an appendage like that of the mink, and eight inches long. The length of its body was 18 inches, and it was covered with a fur of a dark brown color, with a black stripe running down the center of the back. To complete its contradictions the animal had teeth like the beaver, with front feet semi-webbed and hind feet fully webbed.

The animal could not run very fast on land, and Mann had little difficulty in capturing it. He brought it to town in a box, and quartered it in F. D. Taylor's pool room in an effort to determine its classification and origin. Every trapper in the city was induced to inspect the animal, but each declared it to be the first of the kind he had ever seen.

To settle the matter F.D. Taylor wrote to F. Kermode, curator of the provincial museum at Victoria, submitted the best description of the animal he could give, but it was too much for Mr. Kermode and he admitted his inability to solve the riddle. He said the animal had some of the characteristics of the marmot, but others which put it out of that family altogether. Given a chance to make a personal study of the animal he might be able to classify it but this was impossible since Mr. Mann had taken it back to its habitat, and turned it loose. There is a sluggish stream on the property, and Mr. Mann is of the opinion there are at least a pair of the animals living in it, and a chance he might be able to recapture it should it be desired.

Meantime the trappers of the district are invited to figure out the animal's species, if they can, from the description secured while it was held captive in a box. There is a chance it may be a hybrid, or an animal from some foreign land which having been brought to British Columbia in a vessel, made its way up the waterways to Pineview. They can have as many guesses as they like as to where the contradictory little cuss came from and how he got to Pineview.

3

GRIZZLIES

"The haunting calls of wild geese filter down through the gathering snow clouds and echo among the mountain peaks. Sitting alone on a mountaintop in a remote wilderness area, I listen to the music of cascading streams far below on their eternal rush to the sea. Sometimes they fade away until I can scarcely hear them, and other times they sound so near that it seems I can reach out and touch them. One-half mile below me, a mother grizzly tries to entice her small cub into a glacial lake but the silver-hued little tyke will have none of it. She wades out into the water and swims around in a few circles, then comes ashore to find her cub lying on a large rock at water's edge watching with keen interest. Out of the lake she comes in a spray of water, and proceeds to chase her cub around an island of subalpine fir trees a few times. Then she returns to the water. Several times this performance is repeated until at last they tire and move along to new adventure.

Overhead, an eagle wings its way home on the last remaining updrafts of the day, while in the distance I hear the lonely sound of a coyote's cry as it begins an evening hunt."

Jack Boudreau's diary

MY FIRST TRIP ABOVE TIMBERLINE WILL ALWAYS BE SPECIAL TO ME. I was 13 years-old at the time and had already developed a tremendous love for the outdoors. My brother Joe, sister Evie, and her husband Jack McKinley, were planning a trip into the mountains and after a good deal of pleading on my part, they agreed to take me along. There were no trails in those mountains at that time, so what with fighting our way over downtrees, plowing through devil's club and alder, I was utterly exhausted by evening. To make matters even worse, we had climbed too high before picking a camping spot and so we could not find any level ground. We were forced to camp on a

15 percent slope, and this led to problems during the night. Several times we slipped out from under the tarp we used as a tent and found ourselves alone in the dark, then scurried back uphill under the tarp.

The following day we were walking along the edge of a canyon that dropped off near vertical for about 1000 feet when we heard a whooshing sound. We looked up to see a bald eagle coming down in an incredible dive. With its wings almost completely tucked in, it went by us at great speed. A few seconds later we heard a small animal screaming far below; a ground squirrel I suspect, that had virtually no chance of escape, such was the speed of the eagle's attack.

For most of the second day, we fought our way through alder swales and up steep slopes until I found myself wondering why people were stupid enough to climb mountains. It seemed to be nothing but flies, sweat, and darned hard work. But by late afternoon of the second day we reached timberline, and walked right into a world that I never imagined existed. A beautiful sight that made me stare in wonder. I questioned the others no end: "Where did all the flowers come from? How did all the ground squirrels get here? Why did the trees grow in straight lines? Why are the trees only a couple of feet tall?"

As we stopped to enjoy the scenery, I took off my heavy pack and got the surprise of my life: the reflex action of my leg muscles made me feel like I was going to fly away, so I quickly grabbed at a small tree. This brought a few laughs from the others.

That evening we made camp by a small stream and while we were eating our meal, we spotted a cougar walking across a snowfield high above us. As it stepped from the snow into the wildflowers, it instantly disappeared from view—so complete was its ability to blend into its surroundings.

We spent a few days wandering around this paradise, where we saw moose and deer. But most important of all was the abundant grizzly bear sign. A lasting respect was born in me for these huge beasts. I was extremely impressed by the size of the rocks they moved in their relentless search for food. As we left the high country I knew one thing for certain: I was hooked and hooked good: I would return.

It was the long weekend in September when we came off the mountain, and a picnic was in progress in the community. We joined the festivities and while there, I spoke to an old woodsman and trapper named Jack Evans who had first trapped this area before 1900. I told him that we had seen a cougar on the mountain and he let me know in no uncertain terms that I was mistaken. I described it to him and mentioned the long tail, but he refused to accept it. He informed me that he had spent his life in the woods and never saw a cougar. Then I got brother Joe to tell him and he still wouldn't accept it. I guess I don't blame him, I mean how could I go on my first trip and see a cougar when he hadn't seen one in his entire life?

I think there is a message to be taken from this—it shows how much we are slaves to our own experiences, and why there are so many different points of view about the wilderness.

Two years later I was back in these mountains with two school chums—Roy Sinclair and Alvin Litnosky. Perhaps we were too young to be climbing in the mountains by ourselves, but Roy's father had allowed him to bring his rifle along, so we felt confident. We trudged through the forest all day until we were tired, then decided to camp by a dry creek bed. This was a silly thing to do, as we had no water. After we set up our camp, we took our billy can and started following the dry creek beds, looking for water. We walked for at least twenty minutes and arrived at a stream where we filled the can and then headed back toward camp. This was when we got a surprise: we found that there were many dry creek beds and that they all looked the same. This led to many debates about which bed we should follow. Many times Alvin or I pointed to a stream bed and said it was the one, but each time Roy would insist that it wasn't. In due time, Roy pointed at one bed and said, "That's the one we came out of." We followed it and found our camp.

This wasn't the only time Roy showed his power of observation in the woods. He had previously been on several trips with his father, who had taught him well. Without Roy, I'm sure we would have spent the night under a tree and probably never would have found our camp.

The next day we reached treeline where we immediately spotted a herd of mule deer in the trees a short distance below us. Alvin and Roy took off toward them, hoping to get one, while I sat on the mountainside to watch the show. And a great show it turned out to be. When Roy and Alvin got close, the deer split up, each one hiding behind an island of trees until the boys got close to them. Then they ran and hid behind other islands until the boys got close to them again. For perhaps half an hour these deer played tag, without the boys once getting a glimpse of them. I kept them informed of the movement of the deer by pointing, but even with that advantage, they were forced to admit defeat. Then I ran down the mountain to join them and showed Roy where a deer was hiding behind some trees right at the edge of a canyon. As we approached, the deer broke cover and Roy brought it down with a perfect shot. Man, were we ever proud of ourselves! Three little boys out in the mountains by ourselves and we managed to bring home a deer. Our parents never complained about us going into the mountains after that.

The following year I was back in this same area with my brother Clarence, sister Josie, and her husband, Bud Proctor. It was a sunny day in early June when we worked our way up onto a mountain ridge. We made camp and proceeded to erect our pup tent in an island of subalpine fir trees only a few feet tall. We had picked a campsite where there was no firewood and where we were completely at the mercy of the wind. Our ignorance was almost our undoing that day, as Mother Nature was about to teach us a lesson we would not soon forget.

Unaware that we were in any danger, we proceeded to climb a nearby ridge. At the top, we took several pictures. Then Josie and Bud returned to the tent while Clarence and I decided to climb a nearby peak. Just after we reached the summit, we noticed a storm approaching at great speed. We made a run for our tent and got about halfway back when the storm struck. A very heavy, wet snowstorm it was, such that we were drenched before we reached our tent. Our warm sunny day had returned to winter, with a considerable drop in temperature. Inside the tent we huddled, where Josie had both our woolen blankets wrapped around her and yet she was cold. We three men sat wet and shivering as the storm raged outside. Finally we realized that if we did not get off the mountain, we would not survive the night. We gathered up our equipment and stumbled off through the storm, not certain which direction to go. Then Josie drew our attention to some tracks in the snow. It was our footprints still visible under the fresh snow where we had crossed a snowfield that morning. If Josie had not noticed our tracks, we would have gone down the wrong side of the mountain, as we were already about 90 degrees off course. We slipped and slid down the steep mountainside, finally finding a timber-covered ridge with lots of firewood just as darkness fell.

As I look back, I am most certain that if we had stayed on the mountain, we would not have survived the night. At that time we didn't have the sense to bunch up and use the two blankets around all of us to keep the heat in.

Every year since then I have returned to the high country. The first few years we had trouble spotting grizzlies, but that changed to where we counted 24 definitely different grizzlies in a two week period in an area only two miles long by one mile wide. On another occasion, we saw and photographed 17 grizzlies on a mountainside at one time.

It has been 54 years since my fascination with these magnificent beasts began. However, I decided around 26 years ago to stop hunting, and have since spent my time simply watching and photographing them. Many of the animals were seen from helicopters during my years with the protection branch of the BC Ministry of Forests. I have found that the old saying 'familiarity breeds contempt', doesn't apply where grizzlies are concerned; rather, respect builds and grows among those who spend a lot of time around these animals.

In an effort to make people understand why we once hunted grizzly, it is necessary to know that when we were young men there was not a great deal of entertainment in our area. Consequently, we had to make our own. My brother Joe was the first of us boys to get a rifle. It was only a .30-30, but it sure made him important in our eyes. I used to follow him around, begging to be allowed to fire a few shots now and then. When I was allowed to, I was convinced that I was going to be another Daniel Boone.

Not long after Joe got his rifle, he went moose hunting with a school chum named Lindy Chambers, who was always wandering the woods with us. They shot a moose about two miles from home, butchered it, and each tied a quarter of the animal on their pack-boards. As they headed toward home on their snowshoes, Joe lost his balance and slid head-first in under a downtree. With the quarter of moose on his back and his arms in the straps of the pack, he was unable to move. Lindy came to his rescue and dug him out, but there was no doubt in Joe's mind that had he been alone that day he surely would have perished.

The following year, Joe was back moose hunting again and managed to bag one. Knowing that he needed help to butcher and pack the animal out, he headed toward home to get help. After he had gone a short distance, he heard a gunshot in the forest. He hollered and a minute later he was joined by Lindy, who was also hunting in the area. Together they returned to the moose, where they proceeded to butcher it. As they worked away on the moose, their attention was drawn to a noise in the trees beside them, where a mother grizzly with two cubs approached. The two lads fired several shots, but in their excitement their accuracy left something to be desired. The grizzlies disappeared into the forest, and somewhat shaken, the two lads continued working on the moose. Just as they were finishing up, they heard something approaching—it was the three grizzlies returning; this time determined to claim the moose. A great volley of shots rang out and when the smoke cleared the bears were dead. A short time later the two thoroughly shaken young men returned home. Later on, when some adults returned to the scene of battle, it was obvious that the mother bear had no choice but to attack; she was nothing but skin and bone, right at the edge of starvation.

This confrontation was only the beginning of many we would have throughout the years. In fact, it was just a couple years later that I would experience the most terrifying few days of my life.

It happened when my brother Joe and I were hired by the BC Forest Service to cut out a fire-access trail on the opposite side of the Fraser River and upstream several miles from Penny. As we didn't know how long the job would take, we were taken across the river in a boat by a patrolman and given a rubber raft in which we were to recross the river when the job was done. After he let us off, I climbed up into a big spruce tree and tied the raft about 20 feet above the ground to protect it from animals. Then we continued on toward the mountain about four miles away where we intended to start cutting our trail.

As we neared the mountain, we were moving through an area of large cedar trees with Joe in the lead. Suddenly a grizzly came out from behind a large tree right in front of Joe. This was the first grizzly that I had seen close up and as it slowly ran away into the forest, I thought it looked much like a large hog and I was not impressed. When it got about 100 feet away, it whirled and started back toward us at a gallop. Then I was impressed. Joe, who was carrying a cross-cut saw over his shoulder, waved the saw and hollered at the top of his voice, "Shoot, shoot!" (This hollering should have been enough to scare off any bear, because Joe had a powerful voice. In fact, he is the only person I ever heard of that killed a cat just by sneezing.)

I had been carrying Joe's .303 British rifle, and I quickly worked the bolt to throw a cartridge into the firing chamber. I was just about to shoot when the bear stopped and came to an erect position so fast that if I had shot, I would have shot in front of it. I aimed at its neck and squeezed the trigger, but the trigger pull was much stiffer than I had expected, with the result that if the gun had fired, I would have wounded the grizzly instead of killing it. Fortunately perhaps, all I heard was a dull click. I worked the bolt a couple times but the cartridges were jammed just below the travel of the bolt and would not pick up. Stunned, I walked the few steps to Joe and handed him the rifle, which he took and immediately began working on. I then turned my attention to the grizzly which was standing erect only about 15 feet away looking down at us. Never have I felt such a feeling of utter helplessness. I looked up at his cold, unblinking eyes and I felt a coldness run through me that is far beyond words. Then I looked around to see if there were any cubs or perhaps a carcass that it was feeding on, but I noticed nothing. For what was probably a couple minutes but seemed like hours, the bear stood gazing down at us, and I felt certain we were going to be killed. Then it let out a soft cough, got down and very slowly wandered away through the trees. Just as it disappeared from view, Joe managed to get a cartridge into the firing chamber.

For at least 20 minutes we sat there shaking, devoid of strength, and I felt as though I had just finished running the four-minute mile. As we sat there, we finally figured out what had gone wrong with the rifle: Joe had forced 11 shells into a 10-shot clip and they had jammed just below the travel of the bolt.

As for the grizzly, it was in an area that was almost never frequented by people and our scent may have meant nothing to it. The fact that we didn't run may also have puzzled the bear and prevented a disaster. And a disaster it would have been, for if we had been mauled, our chances of ever getting out alive would have been nil, as we shall see.

We carried on to the foot of the mountain where we were to build a shelter in case firefighters would ever have to overnight there. No sooner did we arrive, then a mighty wind came up. Trees started falling all around us and all we could do was watch and try to avoid getting hit. For hours we stood there watching, wondering if all the Gods were plotting against us. As darkness fell, we crawled in

John Humphreys, Edith (Penny) Lammle and Joe Boudreau in the mountains, 1949.

under a huge cedar tree that had been blown over, and for half the night we huddled in fear as the winds continued to topple trees. Sometime in the wee hours the wind let up and allowed us a little sleep where we lay under that cedar downtree.

Three days later we had constructed the shelter and finished cutting the trail, so we headed back out to the river. When we went to get our raft, we found it lying at the bottom of the tree. A close look showed there were about a hundred teeth marks in it, and fresh tracks of a black bear with cubs all around. We had already endured enough excitement to last us for a year, and now we had no way of crossing the river which was in flood stage.

As we had no alternative, we started walking downriver and had gone just a short distance when we reached a stream. The river had flooded the stream and backed the water far inland, so we had to walk some distance before we were able to cross. We followed the stream back to the river and went only a short distance before we hit another flooded stream and had to do the same thing over again. Toward evening a bit of much needed luck came our way when the local bush foreman, Buster Van De Reit, happened along in a riverboat. A couple shots were fired and he came to our rescue and gave us a ride back to Penny. As Joe walked in the door of his house, his wife took one look at him and asked, "What happened?"

When I got home mom looked at me and asked, "What's the matter?" The accumulated stress was more than evident.

Well the years passed, and Clarence and I both got rifles. Then we started picking fights with black bears. It was about this time that I learned why it is not a good idea to keep a loaded gun in the house. I was visiting my brother Joe when he decided to show me a rifle he had purchased a short time before. What I didn't notice, though, was that Joe had taken some cartridges out of the gun before he handed it to me. I looked it over, worked the action to be certain it was empty of cartridges, then I handed it back to Joe, who took it into another room and put it back on the wall. Once again, I didn't notice that he had inserted a few cartridges because he had been having trouble with a bear. During the evening I walked into the other room, picked the rifle off the wall, worked the action and then simulated a shot at a clock that sat on the window sill. There was an incredibly loud roar, and the clock disappeared out the window with a shower of glass. To say that I was humiliated is putting it mildly. I just couldn't believe it. I mean I had just checked, and I knew the gun was unloaded.

Well, after having a few showdowns with black bears, Clarence and I decided it was time to try for a grizzly bear. About that time we got word that a grizzly had been seen feeding on a moose only a mile from the community. As we didn't know how to go about it, we went to visit an old trapper that lived nearby and asked his advice. His advice was simple and to the point, "Oh! Just go to the moose carcass and make lots of noise; it will come out."

This was not at all what we had wanted to hear, and we had a time just steadying each other down before we went in. Luckily for us, the bear had gone visiting and had left the moose remains buried under a pile of debris in the center of a cleared area, a common grizzly trait.

The guns that we had at that time were no match for bear—Clarence had a .32 Winchester with a worn-out barrel that couldn't group shots in a two-foot target at 50 feet; I had a .303 British Jungle Carbine that made lots of noise and jammed frequently. I can't help but feel that the bears had an agreement in those days that they would take it easy on us until we grew up.

Well, our first grizzly bear hunt didn't bear fruit, but I decided it was time to become a grizzly-bear hunter. I read everything I could find on hunting in order to become proficient. From the stories I read, it seemed rather odd to me that many of these woodsmen never made an error in their entire lives. It would have been enough to discourage me if I had been dumb enough to believe them. I found out in later years that a trip or two with these people usually show them to be as prone to mistakes and bad judgment as the rest of us.

Some of my early experiences were quite different from theirs. In fact, some of them were full of errors and some even bordered on the ridiculous. Such as the time I mixed up a batch of goodies that no grizzly could refuse. I took it up on a ridge a couple thousand feet above the main valley, where I rubbed it into the bark of several

cedar trees. A couple evenings later I went back to check. It was one
of those rainy, windy and dreary types of evenings when things are
spooky enough without bears. Just before I crested the ridge, I came
upon two large piles of grizzly droppings and realized that I was about
to hit pay dirt. I crept through the trees until I could see where I had
put the goodies, and at a glance I could tell that a lot of bark had
been torn off the trees. I was standing there, using a tree for cover,
when I heard an animal moving around behind the bait. Filled with
anticipation and with my gun at the ready, I was startled to hear
another animal moving to my right. This really bothered me, as I had
only 'ordered' one grizzly and just a medium-sized one at that. I was
standing there trying to decide what to do, when I heard a hell of a
crash in the thicket right behind me. In fact, it sounded like a big
bear slapping the ground with its paw. That did it. I suddenly remembered that I had forgotten to change socks that morning, so I headed for home on the double to do so. Better to change dirty socks
than to change dirty shorts, I always say.

I also recall the time I came upon some extra large grizzly tracks
on a logging road where someone had shot a moose a week earlier.
A quick check showed that the bear had piled the remains up and
buried them. I took a good long look at the size of the tracks, and
the claw marks in the mud, and my feet just kind of went into gear
by themselves and headed for home. A short distance down the road
I stopped and had a chat with myself. I said, "C'mon self, you can
take him; you just got to have confidence. Besides, it might just be
a small bear with really big feet."

Back down the road to the tracks I went, then took a long look
at the tracks and decided that those claws could definitely mess up a
guy's hairdo. I finally managed to work up enough nerve to hide
behind a tree and wait until dusk, but it never returned. It was just
one of many grizzlies throughout the years that buried moose or
black bear carcasses, and for some reason, never returned. They never
bury the carcasses unless they are going to leave the area. Why else
do they bury them? I mean countless times I have seen where they
have eaten entire carcasses without burying them. Some people say
they bury the carcasses to protect them from other animals. I answer
that by saying that they are never covered well enough to prevent

other animals from finding them. It has been my experience that they sometimes bury a carcass early in the spring before their digestive systems can accept meat. Then they will leave the carcass to feed on grass, skunk cabbage shoots, or other greens. After feeding they will return and camp by the carcass.

Other people say they bury them to prevent flies from laying eggs which turn into maggots which consume the flesh. Again, I have never found this to be successful—the maggots always seem to do their job.

All mountain trips leave lasting memories, but some much more so than others. Such as the September 1950 trip I took with Clarence, Bob Harkins, and a school chum named Roy Lammle. We carried extremely heavy packs back into the ridges and collapsed beside a stream just as darkness fell. Soon the cold September downdrafts came off the peaks and prodded us to action. We went to work and constructed a lean-to, then got a roaring campfire going and within a few minutes we were snug as could be. Then a full moon came over the mountain to paint the valley and peaks with the most magnificent colors and shadows. As we sat around the campfire, a large pack of wolves began howling in the timber far below us. I experienced a special feeling that I will never forget—a sense of what the wildness in wilderness is really all about.

The next morning as we made our way along the dew-covered slopes, I became familiar with the fleshy plant—Indian hellebore. I was making my way down a steep grade when I made the mistake of stepping on one. Before I knew what was happening, I went scooting down the grade on my back—just one of a thousand falls I've taken because of this plant that turns to slippery slime after it has been hit with frost.

In September 1954, Clarence and I decided it was time we headed into the mountains to get some grizzly bears. At the last moment, the local bush foreman, Buster Van De Reit, decided he would come with us, and it was lucky for us that he did.

On our second day back in the mountains we spotted a grizzly feeding just below timberline. After circling to keep the wind in our favor, we moved in and fired, then watched the bear go rolling down the mountain, roaring continuously. As I tried to reload, my gun jammed. At the same moment, Clarence found his new 30-06 was out of shells. He had fired from the prone position and a rock had bumped the clip release button, dumping all his shells on the ground. As soon as we got our rifles operational, I walked out into the open, as I assumed that the hunt was over. Then I was surprised to see a bigger grizzly come bounding out of an island of alpine fir. We fired a few shots and the bear turned and ran back into the trees. At the same time, we realized that this was a mama bear and the one we had shot was her yearling.

Again I made a wrong assumption by thinking the mother had ran away, as I had only taken a few more steps when she came galloping out the bottom of the island of trees. She wasn't running away—she was looking for us. Suddenly the movement of my walking caught her eye and she charged—her claws throwing vegetation into the air as she turned. This is a sight that I will never forget—with total disregard for her own safety, she bore down on us at breakneck speed. Between us and the bear, was a slight depression, and as she dropped into it, Clarence and I each got away one shot and only nicked her. In the 100 yards that separated us, Clarence and I never had time for a second shot. Buster fired his first shot at 30 feet and broke her neck.

As the bear bounced away down the mountainside, I was in a state of shock. I had never suspected that this was a family, and if Buster knew, he sure never let on. Then, as if nature had been holding its breath, an incredible rainstorm hit. We watched as dry creek beds on the cliffs of the adjacent ridge filled to overflowing in what can best be described as a cloudburst.

As we skinned out the bears, I couldn't help but wonder what would have happened if Buster had not been with us. I think there is a good chance that we would have both been killed that day. No question about it, we were in over our heads.

This was my second confrontation with grizzlies, and in both cases the rifle had jammed. This led me to lose all confidence in guns, and resulted in nightmares that persisted for several years. In the dreams I would find myself being attacked by bears and unable to run away because my feet would always be stuck in the mud. I didn't give up because of this, though; in fact it made me more determined than ever to carry on.

As I had spent a lot of time hiking the forests and mountains, I got to thinking I was a pretty good hiker. This was put to the test in October 1954. I had been doing some prospecting with a geiger counter and had left it in a tent back in the mountains. One day I told my dad that I had to get my equipment or else it would be snowed in for the winter. I asked him if he wanted to come along with me, but he declined with the comment, "I'm too old for that stuff." Dad had been a trapper among other things, but had retired from work the year before and had not hiked for many years.

Just as I was getting ready to leave, dad changed his mind and decided to come along. He went to a shed and got 200 feet of rope which he tied on his pack. Rope he wanted to use to explore a cave he had found in these same mountains 30 years earlier. As we left the house on our nine-mile hike with its 3,000-foot rise in elevation, I felt sorry for dad. I told him to lead the way and stop for a rest whenever he felt tired, and he agreed. About two hours later we hit the steepest pitches of the mountain and I got my first surprise. Instead

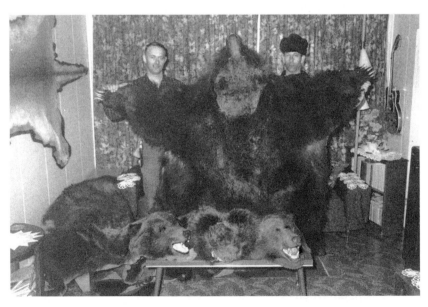

Jack and Clarence with some grizzlies, 1966.

of sitting down for a rest, dad just rested with his arm on his knee
for a few seconds, then continued on. When we arrived at my camp
I was ready for a lengthy rest, and I was very grateful that dad was
64, and not 30 years of age.

The following September, I was back in the mountains once again
looking for grizzlies. With me was Herb Metzmeier, who also had
his heart set on getting a grizzly. We left camp early the next morning and walked about five miles through the mountains to a point
where we split up—Herb going around the mountain one way, and
me the other.

After an uneventful walk, I arrived back at camp just before dark
and a few minutes later, Herb came in. He had a rather concerned
look about him so I asked him what happened. He grabbed a cup of
coffee, sat down on a log and began, "When I left you I went around
onto the opposite side of the ridge, and right away I spotted a big
grizzly about half a mile below me. I crept toward it going as quietly as I could and before I got to it I ran into another grizzly which
I hadn't seen. It stood up and looked me right in the eye from about
15 feet and I was so surprised that I didn't know what to do. Then
before I realized what was happening, it got down and jumped into
the trees so fast that I didn't have time to shoot."

I watched Herb in silent thought for a moment and then asked,
"Well Herb, you looked a grizzly right in the eye. What did it look
like?"

He thought about it for a minute and then answered, "Just like the
devil himself."

Herb did get his grizzly a short time later and several more after
that. In fact, he was one of only a handful of people in our area that
hunted them to any degree. A few times when we came in from
hunting just at dark, we met Herb going out to hunt. I often wondered how he hunted in the dark. He never offered an explanation,
but he often produced the goods.

It was about this same time that Herb Metzmeier got tangled up
with a sow grizzly and two cubs. It was almost inevitable that this
would happen when a person was repeatedly sneaking in on moose
carcasses. With no other choice, Herb was forced to shoot the sow

when she attacked him. Then he and a neighboring trapper, Joe Pastor, managed to capture the cubs and put in a cage. While they waited for a wildlife officer to come and take possession of the cubs, Herb decided to feed them. He opened one end of the cage and lowered a dish of milk for them to drink. Quick as a flash, the boar cub flew across the cage and struck his hand, its claws laying his hand open. The speed and ferocity of this little three-month-old cub had to be seen to be believed. I recall thinking, "If this is what a cub can do, imagine what an adult grizzly can do."

After traveling the forests and mountains for several years, we were forced to accept the fact that we were doing something wrong. Through trial and error, we learned that we were being far too noisy. For some reason the few grizzlies we did see were usually heading over the mountain to distant territory. At times we noticed that we could hear our hiking or hunting companions talking in low voices when they were nearly half a mile from us and the wind was in our favor. One only has to listen to the sound of mountain streams to understand this: some times they sound so close that you feel you can reach out and touch them; a minute later the sounds fades away until you scarcely can hear them. The answer, of course, lies in the restless mountain air that is forever on the move.

Determined to outsmart these great bears and get in closer, we refrained from talking above a whisper. This helped a lot, but we were still more than a little dismayed to find that the bears were leaving the area at our approach. Sometimes we would see them leaving the area when we still a great distance away and had a steady wind in our favor. We asked many guides and woodsmen how these bears could be detecting our presence, but none offered a reasonable solution. Some suggested a sixth sense, but the answer when it came, proved much simpler than that.

Clarence and I had hiked into the subalpine and spotted a grizzly with two cubs feeding on a ridge about half a mile from us. We stopped, took off our packs, and began watching the bears. As I was quite tired after carrying my pack and rifle for many miles, I stretched out on the ground for a rest. No sooner did my head hit the ground, though, then I picked up a thumping sound something like a heavy heartbeat. Puzzled, I took my own pulse and quickly realized that it was not the cause of the thumping sound. Right then, the sow grizzly led her cubs over the mountain at a fast run and disappeared. I put my head on the ground again and immediately picked up the sound. This caused me to get up and walk to where Clarence was standing. I asked if he had heard a thumping sound and he said he had not. At that moment we heard a whistle and turned to see a friend, Guenther Peemoeller, who had decided to join us. Suddenly it all fit together—the thumping sound had been made by our friend's boots hitting the ground. This sound had been picked up by the sow grizzly at least half a mile away, probably by sensory nerves in the pads of her feet. Since that time I have proven this to myself on many occasions and noticed that they pick this sound up at greater distances when they are on the same ridge or mountain. This also explains why it is so much easier to get close to bears on horseback, as the horses have four feet and therefor a totally different rhythm than man with only two feet.

By walking lightly, this helped us get closer to these bear when the wind was in our favor. When we were moving with the wind, we often had grizzlies pick up our scent and leave the area when they were well over a mile distant. Just how much further these bears picked up our scent and departed, we did not know because of our limited range of vision in the areas we traveled. Although the eyesight of grizzlies leaves something to be desired, their sense of smell is beyond belief and I wouldn't be surprised if it is as good as any in the animal kingdom.

On one of our trips back in the mountains, Clarence shot a moose which rolled down the mountainside and came to rest in an alder thicket. After packing home most of the meat, we returned several days later with Guenther Peemoeller. The next day we decided to check the moose remains, knowing full well that the biggest boar grizzly in the entire area would be on it. We moved into the incredibly thick alder swales as silently as possible and had a hard time finding the remains. Suddenly I spotted the remains only a couple feet away and noticed the blood-red meat where an animal had just eaten. Then I saw a patch of grizzly fur right behind it—not 10 feet from me, so I quickly aimed and fired at it. After the shot there was only silence, and then Guenther fired at something in the alders right beside him. Within seconds, a wounded cub grizzly came bouncing down and stopped right at my feet—roaring steadily. As the hair rose on the back of my neck I realized that once again we had made a terrible mistake: this was not a big boar, this was a mother with at least one cub and we were in trouble. I quickly dispatched the cub so that we could hear what was going on. Then followed a few minutes of pure agony. I didn't understand the silence. I felt that the mother should have charged or else ran away, but there was only the silence. Clarence was only about 15 feet below us but we couldn't see him in the tangle of vegetation. We knew that if one of us was attacked, the others would be unable to assist, because it was impossible to even swing a rifle around in that tangle of alders. After a few nerve-shattering minutes, we agreed to back slowly out of there, which we did. When we arrived at an opening, Guenther spoke for all of us when he said with much emotion, "I will never go into a place like that again; nobody will ever talk me into going into a place like that again!" I silently mouthed his exact words.

Back at camp, we discussed the situation. Clarence informed us that just after I fired the first shot, he thought he heard something sliding down through the alders. We assumed that I had accidentally killed the mother with a lucky shot. If I hadn't, I have no doubt that some of the blood on the mountain that day would have been ours.

Three times in my short career of hunting grizzlies I had made assumptions, and every one had been wrong. I knew that I had to do better or my hunting career would be a very short one indeed.

On this same hunting trip, Guenther and I were sitting on a ridge watching a black two-year-old grizzly digging at the base of a cliff. Suddenly a movement in the alders caught our attention and we watched as a big brown grizzly emerged. We knew that we wanted this bear so we immediately set off in its direction. After going only a short distance, we came upon a cliff that stretched clear down to the main valley floor and it appeared that we were beat. We noticed that it seemed to taper off a bit toward the top, though, so we climbed up for a look. Always the daredevil type, Guenther looked it over and said, "I think I can make it across here."

Then without further ado, he set off and had taken only about six steps when his feet slipped out from under him and he began sliding toward the precipice. Unable to assist him in any way, I stood staring in disbelief while he grabbed frantically at the rock in an effort to stop. Right at the very edge of the steep drop, a fault ran through the rock and Guenther got his fingers into it and managed to break his slide. After he worked his way back to safety, I looked for the bears again but they were gone. And though I couldn't remember it, I'm sure that I did a bit of hollering during the ordeal.

Back at camp, Guenther appeared in deep thought for a time and then offered, "I guess that was a pretty close call, wasn't it?" I assured him that he would never have a closer one, and that even an ex-boxer like himself would not be able to stand a 1000-foot drop into a rock-strewn stream.

Without a doubt my most memorable hunt was with Bill Benedict in 1963. Bill had arrived in the community several years earlier and each year he was barely able to wait for his holidays so that he could

Guenther Peemoeller climbing Baldy Mountain, 1957.

visit Vancouver. In 1961 he made his first trip into the mountains and was immediately hooked. From that time on, he could hardly wait for his holidays so that he could climb mountains and hunt with us.

So, just two years after his first visit to the high country, we were back again on a grizzly hunt. We packed into the mountains to one of our high cabins where we stopped for lunch and a short rest. After lunch we continued on through the subalpine for an evening hunt. We skirted a high ridge, and as we returned on the opposite side, we spotted a grizzly. Just as the shadows of the setting sun hit a pass on the adjacent mountain, this big grizzly emerged and with the ground-consuming pace of a large bear, made his way across the slope. We kept pace as best we could on our side of the valley, then noticed that he was heading right for a cliff. We discussed this and figured that the bear would probably come down when it reached the impassable cliff, in which case we would be in good position. As we stood staring in amazement, the bear reached the cliff and without the slightest hesitation, walked across and began digging for the bulbs of the glacier lily, or mountain potato as it is often called.

Bill inspects Hydrant Creek near Baldy Mountain, 1968.

Because of the steep cliffs that were on both sides of the bear, we figured our only chance of getting close enough for a shot lay in our skirting the ridge and coming at it from above. We didn't believe we had enough time to circle the ridge before dark, so we decided to have a little fun with this bear. I shot into the cliff near him at a distance of about half a mile, expecting to see him go tearing over the mountain in fright. Instead, the bear stood erect and stared down the mountain for a few minutes, then returned to his digging. This was surprise number two in the first twenty minutes.

Bill and I had another discussion, then decided that we would try skirting the mountain and hopefully get a shot at the bear before dark. So with the energy born of excitement, we almost flew over the ridge to stare down where we had last seen the bear about 30 minutes earlier. It was nowhere to be seen. Thinking that it may be hiding in the short fir trees at cliff's edge, we worked our way down until we came to the fresh diggings. Once there, we sat down and discussed the situation in whispered voices, and decided that the bear had moved down the mountain to get water in the stream far below. Bill moved across the mountain to the next cliff, and after giving him enough time to get in position, I started downhill, knowing he would be doing the same.

I had only taken a couple of steps when I heard a faint snap behind me and whirled to find the grizzly coming at me from behind. At a distance of 15 feet I raised my gun and fired, and I remember that I didn't even have to aim because his head appeared so large at such close range. At the shot, the bear lunged ahead and disappeared behind several stunted subalpine fir trees. I shouted to Bill, "Wounded grizzly!" Then I took a few steps forward and spotted the bear. He had his head on the ground but his hind end was still up. He was making strange noises and attempting to lift his head. I fired again and then watched an incredible sight. The bear started rolling and then bouncing, soon going hundreds of feet to each bounce, until it went over a cliff and disappeared from view.

Then Bill came running out of the trees, turning this way and that, and exclaiming, "Where is it? Where is it?"

I pointed down the mountain and then we went to the edge of the cliff and spotted the bear where it was lying in a dry creek bed 500 feet below us. I then told Bill about how the bear had bounced down the mountain like a rubber ball, appearing to have 16 legs as they seemed to be sticking out in all directions.

Then a strange awareness came upon me. I realized that I had just had my closest call from a grizzly bear, and yet I wasn't the least bit scared. Perhaps it was because everything happened so fast that I didn't have time to get frightened.

Bill and I worked our way around the cliffs and got down to the bear just as darkness came upon us. Then we removed the entrails and propped the chest cavity open so it would cool quicker and not cause the hair to slip. (If a bear is left too long before skinning, the inside hooked edge of the hair can release—rendering the trophy worthless.) By the time we finished it was dark, and we were caught on a mountain two miles from our cabin, without a flashlight, food, or available firewood. Being exhausted, and with our clothing drenched with sweat, we knew we could not survive a cold September night around timberline. With no other option, we headed down the mountain moving as slowly and carefully as possible. Once we were into the creek bottom, the moon came out and gave us just enough light to make our way along the stream, slipping and sliding as we went. After following the main creek for over one mile, we found the side creek that led to our cabin. At that point the moon deserted us. The excitement of the hunt had worn off by then, leaving us so utterly spent that we crawled the last distance on our hands and knees. Once we got up into the area of the cabin, we couldn't find it. A bit of luck came our way, though, when Bill put his hand on the stump of a tree that had been used to build the cabin. A few minutes later we stumbled in through the door.

No sooner had we entered the cabin than a tremendous hailstorm hit. So loud was the sound of the stones hitting the metal roof, that we could not make each other heard over the din. As I sat sipping coffee, I felt deeply grateful that the storm had not hit earlier.

After the hailstorm passed, we went over the events of the evening. Once again we realized that though the wind was in our favor, the bear had detected our presence before we topped the ridge. Obviously, the bear had picked up our sound through the ground.

As we lay totally exhausted on our bunks, we realized that we had not eaten since noon but we could not bring ourselves to eat a bite. That night as I tried to sleep, visions of mountains and grizzlies in living color danced through my mind, probably brought on by extreme fatigue.

Next morning Bill and I returned to the bear to find more flies than I thought existed in the entire country. After a futile attempt to drive them away, we skinned the bear and then examined the body. Only one bad bruise on an upper leg could be found, leading us to wonder if this bear might have survived his 500-foot fall had it not been for the bullets.

This old boar's teeth were almost all rotted away and there was no fat on its hind quarters. With only about a month to go until den time, it seems apparent that this bear would have died in its den; perhaps the most common cause of bear deaths, especially among black bears. Its poor physical condition may also have been a factor in its attack on me.

As I look back on that evening when I fired into the cliff and the bear didn't run away, I realize that it probably thought the shot was thunder and lightning—a common occurrence in the mountains.

Most notable to me was the fact that I never experienced any bear nightmares after that. It was as if I had slain the dragon.

The following September a friend named Virgil Brandner and I were back in this same area. We had an agreement when hunting that whoever spotted a boar first had the first shot at it. On our second morning out, we had just started glassing when I spotted an adult grizzly about half a mile away. We moved in carefully and got within what I guessed was a couple hundred yards. The bear started looking in our direction and appeared quite nervous, so I decided to try a shot. At the shot, the bear rolled up in a bundle and bounced down the mountainside out of our view. We moved to the spot where the bear had last been seen, but there was no sign of it. In fact, there didn't seem to be any blood—although finding drops of blood on the red colored leaves and vegetation of fall is a very difficult thing to do.

Unable to track the bear, we just started making big sweeps through the endless islands of fir trees, hoping to stumble on to it. After an hour of futile searching, we were coming back from a sweep along the mountain when I ran into some real tough going. As I had already given up on the bear, I moved up and followed Virgil through an opening in the trees. I was absolutely certain that he knew I was behind him, as I had made no effort to be quiet. About halfway through the row of trees, I coughed, and that's when I found out that he didn't know I was there. He made some strange sounds, something like, "Uba-uba-uba", and then brought his rifle around over his head.

Just as he was bringing it into line with me, I threw myself to the side and yelled, "Virgil, don't shoot! It's me!"

The look on his face plainly showed that he figured it was all over except for a bit of chewing. I then spent several minutes trying to convince him that I didn't scare him on purpose. These are the types of scares that are inevitable when dealing with grizzly bears.

As for what happened to the grizzly—we paced off the distance I had shot and found it was over 300 yards. I had tried for a neck shot and shot low, a mistake I never duplicated. The bear simply rolled down the mountain a short distance and then made its getaway. Two weeks later it was back in the same area—Just one of several grizzlies that escaped by rolling down a steep mountainside.

One particular scare that could have ended in a nightmarish situation occurred in 1964. Clarence took his two young sons, Dan and Larry, along with nephews Barry McKinley and Mark Proctor, into the mountains. They spent a few days enjoying the high country and were on their way home, walking through the subalpine, when they walked right into a grizzly with a yearling. As it was windy, the wind may have prevented the bears from hearing their approach. When the sow saw them, she charged, and in response Clarence fired a shot from his 30-06. The noise of the shot caused the bear to turn and run down the mountain. In the state of confusion that ensued, the yearling attempted to climb a tree. It managed to move a short distance with great difficulty, breaking limbs as it went. Then, unable to hang on, it came sliding back down and hit the ground with a big thump. It then turned and followed its mother down the mountain. Clarence gathered the boys together and headed for home, fully aware of what a bad position the boys would have been in if anything had happened to him.

It must be pointed out that this mother grizzly did not send the yearling up that tree. It went on its own. And I want to stress that this was the only time Clarence ever saw a grizzly try to climb a tree; something I never have seen.

Another scare that comes to mind happened when Clarence, Bill, Tommy Wilson and I were in the high country where we spent several days searching for boar grizzlies without having any luck. Finally Clarence stumbled on four bears feeding behind a mountain in very thick trees and alders. We discussed it at length and decided that the following morning Clarence and Tommy would go one way, while Bill and I went the other. This would improve our chances of the bears running into one of us when they tried to leave the area.

The next morning Bill and I left the cabin and headed around the mountain and as we did so, Clarence and Tommy were getting ready to leave. A few minutes later it started to rain. About half an hour after we left the cabin, we heard several shots in the distance and assumed that they had ran into a bear. Then we heard someone hollering with what we thought was a terror-filled voice. We realized that it was Tommy's voice and concluded that they had been attacked by a bear and that Tommy, who hadn't had much experience with grizzlies, was running away. We headed in the direction of the noise, running just as fast as we could until we were ready to drop. Then we shouted as loud as possible in an effort to determine their direction. Back came an answer, and at last we realized that they were still at the cabin. A short time later two spent hunters arrived back at the cabin to learn that the others had just changed their minds about going because of the rain. All the shouting and shooting had just been done by Tommy to get our attention. Well, they certainly got our attention all right; in fact, Bill and I had both endured enough excitement for one day, so the hunt was called off. Also I have to say that we never blamed Tommy; it just seems that when you are dealing with grizzlies you are always ready to expect the worst.

I doubt that there can be anything more frightening in the forests than to find a grizzly bearing down on you, but sometimes these charges are not what they seem. Only three times have I had grizzlies attack me when I was positive that they meant to do me in. Other times their charges were not aimed at me. One example occurred when Bill and I were exploring some mountains near the McGregor River. With darkness approaching, we were skirting a subalpine muskeg looking for a place to camp. Suddenly some movement off to the side drew my attention and I turned to find a mid-sized grizzly coming straight at us at breakneck speed. Instantly I fired my rifle, and just as I did so, I saw the bear glance back over its shoulder. As the bear turned and raced away, Bill and I discussed what had just happened and we both agreed that our sound had gone over the bear's head where it had been lying in a patch of trees. The noise had then bounced off the ridge right behind it and came back to the bear from the opposite direction: Bruin had only been trying to get away.

A similar situation occurred in this manner: Vic Litnosky and I were on a spring hunt when we decided to check the remains of a large bull moose that had been taken late the previous fall. As we neared the remains, we were making a great deal of noise on the remaining crusted snow. Then I heard Vic say something and glanced in his direction just in time to see him raise his rifle and fire at a grizzly that was charging right into him. The bear went down, then immediately regained its feet, at which point Vic and I both fired. That time the bear stayed down. As we skinned it out, we were convinced that this bear had been out to get us. Most definitely that's the way the story would have stayed were it not for the fact that Vic and I returned to the carcass the next day. As we neared the remains we heard a noise and then spotted a black bear with two cubs. We watched as they scurried up a large cedar tree and disappeared through a hole into the tree. A quick check of the many claw marks on the tree told us that this had been their winter den. It then became quite obvious to us that the grizzly had not been attacking us at all, but only trying to protect its prize from the black bears, which it knew were nearby. This grizzly had buried the remains and had made no attempt to eat. It was unable to accept meat at that point as it had just emerged from its den a short time earlier. This was the 15th of April—the earliest I ever found a bear on a carcass in the Interior.

It would not surprise me if many bear maulings result from similar situations: the bear has been bothered by another bear and doesn't realize what it is attacking. In the final analysis, though, it makes little difference—I mean you're just as dead one way as the other.

Perhaps the most unusual story I have ever heard about a grizzly bear was told to me by a man who worked for the territorial government in Yellowknife. It concerned a grizzly and wolf that traveled together in that area for several years. Many people had seen them together, and it was not considered a big deal. Faithfully each year they would return together and be seen by more and more people. I think it would be most interesting to know how that union came about.

There are so many unusual things that happen in the wilderness setting. One such is the following that caught my attention. It was carried in the *Prince George Citizen* on the 5th of December, 1922:

Quesnel Man Killed by Quills of Porcupine

"Quesnel, Dec. 5—Frank Pierreway, son of M. Pierreway of Prince George, died at the hospital here last night. He, with his wife and small child, had been living on a pre-emption a few miles out on the west side of the Fraser River for the past year. Eight days ago he became ill, but feeling better after a day or two, moved down to his brother's house near town. He became worse again and sent for Dr. G.R. Baker, who had him removed to the hospital, where on an operation being performed, it was discovered that his intestines had been pierced in several places by a porcupine quill. Mortification set in where the quill finally lodged and caused general peritonitis."

Something that was not uncommon many years ago was attacks on children by eagles. I have picked out a couple of articles because they show the great reluctance on the part of these birds to let go of their prizes. The first one is from the Prince George newspaper *The Leader*, dated 28th October, 1921:

Attacked By Eagle

"Vanderhoof, Oct. 25—When the five-year-old daughter of W. S. Gibbs was playing on the verandah of her home here, a large black eagle [bald eagle] swooped down and caught her in its talons. The child screamed and tried to run into the house, but was unable to pass through the screen door. Her cries attracted the mother's attention. She came out and tried to beat the bird off, but was unsuccessful. Matthew Semple happened to be near the house and hearing the screams hastened to the scene and picking up a stick, he beat the eagle to death.

A remarkable feature is that the bird did not pay any attention to its assailant, apparently being entirely taken up with its aim of getting the child away. The eagle measured over seven feet and was powerfully built.

The child's flesh was badly torn, but no serious results are expected and she is now getting over her extraordinary adventure."

This second report is from the *Prince George Citizen* of 4 July, 1946:

Youngster Battles Big Golden Eagle

"Eleven-year old Lorne Rugg fought a battle near here with a golden eagle and won. The large bird attacked the lad while he was herding cows and a well-aimed kick momentarily stunned it. He then picked up a large stick and killed it. The eagle had a wingspread of six feet, six inches. Eagles have caused damage to livestock in the area, attacking young calves and sheep."

So many times I have heard people say that wolves have never attacked a person. When I proved a reported fatality, one gentleman changed the subject to moose and then said that there has never been a case of a moose killing a person. The truth is that we hear of these things but quickly seem to forget them.

There was a fatal attack just a few years ago at the University of Alaska where a man was trampled to death by a moose right on campus.

Another moose incident was carried in the *Prince George Citizen* dated 23rd of September, 1937:

Indian Dies After Being Gored By Moose

"Gored by a supposedly dead bull moose, Portage Pius, 69-year old Yacoutchee Indian, died Monday morning in the Prince George Hospital. Pius shot a bull moose in the late evening of Monday, September 13. He left the animal 'til morning to dress. On coming back the next day he found the moose had not stirred, but when he reached over to cut its throat, the animal reared up and charged him, catching him on its horns and tossing him 10 feet in the air. One prong of the moose's horn entered Pius' abdomen just above the right groin and made a gaping wound, as well as puncturing several of his intestines.

The accident happened 15 miles back in the bush from Stuart Lake and the wounded man had to be packed out on a litter to the shores of the lake, from where he was brought 40 miles by canoe to Fort St. James. Dr. R. W. Stone, Vanderhoof, was called and rendered first aid and rushed Pius to the Prince George hospital by car on Friday, four days after the accident. An emergency operation was performed by Dr. E. J. Lyon of Prince George, but as peritonitis had already got good hold before Pius arrived at the hospital it proved impossible to save his life."

4

ALONG THE RAILROAD

THERE WERE SO MANY ANIMALS KILLED BY TRAINS BACK IN THE
early days. I feel there were two reasons for this, I feel: first, the
snows were so deep that it was almost impossible for the animals to
move. When they got onto the plowed right-of-way with its easy
going, they simply refused to get off and flounder in the deep snow
again. Secondly, there were so many more animals then compared to
now. Some winters, during extremely heavy snowfalls, the number of
moose that were killed by trains was almost past belief. In the spring
of 1966 or 1967—I'm not certain which—Clarence and I counted
148 carcasses in 24 miles of grade. Often there were four or five lying
side by side. I do not blame the railway in any way for this slaughter; they were simply trying to keep the trains moving.

As these numbers were unacceptable to the public, the railway did
a smart thing and made the train crews fill out a separate report for
each moose that was killed. Understandably the totals went right
down, although there were still plenty of carcasses along the railroad
grade each year.

Since it wasn't illegal to bait bears back then, we used this method
to our hunting advantage. It was around that time that we really
began to appreciate what a keen sense of smell grizzlies have. On one
occasion we dragged a beaver carcass behind a bike for three miles,
then hung it up in a tree. Next day we checked and found where a
grizzly had cut our trail and followed it for two miles right to the
tree. The beaver, of course, was all gone.

Similarly, I once dragged a beaver carcass right behind a moose
carcass that two men were camped on. They were sitting by the railroad track right above the moose, waiting for bears to come out,
which they never did: the evening downdrafts were taking their scent
right to the bears, which of course wouldn't come out. The next
night when the bears approached the moose, they cut the drag trail

and followed it right to the beaver that I had tied up in a tree. I was sitting across a gully from the beaver and watched as a blonde grizzly with two tiny cubs came out. In a matter of a minute she tore the beaver down and took it back into a thicket for what must have been an enjoyable meal.

In the springtime after a heavy winter's snowfall, the railroad grade was a feasting area for all the carrion eaters of the forest. In a six-or seven-hour walk along the grade, it was common to see half a dozen bears or more. Sometimes we would see eagles so bloated from gorging themselves that they could barely become airborne. One of the reasons I enjoyed hunting the railroad track was because of the unusual things I saw there. Many times I watched lynx feeding on moose carcasses, and this was at times comical to witness. They would take a bite and then shake their heads, sometimes spitting out the mouthful they had taken in apparent disgust. Then they would move around to a different spot and try again, often with similar results. There seemed to be no doubt about it, they preferred fresh meat.

Greg Saugstead holding a Golden Eagle that gorged itself on a moose carcass until it was unable to fly. It was kept in a shed for several days until it was able to get airborne.

As well as the many train-killed moose carcasses there were to feed on, there were also endless stretches of fresh green grass to devour, and black bears could be seen all hours of the day feeding like so many cattle. At times it would seem that there were no bears around, as the carcasses would remain untouched. Then, when the leaves opened on the deciduous trees, the bears would appear in force.

Something I never did comprehend is why grizzlies return repeatedly to the same carcass when there are three others lying nearby. One would think that they would eat the best parts of one, and then move to another. Who knows why they stick to just one?

When I spent lengthy periods in the forests, my sense of smell would became very acute. This would be apparent when a whiff of false Solomon's seal would waft into my nostrils; one of many pleasant smells that pervade the forest in summer.

Another example of just how sensitive a person's nose can become when they live away from polluted cities was expressed quite well by an elderly trapper and guide when I asked him if he ever went to town to try to get himself a honey. He thought it over for a minute and then offered, "Nope! Some of that pecker-bait those women wear is so strong it burns the nose of an old bush-rat like me."

I had to agree that some of it was pretty strong all right, but that I referred to it as perfume.

Grizzly eating grass along the railroad.

Our sense of smell can be an asset in the woods, in that we can smell bears a great distance away. I proved this many times to many people, but perhaps the most memorable time happened when Clarence and I were moose hunting one fall. After a few hours in the woods, we met back at his jeep for lunch, and as we were eating, I said, "I smell bear."

"What kind of bear?" he asked.

"A grizzly bear," I added.

This caused Clarence to burst out laughing, which puzzled me because we had both smelled bears before without finding it funny.

Finally Clarence let me in on the joke: we had taken a fat grizzly bear about one week earlier and Olga had rendered down the fat. That fat had been used to make cookies, which Clarence was in the process of eating when I smelled bear.

Something else we noticed along the grade was that grizzlies have sometimes, of necessity, learned to accept the scent of man—when it suits them. For instance, when we are in the high mountains these bears will not tolerate our scent. Almost without exception when they get a whiff of us or scent our tracks where we have walked, they will leave the area, often for up to a week. Yet along the railway tracks in spring these same bears would come out and feed on an easy pickings carcass that we had visited only hours before. They seemed to accept that this was the price of doing business, as it were. I also want to point out that I seldom had grizzlies roar at me when they picked up my scent down on the flats; only up in the mountains. I really believe that grizzlies are far smarter than they get credit for.

I find it really strange that grizzlies and black bears will often eat on the same carcass at different times and I believe this happens because grizzlies don't claim sole possession of carcasses along the grade. Somehow they instinctively must believe that these carcasses belong to a large noisy animal that comes by occasionally—namely, a train. Why else did they never bury one carcass in all the hundreds that I visited throughout the years? Although they dragged them away from the grade, they never did what they are so famous for—burying the carcasses. They must feel that they are lucky just to be able to feed on them now and then.

I want to point out that I'm not saying a grizzly won't bury a carcass along the grade. I'm only saying that I never found one. If I said they didn't for sure, then a big grizzly would probably run down from the mountain and deliberately bury one just to make a liar out of me.

I also believe that because these grizzlies never really claimed these carcasses along the grade, they were less aggressive at those kill locations. If we had continually homed in on carcasses in the wild, the way we did along the grade, then we would have been charged many times, and there is a good chance that some of us would have been killed. It also seems apparent that these grizzlies were less aggressive because they were continually being hunted at that time.

It seems to me that grizzlies only bury carcasses when they intend to leave the area for a time. Only once do I remember finding a grizzly on a buried carcass in the forest. Not once did I hear one running away at my approach. I think it's because they leave the area as soon as they finish burying the carcasses, perhaps only to get water or to eat something other than meat. I admit it is possible that a per-

My sisters Josie and Margaret at the mouth of an alpine cave.

son could arrive at the carcass after the bear had returned, but that only happened to me once, and this bear was not eating; just protecting the remains from other bears. Of the grizzlies that did bury carcasses away from the grade, I repeat that many never came back to these buried carcasses, and I've often wondered why.

Of all the sounds that bears make, the one that bothers me the most is when they snap their jaws together. But there are other things they do that are quite bothersome too. I'm thinking of the time that Vic Litnosky and I went to check a moose carcass that a grizzly was feeding on. The bear must have been close by because we could tell by the colour of the meat that it had just been fed upon. Unable to detect any sign of the bear, we left and walked about ten minutes downwind. It was a nice sunny afternoon, so we stretched out on a grassy knoll and rested, as we were tired after walking for many miles along the grade. About an hour later, the grizzly let out a tremendous cough and slapped the ground a wicked blow uncomfortably close to us. Then it was all hands on deck: with our hearts pounding from excitement, we walked toward the sounds with rifles ready, but we neither saw nor heard a thing.

This was just one of several times that bears showed us we were clumsy oafs in the forests compared to them. It also clearly shows how easy it is for bears to maul or kill people if they so desire. I was amazed how that bear found us so quietly and exactly when we were quietly resting downwind of it. The message? He was telling us to get lost because this was his carcass. I'm also quite sure that this was an old veteran that we had hunted unsuccessfully for years in that area. I'm prepared to bet that he died a natural death.

Some people who spend many years in the forest become very observant: they seem to notice things that most of us tend to miss. One such individual was a man named Abe Quinn who was employed by the local logging company in Penny. On a December morning I was on my way to hunt moose when I met Abe who walked along with me. About a foot of snow lay on the ground as we made our way along the logging road. When we got to a point near where two moose had been taken a week earlier, we saw where fresh black bear tracks had moved along the road toward the moose remains. Before we took another ten steps, Abe said, "If you want that bear it will be under that big pile of logs."

Though we could not see the moose remains from where we were and the pile he referred to was still distant, I thought he was joking, so I asked, "What makes you think that?"

"Well," he answered, "it wouldn't be out in the snow unless it was sick, and because it's sick, it can't go far. It'll be under that pile."

As we got close, we could see that the bear had approached the moose remains but had made no attempt to eat. Instead, its tracks could be seen going to the pile. We followed and looked under the pile of logs. There was the bear, and it was just skin and bone. Somehow while running through the woods it had driven the spike end of a dry downtree into its chest and punctured its stomach. The poor beast was terribly injured and starving to death, so we ended its suffering. I marveled at the speed with which Abe had put it all together.

I BELIEVE IT WAS IN 1959 THAT BILL BENEDICT WAS FIGHTING A losing battle with a grizzly. He would go to the carcass by riverboat, and then wait. But the bear stubbornly wouldn't come out to feed. We discussed the situation and wondered if the bear was smart enough to link Bill's arrivals and departures with the sound of his outboard motor. That evening we went to the carcass where Bill took cover, then Clarence and I walked the quarter-mile back to the boat making a considerable amount of noise. At the boat, we fired up the motor and left. Sure enough, a few minutes later Bill had his grizzly.

One of the greatest thrills I've ever had in the woods happened on a spring hunt along the railroad with Clarence. He was at least a mile from me when I found where a grizzly had dragged a moose away from the grade. It was a dead quiet evening as I followed the drag trail ever so slowly, not knowing where the carcass was. It was thick swamp spruce and willows that I was going through, and it was tough going—especially so when I was trying to watch in four directions, look for the carcass, and avoid stepping on fallen limbs or other debris that would give my position away. I had just got to where I could see the carcass, when a grouse exploded out of the willows right beside my feet and went flying away. I stood frozen in shock and could plainly hear and feel my heart beating right up in the back of my throat. Truthfully, I felt that it was all over except for a few slaps and a little chewing.

Did I sit and wait for the bear? Not a chance. I went back out to the grade for a much-needed rest. I mean a person only needs so much excitement in one day. Sometimes after a bad scare, I would stay home for a few days. Then, missing the excitement, I would find myself back after the bears again.

By the Skin of our Teeth

ASIDE FROM THE WONDERFUL SCENTS OF NEW GROWTH IN THE forests, spring was also the time when the forests were alive with end-less birdsong. As well, thousands of frogs would add their calls to the din. At times they made so much noise just at dusk that it was diffi-cult to hear the other creatures of the forest. Then just before dark, it seemed as if someone had thrown a switch and there was sudden silence. If no wind was blowing then the silence could really be spooky. Sometimes we would hear noises in the woods and realize that it was the sound of splintering, cracking bones as a bear tore a carcass apart. If I was alone at such times, it was amazing how I could think of a whole lot of things that needed doing at home.

I doubt that there can be a bigger thrill on this earth than to go sneaking in on a carcass that a grizzly is feeding on in thick brush. When it hears or scents you, then what happens can best be described as an explosion. There is a mighty blast that sounds like air escaping under great pressure, the breaking of brush, and the pounding of big feet as it takes off or heads into cover. After an evening of that kind of excitement, I didn't feel bored for several days.

Quite often Clarence and I would leave home about noon and walk seven or eight miles along the railway grade; then as darkness fell we would start the long trek back. Sometimes we would have to walk miles in the dark, passing right beside moose remains. This would provide us with many heart-stopping thrills when bears would let out coughs right beside us and then go crashing into the forest. Truly, it was the kind of excitement that gets in your blood and keeps calling you back year after year. I don't know how Olga and Ann put up with us—not knowing if we were dead or alive. I'm sure they had several anxious years.

I also recall another time that I got a little too closely involved with a grizzly. About a half-hour after the encounter I was sitting on the bank of a stream trying to eat a sandwich, but I wasn't having any luck. After chewing a mouthful for several minutes, I was forced to spit it out. I was unable to find a drop of saliva anywhere. Surely it is not an exaggeration to say that I had just had the supreme hell (and most of my spit) scared out of me.

Many times I came in close contact with black bears and cubs along the grade. Several times the mothers would fake a charge at me. In every case they stopped and veered aside. I'm not saying they don't attack people; I know they do. I'm only saying what my experiences were. I must add though, the fact that black bears—unlike grizzlies —frequently send their cubs up trees, also relieves the pressure somewhat.

There were so many adventures we experienced throughout those years, such as hiding behind a tree on the downwind side of a carcass waiting for a bear to come in to feed. Even if they had a trail, we were never sure they would use it. This meant that we didn't know which direction they would come from. Many times I would be sitting there, fighting 10,000 mosquitoes, and not see or hear a thing. Then I would glance over at the carcass and find a bear feeding on it. This never failed to make my heart skip a few beats, but that wasn't a problem—because it more than caught up later.

It seems so easy for people to underestimate the power and tenacity of bears. Many of us have no comprehension of just how vicious and determined a bear can be when it decides on a course of action. A scary example was told to me by Dome Creek resident Maurice Schultz, who was involved in the story in 1972. This frightening adventure began on a summer's day at the Highways' Maintenance camp near Slim Creek on Highway 16. The foreman, a man named

Ray Arnett, was with his wife Dorothy in their mobile home. She was busy baking for an upcoming wedding when they heard a noise at their back door. They looked out to find a small black bear with two cubs tearing the siding off their back porch. Suddenly their big dog, a St. Bernard, attacked the bear and received a slap that sent it flying head over heels. Again it went at the bear, but another slap sent it scurrying for cover.

In a matter of minutes, the mother bear had torn through the aluminum siding and the sheeting, and was inside the porch. Here she got down to serious business, by pulling the studs out with her teeth. Next, she went to work on a couch which she tore to shreds in a matter of minutes. Inside the home, Ray and Dorothy huddled in terror, afraid to chance going out for fear of being attacked. Ray, just like too many others, was living in a rural area without the protection of a gun. But now, with his family at risk, that message was driven home with emphasis.

At one point the bear grabbed the window and tore it part way out of the sill; but instead of entering, for some strange reason she wandered back into the woods. As soon as Ray realized the bear was out of sight, he took his family to the home of Maurice Schultz where he asked for help. Maurice got a neighbor, Heller Hreczka, to assist him and they returned to the trailer to find the bear had left. In her wake was a scene of devastation that made the home look like it had been hit by a large truck. As the bear appeared to have left the area, the men returned home. But "Bruina" wasn't finished yet. That evening she returned to the home where she was met with a hail of gunfire from Ed Hale, a neighbour.

Another story of people being terrorized by a black bear went as follows. In early May, 1975, three teenage girls left their native Alberta and moved to Penny. In search of adventure, they had decided to hire on planting trees for the Forest Service. As Clarence's son Dan had moved and left his log house vacant, these young ladies moved in—into what was to be more of an adventure than they had ever dreamed of. Trudy Bouvette, Beverly Burns and Corrine Olson were about to spend a night of terror beyond anything they could possibly have imagined.

Just a few evenings after they moved in, as they were preparing for bed, they heard a noise at the window. They shone a flashlight out and there before their eyes was a large black bear. At once the girls panicked and started screaming. Then they started banging pots and pans in an effort to drive the bear away. It left the window area, but only to go around to the door where it continued to make its presence known. By this time, the girls were certain they were going to die. Beverly and Corrine had crawled under a bed, and were trying to pull Trudy under as well. They didn't manage it, though, because Trudy was standing up. In their effort to drag her under the bed, they only succeeded in scratching her shins to a considerable degree.

Between hiding under the bed and banging things together, the girls found Dan's rifle which they loaded and held ready in case the bear came into the house.

All through the night these girls cried, screamed, and banged pots and pans together, as the bear moved around looking for a way in. Half a mile away, Clarence and Olga found themselves unable to sleep because of some noise in the distance. As well, their dog fussed and barked all night.

Finally, as daybreak arrived, the bear left and the girls got up enough nerve to take the gun and make their way to Clarence's house where they arrived in a state of near hysteria.

The following evening, Clarence and I went to Dan's house where we waited for the bear to come back. Just before dark I heard it cough behind some trees as it picked up our scent and departed. Why the bear was afraid of our scent, yet put up with all the noise the previous evening, I am unable to explain. Perhaps it was braver in the dark.

The next evening I tried a different idea and went well downwind of Dan's house where I hid in wait. About an hour before dark, I saw a big black bear cross the railway tracks and head up the hill toward Dan's house. When I got to the house, I saw that a window was broken, probably by the bear gaining entry after we had left the previous evening. I listened and heard the bear moving about inside. I hollered a few times, and then shot it in full flight as it came bounding out the window. A few minutes later, Clarence arrived with the girls, and they were very relieved to know the bear was dead. We skinned it out and gave the hide to one of them as a lifetime reminder of her night of terror. To another girl, we gave the penis bone on which we inscribed: GBBP. I've often wondered if she ever figured out what those letters stood for.

Even though they knew the bear was dead, these girls gave up the idea of planting trees and living in the woods. A short time later two of them moved back to Alberta.

It sure is amazing how starvation can change an individual black bear's attitude: they can quickly change from timid to aggressive. In July, 1975, Clarence and his son Larry were fishing Red Mountain Creek when they got involved with such a bear. With them was Lloyd Vandermark, an employee of the forest service with many years' experience in the forest. After fishing for a few hours, they stopped and built a campfire, then began frying their catch. A short time later they noticed what they figured was a three-year-old black bear approaching. They hollered, but the bear paid no attention: it just kept coming. Then the men started pelting it with rocks, including big rocks that really hit hard. To their amazement the bear just kept coming. Then they threw the fish into the stream and headed back along the path they had came on. While Clarence and Larry went to get the jeep which was a short distance away, Lloyd sat down to wait for them. At this point they believed the bear was still back at the stream a quarter-mile away. Only a few minutes had passed when Lloyd heard a snap in the woods and turned to find the bear walking right up to him. It was snapping its teeth and showing it meant business. Lloyd looked for a weapon of some kind and had to settle for a big limb that was part of a rotten log. He swung it with all his strength and hit the bear across its back. The limb broke apart, but it was enough to drive the bear back into the woods. A few minutes later the jeep arrived and they left the area.

Lloyd makes no bones about the fact that this bear really had him worried. He agrees that this was a predatory attack, as getting rid of the fish did not deter the bear at all. This bear was in very poor condition, with no apparent fat on its body.

Just a few years later there was another episode with a black bear at Penny. An elderly lady named Anna Mellos was resting in her home when she heard a loud bang. She rushed out into her kitchen to find she had a visitor. It was a bear, and the loud bang had been her door coming down. Several times she screamed as loudly as possible, and this caused the bear to run away. At once Anna got on her bicycle and pedaled to Clarence's house for assistance. A short time later Clarence was busy repairing her door when they saw the bear returning. It walked right to him without hesitation; he shot it at point-blank range.

Anna had another problem bear a short time later. This bear would come around at night and slap the side of the house, almost driving the poor woman frantic. It took a while, but Clarence finally managed to bag that one too.

Hunters' Tales

HOW WELL I REMEMBER THE SEPTEMBER MORNING IN THE EARLY '60s, when Clarence, Bill Benedict, and I were on a grizzly hunt. Bill rose first and went outside to glass for bear. A few minutes later he opened the cabin door and whispered, "Hey fellas, I see my grizzly!"

Instantly Clarence and I were out of bed, into our clothes and out the door, where we beheld a truly captivating sight. A fresh snow had fallen overnight, painting the valley and mountains a brilliant white. On an adjacent ridge about 700 yards away as the crow flies, a boar grizzly was digging up roots and the bulbs of the glacier lily. As we watched, he kept turning over sod, and the fresh black earth would go tumbling down over the new snow. He seemed to epitomize all the strength, freedom, and wildness inherent in nature; a gallant warrior whose abundant muscles rippled through his new coat. For several minutes we stood transfixed, and then Bill remembered that he wanted this magnificent beast.

Bill and Clarence decided they would circle the ridge and then try to come at the bear from above. I was to stay put and motion to them with hand signals which way the bear had moved when they finally topped the ridge. As they disappeared into the trees, I again turned my attention to the bear, who was digging away with such vigor that he had an area the size of a large room excavated. For about another 20 minutes he dug away, then he lifted his head to scent the early morning air. A minute later he continued digging. Suddenly the bear lifted his head again smartly and looked in the direction the men had gone. For about 30 seconds he stood motionless, then returned to his digging. About two minutes later he swung his head to look in their direction again, then whirled and headed down the mountain at a full gallop for the forest far below. At one point he jumped out over a ledge covered with small subalpine fir trees, and when he came down the angle of the slope had changed to near vertical. Rather than say he lost his footing, it would be more accurate to say that he just didn't find any. At any rate, he turned over onto his back in mid-air and slid down the steep portion about 50 feet. When he hit the bottom, he rolled back onto his feet and kept galloping without missing a beat.

What a sight! Anyone who thinks bears can't run fast downhill should have got an eyeball full of that. I would say that within 30 seconds that bear was out of sight in the timber nearly 1000 feet below the spot where we first noticed him.

About 20 minutes later Clarence and Bill appeared on the ridge top and I waved them back. We then spent a great deal of time trying to figure out how the bear sensed their presence. This incident happened before we had realized that bears detect distant motion through ground vibration, so at that time the mystery remained unsolved.

It was back in the '50s, that we got involved in some real harebrained adventures, which started when Bill and I were unable to nail a huge black bear that was feeding on the local garbage dump. This wily old bear was what we called an 'educated bear', meaning that it had been wounded at one time and would not feed during the day. One day I saw this bear from an aircraft and realized that it was indeed a beauty.

Back at the lab, Bill and I figured out how to get this giant. We secured flashlights on top of our rifles and lined them up so the bullet would hit right in the center of the spot. That evening we intended to go to the dump about midnight, wait until we heard a noise, and then start a war. Something came up, though, and our plans were put off.

The next morning, a fellow hunter, Herb Metzmeier, stopped by and told us how he had spent a couple hours at the dump the previous evening, just sitting in the dark and listening to the bears. Bill and I looked at each other and felt a bit sick—the noise that may have caused us to open fire could have been Herb. The flashlights immediately came off the rifles for good.

We didn't learn much from this, though, because a year later we did something even more foolish. This fiasco started when we were unable to get a smart grizzly that was feeding on a moose, because it only fed at night. Clarence and Bill went to the carcass, then followed the bear's trail a short distance and put up a set gun with the string across the bear's trail: this bear was going to commit suicide. That

Grizzly with salmon.

night we fussed and worried that someone might happen to walk into it. Even though no one else ever seemed to hunt in that area, the possibility was still there. The next morning Clarence and Bill went to take it down. As soon as they arrived, Clarence made a big circle behind the bait in an effort to surprise the bear. As he came back out, he followed the bear's path and walked right into the string. Fortunately, Bill had already removed the cartridge.

Now if the reader suspects that these antics were a bit crazy, you won't get any argument from me. But wait—we weren't finished yet.

Determined to get the bear, we got another chance a few evenings later with the help of a full moon. Clarence, Bill, Herb, and I set out on what was to be our first and last grizzly hunt by moonlight. We headed out along an old logging road, with Bill and me in the lead. As we approached the moose carcass, we saw something moving. Just as we were getting set to shoot, we caught the reflection of moonlight off Clarence's aluminum hard hat. He and Herb had taken a shortcut through the woods and had arrived at the moose carcass ahead of us.

Finally the message sank in and we vowed that there would be no more dumb deals, but despite the best of intentions, things still went wrong. Another dangerous situation developed when Bill went to hunt on a horse carcass, where he hid behind a tree and waited for a few hours for a bear to come out. Just as the shadows deepened, he noticed something coming out from under a large pile of brush right beside the horse. He took aim and was about to shoot when ranger Fred Baker suddenly stood erect right beside the carcass. Dressed in dark clothing, Fred was unaware that anyone else was around. Bill walked up to him and let him know in no uncertain terms that he had just came within a whisper of meeting his maker.

Sometimes we got ourselves into binds that we should have seen coming, and then couldn't believe it when it happened. I'm thinking of the time that Bill Benedict and I went up the Fraser River for an evening's hunt. Bill dropped me off in a spot where the river and railway tracks came close together and then he carried on up the river. I stopped in this spot because a grizzly had dragged a train-killed moose down the bank and was feeding on it. I knew that toward evening the downdrafts would come off the snow-clad mountains and take my scent away from the bear out into the river. As I moved in behind a downtree for cover, with the river at my back, I felt sorry for the bear because I knew this would be like taking candy from a baby. Well, the evening wore on and the bear didn't show up, and as darkness approached I felt a little bit sick. Suddenly the bear was holding four aces and I just had a pair of deuces. I still had one hope, though, and that was that Bill would return with the boat. But things went from bad to worse when darkness fell and Bill didn't arrive. Without a flashlight, I felt as helpless as a baby. The only way out was right beside the carcass and I wasn't dumb enough to try that, because the bear could have been in the willows right beside it. Then I heard bones breaking and knew that the bear was on the carcass only about 50 feet from me. Never have I cursed myself out like I did that night; I just couldn't believe that I didn't see this coming. The next hour was pure torture with countless mosquitoes buzzing all around me. I didn't dare slap at them, as I sure didn't want the bear to think that I was another bear trying to take its food. Finally I heard Bill's outboard motor running and I don't think I have ever heard a sweeter sound in my life.

About 15 minutes later he arrived, using a flashlight to find his way. Then, after he had picked me up, he explained that he too had been arguing with a bear.

I wasn't the only one to get sucked in this way. A similar situation developed with Bill when he spent several evenings waiting on moose remains for a grizzly. In desperation, Bill went to the carcass early in the afternoon and climbed a tree, then remained silent as the hours went by. As the shadows started deepening he heard the bear coming through the thickets, and then a strange thing happened. The bear stayed in the thicket and wouldn't come out. With darkness approaching and the temperature rapidly dropping, Bill knew that he could not stay in the tree all night. Finally he did the only thing he could think of and hollered in a loud voice, "Okay bear! You win! I'm coming down now!" Then making as much noise as possible, he came down the tree and took the painful walk back out to the river, with every shadow resembling the bear.

Another time, two buddies of mine—Ed Priebe and Frank Davies—were having a grizzly adventure not far from where I was hunting. Ed had climbed up a rock face and had met a grizzly bear—head on. Ed escaped without any trouble but after he returned home he drew a sketch in which he portrayed Frank as a super hero who had risked his life in order to save Ed. The sketch is so well done I had to include it here.

One trick we frequently used was to move close to a bait and then walk away, whistling as we went. After walking perhaps half a mile, we would sneak back and often catch a bear busy feeding. Boy! Do they get upset when you trick them.

Over the years, Frank Davies' account of the Green Mountain Grizzly Encounter became embellished beyond all recognition.

Call of the mountains, age 9.

Quite often on these hunts the bears ended up with the last laugh, such as the nice day in May when Clarence and I made a big lunch and left home about noon. We walked about seven miles along the railroad grade and then separated. About an hour later I heard a shot in the direction he had gone, so I dropped the pack with our lunch in it and hurried to meet him: we had a deal that when one of us fired a shot, the other would come to his aid. About a mile further along the grade I met him and he informed me that he had missed a shot at a bear. Then we headed back to get the lunch as we were both starved by this time.

When we arrived at the spot where I had left the pack, it was gone. A short search turned up the empty pack, but all the lunch was missing. In its place was a fresh pile of black bear dung, just as if the bear had said, "Here—this is for you guys!"

About midnight two starving, sad-faced, tired hunters arrived home carrying a deep grudge against bears. And one of them was feeling pretty stupid because he hadn't had enough sense to at least put the pack up in a tree.

When we used to hunt along the railroad, one of our favorite tricks was to use passing trains to our advantage. If there was thick brush on both sides of the grade, the bears would hear us as we tried to sneak up on them. If we walked on the grade and they were close by they would see us coming and depart. We solved that problem by waiting a short distance away until a train came by. Then we would run like blazes beside the train and flop into cover on the downwind side of the carcass. The bears would only move back into the trees a short distance, then return as soon as the train went by. Sometimes we would lie and watch them feed for hours.

One incident that took place along the railroad started when a hunter was with us to try to get himself a bear. As we were walking along the grade about five miles from home, we heard an animal running in the forest nearby. This fellow got a glimpse of it and fired a shot, then we heard it gallop away through the forest. I mentioned to the guy beside me that it sounded like a horse running, but he disagreed. The next day, word got out that a logger's horse had been hit by a train. The horse was in bad shape, so it was taken a mile into the woods and disposed of. The railway was more than fair about it, and the owner was paid for the value of the horse. This is the way things would have stayed, except that I walked out to check the horse carcass several days later, to see if any bears were feeding on it. The horse had bloated up during this time, and this allowed me to notice a bullet entrance hole right near its anus. As I headed back toward home, it struck me that this was probably the only horse in history that had ever been killed by a sharp-shooting train.

Some people think they are cut out for grizzly hunting, but only when they come face to face with a bear do they really know for certain. I'm thinking of a friend named Jim Rahotsky, who asked to come with me on a hunt. I agreed and he brought along a .338 magnum—a real bear breaker. I left him sitting on the edge of the grade, above and just downwind of a carcass that a grizzly had visited a few times. Then I carried on along the tracks for a few miles. A couple hours later when I was returning, I met him over a mile distant from the spot where I had left him. As I walked up to him he said shakily, "It came!"

When questioned he continued, "I was sitting on the bank watching when this big grizzly walked out to the moose. It grabbed the moose with its teeth and just dragged it away into the trees."

I didn't bother asking why he didn't shoot, because the look on his face made it quite clear—he felt he was outgunned. Jim was not the only person that got close to a grizzly and experienced a quick change of heart. In fact, he was just one of many.

Some of the adventures we had along the grade were very exciting, such as the evening Clarence and I were returning home just as it was getting dark. We thought we knew where all the carcasses were, but somehow we missed one in a depression right beside the grade. As we walked along with our rifles slung over our shoulders, a grizzly stood up less than 15 feet from us. We both whirled and fired at the same instant, and that is one of the few times that I saw a grizzly drop without even a wiggle. Both bullets had hit it in the neck and severed its spine.

Just how tough these grizzlies can be, was shown the evening I shot a grizzly and it ran away into the forest. Clarence and Bill, who were hunting just a short distance away, joined me in the pursuit and we found it a few minutes later. This bear's heart had been blown to bits, yet it had run 200 feet further before collapsing.

Things didn't always go our way, though, as sometimes the bears made fools of us. I'm thinking of the evening we were heading back toward home, checking out carcasses as we went. Clarence had moved some distance ahead of me and when I caught up with him, I noticed he was hiding behind a couple of small spruce trees. He was waiting for a grizzly to come out on a moose carcass it had adopted. Not wanting to spoil his hunt, I went to sit down on the rail a short distance from him to wait until the bear came out or darkness forced us to give up. Just as I moved to sit down, I spotted a grizzly just above and about 30 feet behind Clarence. It had its front feet up on a downtree and was studying him with great interest. No sooner had I noticed the bear than it caught my movement and in two strides disappeared into the willow thickets. I moved up to Clarence and whispered, "Can you tell me something? Who is the hunter, and who is the hunted around here?"

"What do you mean?" he asked.

I then explained to him about the bear and showed him where it had been standing right behind him. As Clarence looked around, his eyes appeared somewhat larger than usual. A moment later we heard the bear moving away through the willows.

Other Mountain Tales

There is a call from the mountains that pulls at those who have spent a great deal of time there. Just as the wild geese head north in spring and the salmon head for their spawning beds, so do the mountains call back those that have known them. There is a bond—an invisible cord that forever ties them together.

Glorious, immense, and mysterious they stand, amid unparalleled beauty and grandeur, locked in a kind of timeless silence that touches the depths of our souls.

from Jack Boudreau's diary

HAVING BEEN BROUGHT UP IN A SMALL ISOLATED COMMUNITY WHERE we had to make our own entertainment, I guess it was only natural that my brothers and I took an avid interest in fishing, camping, and hunting. The first years that we traveled the mountains, we just camped wherever night found us. Usually we only had a tarp for cover and a couple wool blankets that the wind seemed to blow through. This meant that we had to keep a campfire burning all night for warmth. When the wind would blow the smoke right at us, it would be only a matter of time before we were forced out of the shelter to the upwind side of the campfire. After a few days of carrying heavy packs around the mountains with little or no sleep, we would return home utterly exhausted.

Some of my sweetest memories of those years were the sounds of the steam locomotive whistles as they echoed and re-echoed throughout the mountains. It was a lonely, haunting call that was special to me beyond words.

Without a doubt though, the most memorable sound of all was the combined howls of a large wolf pack. If I was alone in the

My sister June Vandeemark near timberline, 1968.

forest when they were howling, armed or unarmed, I always felt shivers run up and down my spine. Their howls seemed to represent more than anything else in nature what is really meant by the word wilderness.

As well as the many sounds one hears in the mountains, there is so much to see and enjoy, especially if one takes the time to stop and do so. Unfortunately too many people do what we used to do: they suffer from the nomad's disease—'wanderitis'. This means that they are continually on the move, spreading their scent and sound far and wide, and then wondering why they seldom see any game. Obviously, they cause more animals to run and hide than they ever see. There is so much more to be seen and enjoyed high in the mountains when a person can rise above the ego that pushes them to be the first person to arrive at the top of the next peak. When we can sit in silence, taking advantage of the prevailing winds, updrafts and downdrafts, a whole new world opens before us. Only then can we begin to understand what it means to become one with nature. In the high open country around timberline it is possible to watch animals for hours and even days on end without scaring them away.

Rhoda Boudreau challenges any takers to an alpine snowball fight, 1970.

For those with the patience to sit still and remain silent, the rewards can be countless. There are endless sights to see and memories that never die. To me they are the real "gold in them thar hills".

The beauty of glassing game in the high country is that we can observe and draw conclusions on things that would be impossible in the thick timber and brush found at lower elevations. Moose, for instance; I wonder how many people have watched a bull moose follow a cow moose for an hour and have had them in full view the whole time. Clarence, Olga, Virgil Brandner and I were able to do so. This was in late September and the bull was in rut and grunting continually. The cow, which still had her calf with her, was not in the mood and was trying to make its escape. Though the cow and calf were always out of sight of the bull, he followed them across the mountain. Every patch of subalpine timber that they went through, the bull took the exact path between the same trees that they did. There was no snow on the ground to leave tracks for him to follow—and he didn't need them.

Again, regarding moose, I would like to deal with something we have been programmed to believe—the idea that moose go galloping blindly through the forest when a wildfire threatens. This is not always true. A case in point occurred during the Pink Fire in 1985. (This was a huge fire, a forerunner to the Bowron clear-cut that gained infamy as being so large that astronauts could see it from space with the unaided eye.) During the peak of the fire, I was patrolling the fire with another forest officer—Jeremy Campbell. Suddenly we came upon a bull moose in the endless sea of fire and smoke. It was standing in the water, near the shore of a small lake, feeding contentedly on some willows. Not more than 30 feet from it, flames were running up the full length of a standing spruce tree. I admit I was surprised at how unconcerned the moose was.

Another thing about moose—I've never seen a cow moose with more that two calves. Yet I have had people tell me that they have seen cow moose with three newborn calves. But if you ask if they've seen cow moose with three big calves, they admit that they haven't. An old woodsman told me that mama knows she cannot adequately feed three calves, and so she starts walking and continues until the weakest calf is left behind. I do not profess to know whether this is true or not. There is another thing this same observant woodsman once told me. If you jump a moose in its bed, scaring it off before you know its gender, then check the bed. If it is a cow, it will urinate in its bed before leaving. I have personally checked this on a few occasions and found it to be true.

We once had a baby calf moose wander into our yard at Penny. During the three days that we had the calf moose, we fell in love with it. My son Kelly, who was about six years old at that time, spent a great deal of time with it. The calf adopted our garden tractor as its mother, and would suck on the handles for a while and then lie down beneath it.

I have never found a sweeter and more trusting pet than a baby moose. Because of their trust they are very vulnerable, and we found we had to lock it up in a shed to protect it from town dogs. We also had a billy-goat at the time, and I wondered if they would take a shine to each other. I took the goat into the shed to meet the moose calf, and held it by a rope so it couldn't injure the calf. They touched noses and appeared to be getting along quite well, when suddenly the goat lowered its head to attack. Quick as a wink, the moose played a rat-tat-tat on the goat's head with its front feet. Then I took the goat out of the shed. The speed of that moose's front feet amazed me, and the

The Pink Fire runs at midnight, July 31, 1985.

goat seemed impressed too. On the third day this calf was picked up by the conservation officer, George Vincent, of Prince George.

Moose were always in abundance during my early years, and some places were literally crawling with them. Before logging hit the area, the Torpy River was absolute heaven for them. It was a common sight to see several of them standing along the edge of the stream at any given time. While we were logging in the valley in 1963, a lot of huge fir trees were taken off a ridge adopted by the big bulls. Some of these big fellows did not take kindly to people coming into their domain and would show it by putting the run on them.

I was there one day when the local forest ranger, Carl Rohn, came by to check the logging. I heard the woods foreman, John Humphries, tell him to be careful up on that ridge because the bulls were dangerous. "Yes! Haw haw!" came the reply, as Carl headed out

*Kelly Boudreau
with calf moose.*

to do his inspection. I was also there when Carl came back several hours later; when he wiped the sweat off his brow, threw his cap on the floor, looked at John and said, "Whew! I see what you mean!" Carl, just like many others before and after him, found that there is no humour involved when a huge set of antlers on the front end of an irate bull starts heading in your direction.

Moose have so many enemies, what with trains, highways, wolves, and grizzlies, but their worst enemies, I think, are the black bears that are forever after their newborn calves. Another natural hazard for them is the frozen streams they try to walk on when the ice is not strong enough to bear their weight. It used to be a common occurrence along their migration routes to see several of them trapped in the ice at the same time, while others walked on and broke through right beside them. They simply could not comprehend the danger.

Arne Jensen, who trapped the upper McGregor River for many years, told me that he once counted 27 moose along 30 miles of river. All had broken through the ice before it had formed strongly enough to bear their weight.

Though they are unable to sense the danger of thin ice, these moose sure comprehend the danger when they have a big grizzly bear breathing down their neck. When Frank Novotny was logging across the river from Penny, he and his crew had a grizzly run a moose right toward them where they worked on a landing. When the moose spotted them, it ran around behind them and stopped, using them for protection. When the grizzly spotted the men it broke off its attack and departed.

In Crazy Man's Creek, Ole Hansen tells the story of an injured moose that was being pursued through the forest by a grizzly bear. He described the mournful moaning sounds that the moose was making. Only once in my life have I heard this moaning sound and it was made by a wounded moose making its escape. Never have I heard a moose make this sound when it is lying down wounded— only after it escaped. Ole had it right, and it is the most mournful sound that I, too, have ever heard.

The endurance of moose is legendary, and nowhere have I heard a more glowing example of this than I did from my father. This event took place right on the Fraser River at Penny. One morning my dad went to work on the log boom, where he was helping to move the logs to the sawmill. Immediately upon arriving he noticed a cow moose with a calf fighting a fin-boom in mid-river. The cow had made up her mind that she was going to climb over the boom which was blocking her way. Unable to assist in any way because the river-boat was gone, dad watched her fight the current for over two hours before she went under. The calf, which had been swimming in the eddy formed by her body, then drifted downstream about a mile and climbed up the bank to safety.

Perhaps the neatest story I've ever heard about moose occurred in Penny. It all began after the Michaylenko children lost their parents. Bill, the oldest son, quit school and went to work for the local sawmill, while Nettie, the eldest daughter, took on the role of mother to raise her younger siblings. Forced into the role of provider, Bill set off on a moose hunt to help with the family provisions. As he snowshoed along through the forest, he came face to face with a bull moose. He took careful aim, fired and dropped the moose, then approached and stepped over the moose's neck to cut its throat. Right then, the moose jumped up and tore off through the forest with Bill riding on its neck—afraid to hang on and scared to jump off. For some distance they rode through the trees, until Bill, in desperation, jumped off and headed for home. What a start to a hunting career! Nettie told us that it took Bill three days to work up enough courage to go back for his gun and snowshoes.

That was the first time I ever heard of a person riding a moose, but it was not the last. Clarence has a video of people in the Chilcotin riding moose. It was surprising to me to find just how easy they are to ride. They don't buck; they simply run around until they get tired.

Another point of interest concerning moose was told to me by a forest ranger that worked in the Chilcotin. He told me that Chilcotin Indians used to catch young bull moose and castrate them. The surgery guaranteed them excellent eating in late fall when these moose were easily identified by their deformed antlers. The deformities were directly caused by the damage to their genitals.

An unusual moose story took place in Sinclair Mills, BC, during the winter of 1964/65, when a moose ventured into the community, moved into an old shed, stayed there for several days and then died. This moose was definitely injured, and some people blamed wolves.

On a hunting trip along the railroad, we once had a strange, near-impossible experience with a moose. Two fellow hunters, John Humphreys and Bud Proctor, were with me at the time. We camped where the railroad and river met, and went hunting for moose and deer. Just at dawn one morning we split up—Bud walking the railway, while John and I drifted down the river in his boat for three miles—where we intended to meet up with Bud again. About halfway along the river, we heard a rifle shot, and assumed Bud had connected. We arrived at the meeting spot where the railroad and the river merged, only to find Bud was not there. We headed back to meet him, and after a short walk we found him sitting by the rail. At a glance, we saw that he was white in the face and had obviously just received a scare. He filled us in: "I left you guys and walked right to

Riding moose Chilcotin style

this spot and then nature called. I pulled down my pants and was doing a job when I heard something bellow right behind me. At the same time some water went flying up in the air and landed on me. Without even pulling up my pants, I managed to run right across the tracks, then I grabbed my rifle and went for a look."

Bud then showed us the moose he had finished off, and we were able to piece together what had happened. A train that had passed by about three hours earlier had struck the moose and thrown it over a pile of willows into a pool of water, breaking its rear legs in the process. Bud had happened along and was doing his thing within 10 feet of the moose when it broke radio silence. We all agreed that it defied all odds that out of three miles of grade, that Bud would stop right in that spot. I mean what are the odds?

Something that is not generally known about moose is that cougars will on occasion attack and kill them. This was confirmed by Maurice Schultz of Dome Creek, BC when he and a crew of men were working on the Highway 16 right-of-way in 1965. One morning they came to work and found a freshly-killed cow moose. The snow was so deep at that time, that the moose had been floundering neck deep. The cougar attacked and tore out the top of the moose's neck. It died standing upright in the deep snow. A fresh snow had fallen overnight and the cougar sign was unmistakable. There was no question about it; the cougar had killed it.

Another unusual moose story took place when a Penny resident named Victor Mellows and a friend, Jack Clements, were on a mountain hiking trip. On a slope above timberline they found a moose trapped on a snowfield. The poor beast had walked above a spot where a stream had undercut the snowfield and its legs had broken through, leaving it suspended on the snow. Unable to assist, the men continued on their way, leaving the moose to face a lingering death unless a grizzly or some wolves happened by.

While I'm on the subject of wolves, I must say that I agree with many others who have stated that wolves are among the smartest animals in the forest. Just going by my own experience, I do not recall ever seeing, or hearing of, a wolf getting killed by a train. Yet all other animals lost battles with trains. Moose, grizzlies, black bears, wolverines, coyotes, deer, caribou, domestic dogs, cows, horses, and a host of smaller animals were common casualties of the trains—but not wolves. They seem to be more intelligent than most other animals.

Tommy Wilson of Prince George, who spent the greatest part of his life working as a train man, assured me that he never knew any case of a wolf being killed by a train.

While I'm on the subject of wolves, there is one story that demands telling. This concerned a perfectly delightful individual named Bob Beard. Bob was one of several people that used to meet with us regularly for a session of storytelling and coffee. Then we got word that Bob was dying of cancer. Just a few weeks before his death at the age of 83, I was at home one evening when the phone rang. It was Bob, who informed me that he didn't have much time left and he wanted to tell me something that he had never told another soul. Quickly I grabbed paper and pen and began taking notes as he began: "I've never told anyone about this because most people wouldn't believe it anyway…This happened down in the Chilcotin during the '30s when I was doing a bit of trapping down there. One day I was walking the line on snowshoes when I heard a pack of wolves howl-

Penny pioneer Victor Mellows at 95. Victor often roamed the mountains with us.

ing in the distance. I kept walking but they caught up with me. When they got close, I was so frightened that I climbed a tree with my snowshoes on. Well, I must have been up there for at least two hours when I knew I had to do something because my legs were starting to freeze."

When I caught up with my notes, I asked, "What the devil did you do?"

Back came his answer: "The only thing I could have done, I took off my snowshoes, tucked one under each arm and flew home."

There was a few seconds of silence, and then he added, "Gotcha!"

There was no doubt about it; he got me all right.

SINCE THIS BOOK DEALS WITH MOUNTAINS TO SUCH A DEGREE, THERE is something I want to bring to the attention of the reader— something I was unaware of until recently. This concerns the existence of wild horses throughout the Interior mountains many years ago. While searching old newspaper articles for my book, I stumbled upon several that dealt with wild horses running at large in the Interior of this province. The one I have chosen was picked up from the *Edmonton Journal* and reprinted by the *Fort George Herald,* dated April 5, 1913:

"Bronzed and weather beaten from long months of back-packing in the interior of British Columbia, Jim Bradley and Gus Riemland, two well-known western prospectors, arrived in the city with their pack train of five horses.

> "...Leaving Tete Jaune Cache in June last, Bradley and Riemland started with a pack train from Mile 125 and went up along the Little Smoky River making temporary camps as they went along and prospecting every inch of the country.
>
> "In the two months that followed, the two men covered about two thousand miles of the interior in their search for the precious yellow metal, but without success. But in the region of the Big Smoky River, at its headquarters and country tributary to that, they discovered rich galena and copper ore.

"...Probably the most interesting part of Mr. Bradley's story of his trip is of the great bands of wild horses that roam the country they traveled through. These animals have been the subject of much discussion and argument among the people of this western country, but Mr. Bradley, fresh from their haunts, is in a position to vouch for their numbers and their existence.

"Without a word of a lie, there must be easily three thousand of these animals roaming in little bands through the country which we passed through. The Indians and white prospectors and pack train men value these horses more than an animal of the best breeding," said Mr. Bradley.

"They are the descendants of horses that were turned loose by disgusted or dying men at the time of the famous Cariboo Gold Rush. At that time thousands of tenderfeet stampeded to the Cariboo, and like in all gold rushes, a great many of them were utterly incompetent to get along in that wild country. Many of their horses got away or were turned loose by them, and for many years these animals made their feeding grounds near Barkerville. As the years went on the bands increased in numbers, and the descendants of these early animals are to be found through all the mountain country of Northern BC. They make trails in the mountains much after the fashion of deer and the buffalo, and also in the timber country, where the Indians and packers set snares for them in just the same way as a lynx trap. The horses in most cases are easily broken in. We lost animals from our pack train from time to time and were able to capture animals to replace them. And in fact the wild horses are better for this class of country on account of their hardiness and sureness of foot on mountain trails."

At this point I would like to mention that Stan Hale, who packed with horses for many years, confirmed this story. In 1935, he took a hunting party into this same area. The trip was financed by Stan Clark, the game commissioner out of Edmonton, Alberta. During their 42-day trip, they saw many herds of wild horses, especially around what is now the Willmore Wilderness Provincial Park. Stan explained that there were many windswept ridges along the Little and Big Smoky Rivers and along the eastern slopes that allowed for good winter feeding areas for these horses. They also noticed many small herds of caribou in that area.

It seems obvious that the horses in the Interior mountains perished, probably during severe winters when they were unable to obtain forage due to heavy snowfalls. The horses that moved out to the windswept eastern slopes managed to survive.

Bear Habits & Behaviour

THE THING THAT HAS AMAZED ME THE MOST ABOUT GRIZZLIES IS THE places they go in the mountains. Many times I have seen them climb very steep places where they have negotiated cliffs, snowfields and glaciers, yet never did I ever see one lose its footing and fall. Though I have seen their back ends swing around a few times, their front claws always held.

Clarence watched a grizzly go up a mountainside until it reached a cornice, or snow overhang. For several minutes it appeared to be standing still while its four legs kept moving. Finally it got its front paws over, then slowly started moving and inched its way over the top.

Virgil Brandner and I watched a grizzly climb up a very steep talus slope and as it neared the top, it began sliding back with each step.

Grizzly at timberline

Not once did it look around or even hesitate. It kept its legs going and moved an enormous amount of rock before it gained the top. Are they bull-headed or what?

A few days later, Virgil and I were back in the same area trying to get pictures of grizzlies. It wasn't long before we picked up a sow with two yearlings on a distant mountain and the pursuit was on. When we got within 200 yards of them, Virgil stopped to watch while I moved in alone to get some close-ups. I used a large erratic boulder as cover and managed to get nearer to them, then I watched as they began a major excavation business. Within minutes, the sow and one yearling, working side by side, had dug down to where their legs were out of sight. The other bear, obviously the foreman, watched and did nothing. I took a few pictures of this performance and suddenly the sow stepped out of the hole and looked right at the rock I was hiding behind. A steady breeze was in my favor so she never got my scent, yet somehow she seemed to know I was there. Slowly she moved away, stopping every now and then to stare at the

Clarence and Olga Boudreau atop Grizzly Bear Mountain, September 1967.

rock I was hiding behind. At that time I was bewildered; I couldn't understand how she sensed my presence. As I look back at it now, I think she must have heard the click of the camera's shutter, even though she and her cubs were busy digging at the time.

In the fall of 1965, Clarence and his wife Olga were watching a big grizzly digging on an adjacent mountain. A few hundred yards above it a two-year-old was digging, each bear seemingly unaware of the other. After feeding for a few hours, the big bear suddenly ran up the mountain to where the two-year-old was attempting to flee. At the last minute, it turned to face the big bear and received a slap across the head. For several minutes they stood facing each other— almost as if they were talking things over. Then the big bear walked back down the mountain and resumed feeding. The two-year-old walked away over the mountain and did not return.

The day following the bear fight, Clarence and Olga were back at the same viewing spot, while Guenther Peemoeller and I circled around several mountain peaks. By late afternoon we were on the mountain ridge adjacent to them. Suddenly they saw a grizzly come galloping over the skyline and down the slope where it jumped into a thicket of fir trees and disappeared. A few minutes later, Guenther and I appeared on the ridgetop where the bear had been minutes earlier. We dropped down the slope until we came to a cliff, where we stopped for a much-needed rest. As I sat glassing with binoculars, Guenther took a nap on a narrow ledge of the cliff. Unknown to us, the grizzly was hiding in a clump of trees only 100 feet away. A couple of hours later we dropped to the valley floor and then climbed up to where Clarence and Olga were sitting. They pointed out where the bear was hiding, and though we watched until near dark, it never moved. Judging from other experiences we have had, I'll bet that right after dark that bear left the area and didn't come back for several days.

One thing that has repeatedly surprised me is that bears run from dogs. If they even had a clue as to their own power I doubt that they would ever run again. My parents watched a meeting between a bear and their dog, and were quite surprised at the outcome. Somehow a tiny cub black bear had been separated from its mother and was walking alone along the railroad grade when their big dog spotted it and gave chase. As the dog pulled up behind it and went to bite it, the cub spun around and slapped the dog across the face. Head over heels it went, as the cub sped away. Dad said it was difficult to believe because the dog was three or four times the size of the bear.

Some of our own experiences with dogs and grizzlies have been quite surprising as well. Often the dogs would lie down and be quiet when they scented or saw a grizzly. They seemed to sense that they were in over their heads. Yet those same dogs had little or no fear of black bears.

Black bears are funny creatures, often being timid to the point of shame. Such were the black bears that frequented the Purden Lake garbage dump in 1981. Bob Fretter, co-owner of the resort, had a Norwegian elkhound that weighed, at most, 50 pounds. Many times I had heard rumours that it used to chase the bears every day. One day I happened to be there when it took off on its daily trip to the dump, so I decided to follow it. It slowly trotted along until it got about 100 feet from the dump, then it turned on the jets and rushed, furiously barking, right to the dump. It was hard to believe that four bears feeding on the dump and another that was in the woods went tearing away in total fright, the biggest bear even climbing a tree. Satisfied, the dog went trotting back toward the resort just so darned proud of itself that it sort of swaggered. Apparently this dog chased those bears every day all summer and they never once called its bluff.

When black bears feed on garbage dumps, they seem to lose the innate wisdom that goes with wildness. Not only do they lose their fear of man, they just become really stupid. I recall the afternoon I was walking the railroad tracks when I came to a garbage dump that had recently been used by a railroad work gang that had just departed. I didn't see any bears, so I took a stick and stirred up the garbage, moving tin cans around and making as much noise as I could. Then I moved about 100 feet away and hid behind a tree. Within five minutes a big black bear came out and began feeding. Several minutes later, the wind changed and took my scent right to it. As soon as it got my scent, it laid down and didn't move, yet when the wind changed direction, it got up and started feeding again. Three times this sequence was repeated before I tired of it and stood up to holler, "You stupid bear! Don't you recognize a person when you smell one?" It left amid huffs, puffs, and flying tin cans. In its natural state in the wild, this bear would probably have departed with the first hint of the presence of man. This is just one of many incidents that have convinced me that garbage dumps create more problem bears than anything except outright starvation.

When black bears age and their teeth rot away, then trouble is close at hand. We have seen so many examples of this that many are gone from my memory. My mother had a session with one after she heard her chickens fussing in their pen. Assuming it was a hawk or weasel, she went running and opened the gate to the pen, only to come face to face with a bear. It stood up right beside her and mom took off her boot and hit it across the face. Then she turned and ran to Clarence's house for assistance. Clarence returned with her and shot the bear which was very thin, its teeth rotted away. It weighed, at most, some 100 pounds.

It strikes me that black bears get into a lot of trouble because of their poor eyesight. They often don't sense approaching danger until it is right upon them. I have stood motionless within 20 feet of black bear and have had them stand up to look around, including right at me, then get down and continue what they were doing without seeing me. I think some of them are almost blind.

I also think that a lot of bear traits are misunderstood. One thing that has been taken for granted throughout the years is claw marks on trees. We have been told countless times that bears put claw marks on trees to mark the boundaries of their ranges and keep other bears out. I think not. When you see 17 grizzlies on a mountainside at one time, which one put the claw marks on the tree? And why didn't the other bears stay away? When you see five different sized black bears in a small cut-block at the same time, which one marked the tree, and why didn't it deter the others?

I have seen a yearling black bear put claw marks on trees. Am I supposed to believe it was claiming a piece of real estate? I doubt it. Cats claw away at trees or posts to sharpen their claws. Is it possible that bears like to sharpen their claws, too? I suspect that these mark-er trees are little more than message posts.

Another thing we learned about bears is that pregnant black bears prefer to den in hollow cedar trees in the western red cedar belt. It is easy to spot their den trees in spring, as there are a great number of claw marks plainly visible on these trees. I cannot imagine a safer place for them to den, as a grizzly is unable to dig them out. They must spend a great deal of time searching because they always seem to be able to find a tree with an entrance hole high above the ground. I find it most surprising how small a hole they can squeeze through.

Some black bears are really stupid about their choice of a den site. They may den up right beside a stream, where high water or an ice jam will either drown or displace them.

In all my years in the woods, I have found many black bear dens, but only one newly-made grizzly den. Bill and I walked onto a newly-dug den in late September, on an east slope, about 2000 feet above the main valley. It went in under the roots of a hemlock tree and then angled upwards.

Occasionally bears get fooled when they den up. I'm thinking of a September in the '50s when the snow fell for several days and the bears all went to their dens. We were hunting intensively at that time, yet we never saw any sign of bear tracks in the snow. Two weeks later it warmed up and the snow melted away: suddenly there were bear tracks everywhere. Clearly they had been fooled.

Another observation we made is that black bear mothers have a habit of crossing an opening to check that everything is safe before returning for their cubs. I'm sure that some of them doing this get shot by hunters who think they are lone bears. One example occurred in 1979, when a fellow admitted to me that he had shot such a bear in error. As he had no desire to get involved with the authorities, he had just walked away. A couple of days later, I was in that area and went to check the dead bear. It stunk pretty high so I didn't go too close. Then, just as I turned to walk away, I heard a noise under the roots of a cedar tree right beside me, and noticed two cubs staring up at me. They had refused to leave their dead mother, thereby sealing their own fate. I called to a hunting buddy a short distance away and when he arrived, I showed him the bears. We then spent some time trying to decide what to do. I told Dave that I had been led to believe that bear cubs could not survive the first winter without their mothers. We thought about it for a while, and then decided to walk away rather than get involved with wildlife people who understandably frown on anyone taking possession of wildlife.

After we arrived home that evening, it bothered us to the point where I phoned regional wildlife biologist Ken Sumanik in Prince George. I explained to him that the bear cubs would not leave their mother. I also suggested that I was willing to take officers to the scene if they wanted to capture them. Ken told me that they were so busy they could not spare anyone, but added that it would be nice if we would catch them and bring them in to him.

That evening Dave and I built a cage, and then a quick release snare from a piece of pipe and some wire. The following morning we set out in my riverboat for the 10-mile trip upriver. Then followed some really hard work as we fought that big cage through the forest for half a mile. We arrived at the scene to find the cubs still under the tree, so Dave lowered the wire loop down and over the boar's neck. It took a minute to snare it, but when he did, an incredible performance followed. The cub braced its front feet against the roots and bawled fiercely. Only when it started losing consciousness was Dave able to pull it up and put it in the cage. No sooner had we closed the door of the cage then that cub came to and started tearing lumber off the cage, all the time bawling steadily.

Then the same procedure started over with the sow cub. She had seen the old 'wire on the neck trick', and she wouldn't have any part of it. Every time Dave lowered the loop she would turn her bum to him and so we were getting nowhere. Finally I managed to fool her by poking a stick at her, and then when she turned, Dave caught her. As he held her, I opened the cage and the boar tried to get out. I'm sure that we could have sold a million tickets to the performance that followed. With both bears bawling and us trying to get the sow in, without letting the boar out, it turned out to be quite a show. We managed to solve the problem, at last, by holding the cage on end and then forcing the other bear in.

When we had them secured, we started the tough job of carrying them out to the river, during which time they both bawled continuously. Once at the river, we were surprised to see several hunters that had been drawn out of the woods by all the noise. They stared in wonder as we headed down the river while the cubs bellowed in anger. During the trip, Dave tried to feed them some chocolate, which the sow readily accepted. The boar refused it, though, and even took a few bites out of his sister in between his attacks on the cage.

A little over an hour later we were driving down the streets of Prince George, while curious onlookers stared at our vehicle. The sow had calmed down, but the boar put up a steady wail. We stopped at the wildlife office where they directed us to the home of a Mrs. Sawitsky on Foreman Flats, and here we found other wildlife including several eagles that had been injured. At Mrs. Sawitsky's direction, we put the bears in a shed and departed.

The following year, we met Mr. Sawitsky who informed us that the bears were allowed to run free. He told us that when the first snow arrived they went down by the river and dug in under a tree where they made their winter den. The following spring they were seen running about in good health. A few weeks later they returned to the wild.

Looking back, it appears that we went to a great deal of work for nothing. The only question I have is whether the cubs would have left their mother's side before they perished.

The often-repeated idea that grizzlies have a huge range to themselves and other bears had better not trespass, is absolute nonsense. As well, the notion that the big boars control their ranges should at least be questioned. I would like someone to explain to me why we have noticed that mothers with cubs have possession of carcasses even though there is sign of a big boar in the area. As well, several times we have noticed that when there are several sets of mothers with cubs on a mountainside, the boars are absent. Possibly the families move there because the boars have left. On the other hand it is also possible that the boars move out because they don't like the continual threats from these irate mothers who will fight to defend their cubs if they have to.

We have seen five sets of mothers with cubs or yearlings on a mountain at the same time. Imagine a boar grizzly trying to get a little peace and quiet around there. After being roared at several times he may very well say, "Okay! Quit the nagging; I'm out of here!"

THERE CAN BE NO DOUBT THAT THE BULBS OF GLACIER LILIES (*erythronium grandiflorum*) are one of the grizzlies' favorite foods. They tear up enormous areas searching for them. One day we ate a batch of them for our evening meal and the next morning I was still full. They are incredibly starchy. In my opinion the grizzlies can have them.

Rather than ask what foods a grizzly bear eats, it would probably be easier to ask what foods they don't eat. When they are eating berries, for instance, it seems that more leaves are ingested than berries by a long shot. Sometimes in late fall their droppings are pure mountain ash berries, and these berries certainly must go through their digestive system in a hurry, because they don't look like they've even been digested. Years ago, we noticed that when grizzly bears were in the berry patches, or anywhere else for that matter, they felt far more secure when they knew that there were other grizzlies around. Emboldened by their numbers, the adult boar grizzlies would feed in the open at midday. Yet some of these same bears were only seen at dawn or dusk when they were alone.

In August 1970, a friend named Marlin Priebe and I were watching a lone female grizzly as she fed on an adjacent ridge just below timberline. Suddenly a large boar emerged from where it had been bedded down in a small thicket a short distance above the sow. After looking the area over for a minute, he crossed the sidehill to where a spring had cut a trough out of the mountain. As it was an extremely hot day, this bear's new coat must have been a bit too hot for it. It sized the situation up for a minute and then rolled down into the stream. Next, it adjusted itself around until its feet were sticking straight up in the air. For about an hour the bear stayed in that position with the cool spring water running around its body. I could not help but think that this grizzly would not have been so unconcerned had the sow not been nearby to warn it of approaching danger.

Another example of a grizzly's personality was displayed when Clarence watched a sow with two yearlings. Mama dug up a ground squirrel which she gave to her smallest yearling. Suddenly the bigger yearling, probably a male, lunged in and grabbed the squirrel, then took off across the mountain with mama in hot pursuit. After chasing the thief a short distance, mama returned to the other yearling, while the thief went off by himself to feed.

When checking diggings where grizzly bears have gone after ground squirrels, take note if there is any nest material in the diggings. If so, then you can bet that the bears were successful. Sometimes the squirrels will attempt to escape by running out between a bear's hind legs. They seldom make it, though, for the speed with which these bears can whirl and grab them, must be seen to be believed. Although they appear to be clumsy animals, grizzlies are anything but clumsy.

Bill Benedict and I watched three adult grizzlies feeding along a mountainside in October, 1994. Shortly after noon the sun came out and it got quite warm. This inspired two of the bears to dig fresh new beds for themselves in the shade of trees a short distance apart. Then they stretched out on the newly exposed cool earth. Occasionally they moved around to cool off different parts of their bodies. A couple of hours later they started moving again and we got some action that we were lucky to catch on film. Because of the updrafts, the bear highest on the mountain knew that the other bears were there, but the bear in the middle wasn't aware of the bear above it. Suddenly the middle bear heard the bear above it. It jumped, and stood up for a good look around. Quite alarmed, it moved uphill until it got the other bear's scent. Then, perhaps upset at being startled, it charged the other bear and the chase was on. Through a row of trees, up the mountain and back through the row of trees they went until the charging bear caught up with the lead bear. Then as it pulled in alongside, it realized that the other bear outsized it. Immediately it turned and tore back across the mountain with the other bear now the pursuer. After running across the mountain for some distance, they declared a draw and both settled down for a much-needed rest.

I strongly suspect that this was just a form of entertainment for these bears, because not once did either bear let out a roar—something I'm sure they would have done if they were playing hardball.

Bears can be capable of doing some pretty clever things, but one thing really stands out in my memory: Clarence and I were sitting on the railway grade watching about 10 ravens feeding on a moose carcass that a grizzly had claimed. They were feeding in a hole in the ribcage made by the bear. As we sat watching, the bear suddenly got up from where it was resting, walked out to the moose carcass and flipped it upside down. As the bear went back and lay down, the ravens sat in the tree right over its head and cussed it out something terrible: they were now denied a hole to eat in.

We had ample opportunity to learn things about bears and we found that there is much to know and wonder at. One thing I had heard from old woodsmen—and I saw proof of it—is that bears will pack their own wounds with moss. They can be bleeding profusely when they reach a swamp or muskeg, yet that may be where you will find the trail ends. Hopefully though, hunters will use great care and try to avoid the dirty and dangerous job of trailing a wounded bear.

Another memory concerns a black bear that was feeding on a carcass. There's no doubt that black bears know their tenancy on carcasses is tenuous at best, especially if a grizzly happens along. Perhaps with this in mind, a black bear that had just finished eating took a good portion of the remains and crammed them into a hollow cedar log nearby. When it finished the task, it then took a large amount of moss and earth and filled up the remaining space to hide the meat, and hopefully the smell, from the keen noses of other bears.

Clarence and I once watched in awe the strength of what was probably a 200-pound black bear as it found a full-grown, train-killed moose. It grabbed the moose by the neck with its teeth, and then it held its head out to one side so that the moose wouldn't get under its feet. In six jumps it had the moose out of sight back in the trees. Another time we saw where a big black bear had taken a full-grown moose carcass up a very steep hillside. They are indeed a formidably powerful animal, but for all their strength they are not invincible.

One grizzly bear that was killed by a train right in the community of Penny certainly took a beating. It was cut up in six-inch slices just as if it had gone through a giant meat-slicer. A local farmer, Joe Pastor, had a field of potatoes ready for digging and that is exactly what the bear was doing when the train came along. When it heard the train approaching, it headed back toward the mountains, with the result that both it and the train arrived at the same spot at the same time. There was no doubt about it, the bear was decidedly the loser.

Another thought about grizzlies is that logging must have a confusing effect on them. It must be a terrible shock for a grizzly bear to go to sleep in a heavily forested area and then emerge from its den the following spring only to find the forest gone.

During my years with the Protection Branch of the Forest Service, I often saw grizzlies high on the mountains during late June, when the boars started following the sows, and early July when they started mating. If two bears were together at a great distance from me, I used to wonder if they were a mother and yearling or two adults together for mating purposes. Then it occurred to me that if they were on the move and the smaller bear was in front, it was a sow and boar mating. Alternately, if the biggest bear was in front, it was a sow and yearling. In both cases, the sow led the way.

Something that became apparent time and again, was the ability of the black bear population to recover quickly after a year of heavy den deaths. With their ability to have cubs every two years, it seemed that within a few years there were black bears everywhere.

It is not uncommon for black bears to have four cubs, and I know of one case where a bear had five cubs. This was at Slim Lanehan's camp on the Torpy River in 1962. Everyone that worked in that camp had seen this bear family. It was common to see them eating on the garbage dump and they did this for at least a month that I knew of. Whether they were all her birth cubs, or if she had adopted some, there was no way to know.

Sometimes the things bears do don't seem to make a lick of sense. Such as the time Bill Benedict and I watched a grizzly with three cubs climb over a barren steep rock ridge, then go down the other side to a lush alpine valley. This involved about two hours of hard work on a hot August afternoon; work that could have been avoided by walking around the ridge in ten or fifteen minutes. This seemed all the more strange when they returned three days later and did the exact same thing again.

Often it is almost impossible for us to find adult grizzlies high in the mountains during late August and early September, with the exception of mothers with cubs. While the other bears are down on the salmon streams, mothers with cubs sometimes stay up high—possibly they stay away from the salmon streams to protect their cubs from other bears. In my opinion, they can get by without salmon, especially when mice are plentiful. Many times I have heard my hiking partners say that grizzlies were chasing ground squirrels when I would have bet my last dollar they were chasing mice.

One of the most interesting sights the mountains can provide is grizzly cubs or yearlings play-fighting; their multi-coloured coats often blending in with the wildflowers growing in such profusion on the slopes. They tear around and knock each other over with such vigour that it seems they are locked in mortal combat. Often it has been this activity that has given away their position and allowed us to watch them for hours on end.

Knowing that grizzlies are capable of great ferocity, I think my biggest surprise was in watching the tenderness they often showed to their cubs. Somehow that just didn't seem to fit with the image that I had built up in my mind.

I recall the September evening in 1965 when Clarence and I were glassing a grizzly with three cubs on an adjacent mountain. They were right at timberline with only a few small islands of fir trees nearby. As we watched, we heard an airplane approaching. Just before it cleared the ridge, the mother took her cubs and disappeared into one of these tiny islands. Then the plane flew directly over top of them and had not cleared the ridge beyond them for more than a few minutes before they were out in the open again. So much for the accuracy of aerial surveys of grizzly bears!

One hot afternoon in August 1973, I watched a grizzly with two cubs as they traversed a mountainside. I had watched them from early morning until almost noon when they moved into an island of trees to rest. A couple of hours later they emerged and I began moving closer to get some pictures. I lost track of them for a while in some rows of trees, and was suddenly startled when the cubs came running out of the trees right in front of me. They were play-fighting, rolling end over end. The bears were much closer than I wanted them to be, so I sounded retreat. Just as I started to move away, the mother came out of the trees less than 100 feet from me. She spotted me at once and let out a loud cough, then stood erect. Instantly the two cubs rushed to her side and also stood tall, one on each side of her. Three blond grizzlies looking me over in silence— it is impossible to describe just how wild and beautiful they looked. Three golden statues, just staring at a man who forgot to take pictures and wasn't even sure if he'd remembered to bring toilet paper. After about 30 seconds the sow let out a soft cough and led her cubs away, much to my relief.

Another small mystery is that sows and cubs will sometimes roll over and over in the remains of a carcass, with the mother being the one to initiate it. I've often wondered if that is her way of telling them that this is something good to eat.

Clarence and I watched a mother grizzly with three cubs meet a mother with one cub at close quarters. First there was a loud roar, then they started moving apart. One cub was slow to respond to the mother's warning, though, and that resulted in it getting a quick slap across the bum. For several minutes we could hear it crying as they moved away through the trees.

During their first year together, mother grizzlies keep their cubs very close at hand. They nurse them, kill mice and ground squirrels for them, and generally just spoil them rotten. During the later part of the second year, although they nurse the entire summer, that dependence has to be broken. This leads to a lot of noise in the mountains. The mother will catch a ground squirrel and immediately the yearlings will try to take it from her. This often results in the mother standing up and letting out a mighty roar, which I interpret as meaning, "Get off your butt and go get your own, you're not a baby any more!" Sometimes the yearlings will respond by crying, but the message is clear, and mama eats the squirrel.

In the many meetings we have had with mothers and cubs, the mothers have always kept the cubs right with them. Mothers are not nearly as protective of yearlings, though, as I have seen the mothers go through a pass or over a mountain as much as a quarter-mile ahead of their yearlings, especially toward the end of their second summer together. I'm sure this leads to separation on occasion, and it may explain the yearlings we have seen alone during the months of September and October.

In the many meetings we have had with mother grizzlies and cubs, not once did they try to send their cubs up a tree. This is a major difference between grizzlies and black bears, which readily use this protection tactic. This is a great pressure release, and a lot of attacks would be avoided if only grizzlies would do the same thing.

Sometimes we can watch a certain thing for a long time before the significance of it sinks in. For instance, I wonder how many people have seen a mother grizzly with two or more cubs spend any great amount of time playing with them. I doubt that I have ever seen them spend more than a few minutes playing with them, although I have seen the cubs play among themselves for hours on end. On the other hand, I have seen mothers with lone cubs spend a great deal of time playing with them. I was watching a grizzly with a lone cub as they played and wrestled around right on the skyline of a ridge one evening when it struck me. I couldn't help but feel a sense of gladness in my heart at how the sow was apparently compensating for her solitary cub's lack of a playmate.

A mountain hiking friend of mine has, however, offered another explanation as to why a mother grizzly will spend more time playing with a lone cub. It may simply be because she doesn't have to spend as much time gathering food when she is only nursing a single cub, and hence she has more time for play.

THROUGHOUT THOSE YEARS OF OBSERVING BEARS, THERE WAS something that stood out time and time again: when bear populations were high the animals would get very aggressive and at times would refuse to run from us. Yet during those years when they were scarce, for instance after a long, hard winter with many den deaths, they were like ghosts that would flee from their own shadows. This trait seems prevalent among most wild mammals, and would seem to be a phenomenon necessary to the survival of a species.

Somehow I never seem to tire of watching grizzlies at work and play. There are times when one is treated to sights never forgotten— such as watching a grizzly walk through the early morning mist and then suddenly step out into full sunshine. As its silver-tipped coat glistens in the sunlight, it presents an overwhelming picture of strength and beauty. Many other people feel the same way.

During the '70s, I made several trips into this same area with a photographer named Lou Siguenza. It didn't take long for him to realize that getting pictures of grizzlies around timberline is a very tricky business. It is different from taking pictures in parks, or along salmon streams. He appeared amazed to find bears running away when we were still a mile distant. Returning from one trip, we walked right into a grizzly on a ridge in the subalpine. At a distance

Betty Kovasic and Larry Boudreau saw 14 grizzlies in two days.

of 50 feet, the bear exploded over the ridge and disappeared in two seconds flat.

In 1972, Prince George artist Betty Kovacic spent two days around Grizzly Bear Mountain with Larry Boudreau and me. During that time we saw 14 grizzlies, and most of them were alone. The respect she felt for these bears was written all over her, and isn't respect what it's all about?

5

BIG GRIZZLIES

"The early morning sunshine spreads its fingers through the mountain peaks and catches movement down by a tiny glacial stream. Then into the sunshine emerges a mother grizzly and two brightly colored cubs. They are sliding down a steep slope on the vegetation made slippery by the heavy September dew. Again and again they climb up the ridge to go scooting down to the edge of the foaming mountain stream. High above, a bald eagle that has been riding the air currents can no longer contain its curiosity. Down it comes in a long swooping glide, where it circles several times in an attempt to determine what manner of foolishness is being perpetrated in its domain. Then satisfied, it finds the first updrafts of the day and within minutes is back among the peaks."

from Jack Boudreau's diary

AT THIS POINT, I WOULD LIKE TO TELL YOU ABOUT THE TWO biggest grizzly bears of the many hundreds that I have seen. These two were large enough to prompt me to measure their tracks.

The first was a large boar that traveled the mountains in the area of Slim Creek, where he used a portion of an old logging road for one of his boundaries. The local trapper, Sid Frank, told me that he could almost set his watch by this bear, as it came by every ten days, almost without exception. During the summer of '58, I was helping with a log drive on Slim Creek, where there had been many reports of grizzly tracks that were as much as 17 inches in length. One morning we arose to find that this grizzly had walked right by our camp and had stolen a beaver out of a trap just a stone's throw from where we slept. The trapper was out getting treatment for an injured eye. Meanwhile this bear was following his line and cleaning up his beaver catches. After eating the beaver carcass, it walked along the muddy road leaving many plain tracks for us to measure. This bear had a front pad width of just over seven inches, and a hind foot length of 12 inches, the longest hind foot I've ever measured.

A few years later, Clarence, Bill, and Herb Metzmeier were hunting near a mineral lick in this same area when Bill stumbled upon a moose carcass that had been shot or taken by the big bear. It was all piled up in a willow thicket. As he approached the carcass he must have made some noise, for the bear came down off a knoll to meet him. At the same time, Herbert had circled and was standing on a downtree when the grizzly went by to meet Bill. Herb took the bear with a well placed shoulder shot and may well have saved Bill some serious problems, as the vegetation was thick and visibility was limited to a few feet around the carcass.

These were, no doubt, the bear tracks that had been guessed at 17 inches, as such large tracks were never spotted in the vicinity again. The pads on this bear were exactly the same size as the tracks I had measured the previous year. Also, this was just one of many cases where we measured tracks and found them to be far smaller than others had said. We found that there is nothing that shrinks bear tracks like a tape measure. I always measured any big tracks that I found, and if I didn't have a tape measure I would cut a stick and use it, then measure it when I got home.

Herb Metzmeier with a big grizzly.

The other big grizzly story started out like this. In September, 1958, Lindy Chambers, my nephew Dwayne Proctor and I decided to explore some mountains that we had never visited before. A report that a helicopter pilot had seen mountain goats in that area was the reason for our trip. Well, we didn't find any goat sign, but we sure found something of interest. Nestled between two peaks on a ridgetop was a grizzly bear's hideaway, and we walked right into it. In a 50-foot area, we found about 20 piles of the largest bear droppings I have ever seen. The scat was four inches in diameter and the piles were equivalent to what you would find behind a large horse.

So help me, if I searched for 1000 years I could never find a better spot for a wise old boar grizzly to have his headquarters. Open alpine peaks above, an incredibly thick alder jungle to the south in which to escape if danger threatened. To the east a sheer drop of about 500 feet into a beautiful subalpine lake. During the day the updrafts would warn of approaching danger, while the prevailing winds would warn of danger from the west—the direction we would have came from to hunt him.

Although we had glassed this general area for years, we had never spotted this bear, and it is my belief that it fed mostly under cover of darkness in the long nights of late fall. As we studied the available sign, we were certain that this was an outstanding bear. Later, on a couple different occasions, we found this bear's tracks on the flats, but it was not until several years later that we would encounter it.

One evening in May 1965, Clarence and Lindy Chambers decided to take a walk to a small dam about one mile from the community. Just as an afterthought, Clarence threw his rifle over his shoulder and took it along. As they stood looking over the dam, Lindy let out a yell and Clarence turned to see a huge grizzly walking right up to them. It paid no attention to their yells, so Clarence took aim and fired. At the shot the bear dropped, then instantly regained its feet, turned and ran. Just as the bear was going into a thicket, Clarence fired a second shot. They quickly rushed over to where the bear had gone into the heavy second-growth trees, where they could plainly hear it moving, but since Lindy was unarmed, Clarence did the wise thing and would not go in alone.

A short while later, I happened to look out the window at home to see Clarence coming on the run. As he came through the door I could tell he was shook up about something. As soon as he said, "Wounded grizzly!", I grabbed my rifle and then he filled me in on the way.

"Are you certain you hit it?" I asked.

"If you seen the size of that bear, you wouldn't ask that, I'm telling you that this is the biggest bear I've ever seen." He responded.

When we reached the spot where the bear had entered the trees, we stopped to listen and could plainly hear it moving in the thicket just a few yards from us. We worked our way in, but could not see more than a few feet in front of us in that tangle of vegetation. As it was getting dark, we decided it would be best to wait the six hours until daylight rather than have someone killed.

Jack and Clarence with grizzly — note size of claws.

Back home I found sleep impossible, so after giving it up as a bad job, I went to Clarence's where I found that he had been unable to sleep as well. We discussed the events of the evening and both agreed that the bear must be hurt bad in order to have remained at that spot.

First light found us carefully following the blood trail into the thicket, where we found the bear dead. It had just died, however, as it was still loose and warm. The first bullet had broken its jaw and lodged in the back of its neck, causing a terrible wound and a great loss of blood. The second 30-06 bullet had broken his hips and had prevented the bear from getting away.

What a magnificent bear—it had four inches of fat distributed over its back, yet it had just emerged from the den perhaps one month earlier. The size of the muscles on this bear were truly something to behold. I tried pushing them in with my thumb and could not do so. They were almost as hard as bone.

The following day, Clarence and I, along with a friend named Victor Mellows, carried a beam scale back to the bear where we cut it up and weighed it, and it came out at exactly 747 pounds. Assuming a minimum weight loss of 20 percent in the den, it appears that this bear must have weighed about 900 pounds when it went to den. An exceptionally large Interior grizzly.

The hide squared eight feet and five inches lying loose on the ground, the largest we ever measured. The front pad was seven and three eighths inches measuring straight across, and the hind foot measured 12 inches in length. The front claws, which grow all winter in the den, were at their full length and were very impressive. We discussed how this bear could easily have broken a moose's neck or back. We also agreed that this bear would not maul a person; it would kill a person, and very easily at that.

Now I must point out that these measurement of grizzly tracks were made straight across the pads, or as they would show on a hard surface. This information was for our own use and it is meaningless to compare this information with that of individuals who want to exaggerate the sizes of bears. Likewise, it should be noted that posing well behind an animal when its picture is taken is also an oft-used modern-day attempt to exaggerate the size.

It doesn't take many years in the mountains to teach a person that not everything is exactly as it appears to be. Case in point? How about a September morning when Bill and I walked over a mountain to glass for grizzly bears. For a time, we didn't have any luck because fog kept wafting up out of the main valley blocking our view. Finally, through a hole in the fog, we spotted a grizzly on an adjacent ridge. It didn't take us very long to realize that this was one huge bear. It was digging away right at the edge of a steep cliff, and we kept whispering back and forth about what a huge bear it was. Suddenly the fog cleared away and we saw another, larger bear just above the first bear. After an embarrassing moment of silence, we were forced to admit that we had been watching a yearling. The fog had somehow distorted and magnified it to such a degree that we

Ben Meisner with a big boar grizzly. Taken along the McGregor River.

honestly believed that we were watching one of the biggest bears that ever graced those mountains. After the embarrassment passed, we settled down for a hearty laugh.

Since that time I have become a little better judge of bear size. I find that the best measure is to compare the body depth to the length of the legs. If they about the same, it is a small bear. Alternately, if a bear's body is much deeper than the length of its legs, you know it's a big bear. As to the sex of the bear, it is best to notice the size of the neck, as boars have much heavier necks than sows.

From the time of my childhood I was led to believe that when grizzlies are in an area, all other animals move out. This is not true. Many animals such as deer and caribou, seem to completely ignore them unless they get very close. I'm sure these animals are quite aware of what each other can do and this saves a lot of unnecessary running on all sides.

While building a cabin back in the mountains in 1966, we found ourselves running low on food, so an amiable young school teacher named Dave Windle and I set out to get a mule deer to add to the larder. We left camp just at daylight, climbed over a ridge, and spotted two mule deer bucks on an adjacent peak. Then we saw two more bucks 200 yards beyond them, and noticed that one of them was a huge deer with an enormous rack. As it was open alpine between us and the deer, there was no way we could get closer, so we decided to try for one of the closer bucks. We flipped a coin for first shot and Dave won, but our agreement stated that if the first shot missed, then it was anyone's deer.

Dave stretched out and was about to shoot when I noticed that his rifle barrel was pointed at a rock only a few inches in front of the barrel. His scope was looking over the rock and had I not noticed it, he would have been in for a wicked surprise. He re-aimed, and with his shot all the deer took off down the mountain with the spring-loaded bounce so typical of mule deer. I jumped up and fired, then saw my bullet hit just behind and below one of the deer. I aimed higher and gave it more lead, and then with the luckiest shot of my life, hit it right in mid-air. As the deer dropped to the ground, Dave whirled and said, "What a shot!" I didn't acknowledge it, but I'm sure that I was more shocked than he was. We paced the distance off at exactly 456 paces.

After we dressed out the deer, I took half and started back over the mountain for camp, while Dave took the other half down into a beautiful little subalpine valley, where he began burying it in a snow-field for future use.

After climbing with the load of venison for a while, I stopped to rest and glanced down at Dave who was busy burying the deer. Just at that instant I saw a grizzly moving up toward him from a distance of about 200 feet. Dave had left his rifle where we had shot the deer, so he wouldn't have to pack it up again—this left him defenceless. I took off down the mountain shouting at Dave, and when he heard me and glanced up, I pointed to the bear which had also heard me and turned away. Dave later said that the bear didn't look too bad going in the opposite direction.

We continued on and carried the venison over the peaks until we came to a snowfield, where we stopped and rested. As we had no drinking water with us, Dave sucked on some snow. An hour later we arrived back in camp where Dave got violently ill, then spent the rest of the day alternating between bed and vomiting.

We hung the deer in a tree right beside the open style tent we were sleeping in, and then we retired for the night. A few hours later while we were sound asleep, we heard a tremendous crash and thought we had a grizzly in camp. Then it was all hands on deck. We rushed out with our rifles and flashlights, and were very pleased to find that it was just a case of the rope breaking under the weight of the deer.

The next morning Dave awoke feeling fine, so he got out the fry pan and did up some steaks. So help me, I've never tasted anything better in my life. We had steaks five times that day, so by the end of the following day, we had used up all the venison.

The next daylight found Dave and I, along with my nephew Barry McKinley, going over the same peak for the other half of the deer. No sooner did we crest the peak, than we were met with a splendid sight: below us, in fact on the same snowfield where Dave had buried the deer, stood the same huge buck, with a smaller buck deer beside him. Less than 100 yards below them, a grizzly was digging up the bulbs of glacier lilies. Aside from the odd glance from the deer, they were perfectly at peace with the world. As we sat watching, a coyote loped across the mountain and passed between the deer and bear. We watched in silence for several minutes and then Dave whispered, "You know, this is the kind of thing that a person never forgets until he dies."

The deer started moving and passed just below us as we lay hidden behind boulders, and though Dave had a licence and tag, he would not shoot. He just shrugged and said, "A magnificent specimen like that deserves to live."

I spotted this deer a few more times throughout the years; a true king that stood head and shoulders above any other deer I've ever seen. In that remote area, I have every reason to believe it died a natural death.

After the deer were lost to view, we riveted our attention on the grizzly, as Dave wanted one. But again he would not shoot because this was a two-year-old and he wanted a big one or none at all.

Well, the heat of the day increased, which caused the bear to start looking for a place to bed down, and where do you think it went? Why it climbed up to the top of the snowfield and dug a hole in the snow right against a cliff. It then crawled in and laid down, and had we not seen it go there, we would never have picked it out, even with binoculars. As we walked along the ridges, we kept watch but it never stirred. Undoubtedly it could not possibly have found a better place to spend the day, for here it found escape not only from the heat, but also from the flies that are a constant source of irritation to animals in summer.

When a person spends many years wandering the mountains they are bound to have experiences that elicit strong emotions. Such as the September evening in the '60s, when Clarence and I sat glassing a distant mountain and spotted two grizzlies. We set off to investigate and when we got closer it became apparent that this was two cubs without their mother. The poor creatures seemed to be extremely nervous and kept constantly moving across the snow covered slope. We watched them move along the mountainside for about one mile until they were swallowed up by the gathering darkness. As we hiked back to camp, I felt a sense of despair for them as they headed into what I thought was a lingering death. Since that time, however, there has been increasing evidence showing that grizzly cubs can survive alone at the age of seven or eight months.

Many times we have had a ringside seat when grizzlies have discovered our presence. Their actions, or rather reactions, are not always what one would expect. Again in the sixties, Bill and I were after an adult grizzly that we had spotted on an adjacent ridge. Between us and the bear lay a subalpine valley which we had to cross in order to approach the bear. As we dropped into the valley bottom, we were confronted with a mother grizzly and two cubs directly in our path. We made a large circle around and downwind of them, and then continued on toward the other bear. A few minutes later we noticed that the three bears had changed direction and were headed toward a stream we had just walked along. This caused us to sit down and watch what would happen when they hit our fresh scent. The sow came down the creek bank and the instant she got our scent, she let out a mighty cough, then cleared the bank and sniffed each cub. Then she started running, but only a few steps; then she turned and brought the cubs back where they sniffed the scent again. Once again she led her cubs away on the run, but only a few hundred feet away she stopped and checked out some old bear diggings. Again she ran off with the cubs and again she stopped to check out some other bear diggings. Finally she was lost to view, and when we turned our attention back to the other bear, it was gone, probably alerted by the mother's cough.

At the time I thought that the mother came back to our scent because she wasn't sure what it was. I now believe that she knew exactly what we were and wanted to make certain that her cubs did too.

Several times I have seen mother grizzlies sniff or appear to sniff their cubs when danger threatened. I've often wondered if they are checking to see if they are all right or if they are imparting a message to them. Something else that seemed puzzling at that time was why the mother would stop to check out diggings when her and her cubs were in danger. I think this was answered by Andy Russell in his magnificent book—*Grizzly Country*. If I understood him right, he believes that grizzlies are extremely proud animals and that by leaving in this manner, they are in effect saying, "It's not safe here, so let's leave, but let's leave with dignity." I think Mr. Russell hit the nail right on the head with this observation. I have seen grizzlies do this several times, but just never put it together until I read *Grizzly Country*.

I also think Andy Russell is the number one writer about wilderness adventures. So many writers give away their lack of experience in the woods, but Mr. Russell really tells it like it is. There can be no doubt—he was there.

There are so many special memories I have of all my years in the mountains, such as the following; just as dawn broke with a clear blue sky one September morning in 1968, Virgil Brandner and I gazed across from a mountain peak to an adjacent ridge and glassed seven grizzlies feeding. A very strong wind was blowing our scent in their direction, and though they were at least one mile away as the crow flies, the morning silence was suddenly broken by the chilling roars of a mad grizzly. Just then we saw another grizzly—a large brown male—erupt from his resting spot in a small subalpine island and head down toward the thickets below at a full gallop, all the while roaring continuously. When it reached the alder thickets, it turned and went along the slope through the incredibly thick alder swales. This is possibly the most impressive thing that I have ever seen: this bear galloped through the alders where a man has a terrible time walking and the alders simply moved out of its way. Only after it was a safe distance away did the roaring cease, and it was a while after that before the chills stopped running up and down my spine.

I believe this was a bear that was wounded several years earlier and managed to escape, probably by rolling down the mountain. Several times in later years I heard it roar out its hatred at the first scent of man. A sound that went right through me, and I doubt that there is another sound in nature that expresses unbearable rage with more eloquence. When the big grizzly stopped roaring, we turned our attention back to the other seven bears but they had all vanished. As for this brown grizzly, we would meet again.

In the summer of 1971, a chap named Gordon Ross asked me if I would assist him in getting a grizzly bear, as it had been his lifetime dream to get one. I agreed to give it a try, on the condition that he would go to the range and practice shooting before we lost a wounded bear, rather than after. He informed me that he had already done his practicing and so we started out with a hunt near timberline in September.

On our first evening out, we worked our way up on to a peak at the 6000-foot level where we intended to glass for bear. There were some clouds in the sky but we had heard no thunder. Suddenly a bolt of lightning flashed right in front of Gordon, who was about 50 feet ahead of me. Instantly Gordon threw his rifle away and hit the ground. I followed suit and had no sooner hit the ground than a ridiculous thought struck me, "That was a $1500 rifle and scope that he threw out onto the rocks—what a waste."

No sooner had we hit the ground, or rocks if you prefer, than a very heavy rainstorm hit us, and in a matter of seconds we were completely drenched. A strong wind had arrived with the rain, which was rapidly stealing my body heat, so I got up and made a dash for some cliffs just a few jumps away. Upon reaching the cliffs, I shouted to Gordon several times before he heard me over the noise of the storm. I motioned for him to come, and after hesitating for a minute he gathered his rifle to follow me. No sooner had he taken a jump, then another bolt flashed right behind him. It was like a still photograph— Gordon frozen in mid-air with a bright light right behind him.

Being an employee of BC Hydro, Gordon understood electricity very well, and this time he refused to move until the storm had gone past. When it finally did, it was two sad-faced, drenched rats that stumbled back to camp just as darkness fell.

That evening as we sat around the cabin drinking coffee, Gordon asked why I had insisted that he not use his variable scope for glassing. I told him about some people that had used their scopes for glassing and had forgotten to put the scope back on low power. Then, when they went to shoot at an animal that was close by, they could not see it.

I also told Gordon that I preferred that he use good expanding bullets, as we had seen several bears lost after being hit well with partition type bullets. In contrast, we used copper point expanding bullets in 30-06 rifles and seldom lost bears. In fact, Bill got his biggest grizzly by shooting it in a hind leg as it ran away through the trees. The massive injury caused such bleeding that the bear only made a 200-foot dash before it collapsed.

Our motto was quite simple: if the bear doesn't stop the bullet, then change ammunition. There is nothing to be gained by blowing up the mountain behind them. The assumption that these bullets will hit bone and keep going, is the apparent reason for their acceptance. But the same thing can be said about military ammunition, which leaves about the same sized exit hole. I have always felt that there is no logic in this argument because if you hit any major bone, you have your bear. It's when you miss bone that you need a good expanding bullet that will open up and do massive damage, even in six or eight inches of flesh.

The next day, Gordon and I spent several hours glassing in vain. Then I accepted the fact that the bears were still down on the salmon streams. We gave up and headed home, and though we had seen no bears, we had seen a total of 35 blue grouse—the most I have ever seen. At least 20 of these birds were seen in a one-mile walk through the subalpine.

The following spring, I spent some time following the railway tracks looking for grizzly on train-killed moose. One day I found where a moose had been dragged back into the woods, so I checked it out and found what appeared to be large tracks. But because of the nature of the ground, I was unable to determine if they were grizzly tracks or not. I notified Gordon who was unable to come out because of a previous commitment. The next day I checked it again and found that there were only about 50 pounds of flesh left. This meant that a 700-pound moose had been almost entirely consumed in two nights. I could not believe that one bear ate that much, so I suspected several bears were eating there. I phoned Gordon and told him that if he didn't get out for that evening's hunt that it would be too late.

By late afternoon Gordon arrived and we took our trail bikes and rode along the grade for six miles, then walked the last mile to the carcass. We positioned ourselves 200 yards downwind of the carcass where we hid behind some small spruce trees. The reason we hid downwind was because a smart bear will sometimes circle as much as 400 yards downwind of a carcass and then scent the area well behind the carcass in order to make sure that there are no surprises waiting for it in there.

Perhaps 30 minutes passed, when out of the woods came a big black bear with a large diamond-shaped white spot on his chest. He faced us and stared right at us from a distance of about 40 feet. Then he made us out and took off for parts unknown.

This left us completely puzzled—did this bear leave the large tracks at the carcass? Or was there a bigger bear feeding there? We decided

Gordon Ross with grizzly, shot April 30, 1972 near Longworth – a possible man-killer.

to wait until dark to see. We settled down again and just before dark we heard a large animal moving noisily through the forest toward us. It made no attempt to be quiet and when it reached the open grade, it came right out like it owned the entire area. At first glance I knew this was the big brown boar that had roared at us so many times in the surrounding mountains.

Now I was really caught with my pants down. The bear had came out on the downwind side of me so I was between it and Gordon. On top of that, Gordon had told me not to shoot, regardless, as he wanted it to be his bear alone. I knew that with a few more steps this bear would get our scent, so I did the only thing I could think of and put my fingers in my ears, then mouthed the words, "Shoot, shoot". I had told Gordon that I wanted him to break a shoulder on the bear and he promised that he would. He was about 10 feet from me on one side, and the bear was about 30 feet from me on the other side when Gordon fired right in front of my face. Instantly the bear threw his hind end up over to land on his back, then commenced bouncing and thrashing about, filling the evening air with the most blood-chilling roars imaginable. In fact, I'm sure they could have been heard miles away. When it stopped bouncing for a minute, Gordon silenced it with a neck shot.

By this time it was getting dark, so I wanted to gut it and prop the chest cavity open for cooling, then return to get it at daylight which was another six hours away. But Gordon informed me in no uncertain terms, "If you leave I'm going to stay all night; no one is going to steal my bear!".

Imagine, if you can, me undressing a large grizzly while Gordon held a dim flashlight. Over an hour later I had the hide off in what surely must have been the worst skinning job in history. I'm sure there had to be at least 100 pounds of flesh and fat left on the hide. Next, we cut a pole and draped the bear hide over it and with much difficulty, carried this 200-pound load back to our bikes.

It was well past midnight when we arrived home and spread the hide out on the ground, then retired for the night—at least I did. Poor Gordon, I don't think he got a wink of sleep all night; he kept shining the light out the window to make sure nothing was bothering his precious bear hide.

As we fleshed out the hide the next morning, I couldn't help but notice that Gordon was elated. I've seen some happy bear hunters, but none ever as happy as Gordon—he just beamed and beamed some more. A short time later, two American hunters stopped by to see the bear. They watched with envy written all over their faces and then one of them said, "I'll buy that bear from you".

Instantly Gordon came back with, "You don't have enough money to buy this bear."

I thought it strange that he would say that without first asking how much money the gentleman had.

That afternoon we returned to the carcass and found that Gordon's first bullet had broken both shoulders. He had used a .375 H&H rifle, which is a good idea because if you miss the first shot, then the recoil will drive you back far enough so that you have time for another shot. As we stood there examining the bear, Gordon asked me what I thought it weighed and I guessed between 600 and 700 pounds. Taxidermist Al Rand thought it weighed more.

*Prospector Harold
Olson in 1965 – killed
by a grizzly bear.*

This bear still had four inches of fat over the rear portion of its body near the tail, which appears to be the last area of fat to burn off. This, in spite of the fact that it had just emerged from the den perhaps a month earlier. This bear was taken only three miles from the spot where Harold Olson had been mauled and killed on October 23rd the previous fall, and I have no qualms about saying that I feel certain this was the bear that did him in. Harold had an axe with him when he was attacked, and an injury compatible with an axe cut was found on the bear's neck. As this bear had been wounded years earlier, I have no doubt that Harold's fate was sealed when he walked right into it in its bed. We never did see that bear again or hear its mad roars echo through the mountains. I firmly believe it was the same bear.

Because of the exceptional visibility around timberline, we are sometimes able to see things that profoundly impress us. Such as the day in July, 1975, when I was in the alpine glassing grizzlies and taking pictures. As was usually the case, I finally managed to spot some grizzlies—a mother with two cubs on an adjacent slope about six hundred yards distant. I watched them for a couple hours as they moved slowly along the slope, with the brightly colored cubs often disappearing among the wild flowers. Suddenly one of the cubs ran downhill through an island of fir trees, obviously chasing something. Then it started pawing by a downtree at what possibly was a ground squirrel. A few seconds later, the animal must have bit its paw, for I plainly heard it cry out. Instantly the mother tore through the island of trees to stand at the cub's side in two seconds flat. The significance was not lost on me, for I couldn't help but visualize what could have happened had a hapless hiker been the one to make that cub cry out.

On that same trip, I was watching a mother with two yearlings when it became obvious that one of them was an albino. I headed toward them to get some pictures and had only gone a few feet when I heard a loud roar come from their direction. I stopped and looked through the binoculars and saw a large boar emerge from some trees just above the other bears. It made a circle and picked up the scent where the other bears had walked only a minute earlier. Then it let out another roar, probably miffed at being startled. I took several pictures as the mother led her yearlings over the mountain and into the next valley.

I must add a footnote to this story. It occurred about five years later when I told this story to a wildlife officer over a coffee at the Purden Lake Café. When I finished, he informed me that he knew where there was an albino grizzly and pointed out that it was about 50 air-miles from where I had spotted it. Five will get you ten that it was the same bear and that it suffered the fate of many two-year-old bears and was driven from its place of birth.

It is nothing short of amazing the amount of effort hunters will put into getting their game, especially if it is a big grizzly bear. Some people just don't know when to quit. A classic example of this was a hunt for grizzly bear on the upper Parsnip River in 1983. This story was told to by the person it happened to, Rick Guenther, who was trapping the area at that time.

"It was early May, and I was trapping beavers at the time. The first day we were there, we found where a tree had fallen across the river, blocking it off, so I had no choice but to cut it out of there. I took my chainsaw and walked out on the tree and started cutting it. Suddenly it let go with a bang, and sent me flying up in

Clarence and I watch a family of grizzlies while sister Isabelle enjoys the view.

the air. When I came down, I landed right in the river. Then I had to swim back to shore.

"A couple of days later, I noticed that the beaver carcasses I had left on the bank of the river had gone missing. That evening I sat in wait, and just before dark a huge grizzly came out of the woods and turned broadside to me at a distance of about 60 feet. I was using 130 grain bullets in my .270 rifle, and so I fired at his heart and he dropped like a log. After he dropped, I couldn't see him, so I waited about five minutes and then moved slowly forward with my gun ready. When I got right close, I threw several sticks at it, then put the rifle to its head until I was sure it was dead. When I was satisfied that it was dead, I went to unload my gun and got a chilling surprise: when I had attempted to reload after firing the first shot, I had not brought the bolt back far enough to introduce a new cartridge, and so I had put the empty back in the barrel again. I had approached the bear with a useless weapon.

"I left it at dark, being unable to skin it because it had fallen into a big hole at the edge of the river bank. The next morning I returned with my wife and we both tried to pull the bear out of that hole, but we couldn't do it. I had a riverboat with a 50-HP outboard engine on it, so I hooked a line to the bear. Then I made a circle upriver and gunned the engine coming back down the river in an effort to pull it out The bear didn't come out, although the boat almost jumped out of the water. About 20 times I tried that without success, then I finally gave up.

"Next I headed downriver to Anzac, where my boat trailer was parked. Once I got down there, I took the winch off the trailer and brought it back up to the bear. This was a two-hour trip in itself.

"I spiked the winch to a tree with four big spikes and then started to winch the bear out of that hole. But again the bear didn't move, instead the spikes pulled out of the tree. I couldn't give up after all that work, so I took my chainsaw and notched the tree, then spiked it again and wrapped a bunch of haywire around it for added strength. This time it held, and at last I was able to drag that bear out and skin it."

Rick had one more story that I feel deserves telling. It confirms what I've always known—that grizzly bears are extraordinarily tough.

"I was glassing two families of grizzlies up near timberline when I noticed they were getting very close together. There was a mother with one cub and a mother with two cubs. At one point, they climbed up a rock face that was almost vertical for a distance of about 100 feet. Once they got on top where there was a little bench, they squared off and started fighting. The mother with two cubs managed to land a good swat and knocked the other bear over the edge, where it fell the almost vertical 100 feet down onto the rocks. I knew for sure that the bear was dead, so you can imagine how surprised I was when it got up, shook itself off, and went on its way just like nothing had happened."

Rick's experience only confirms what I have learned about grizzlies: they are in fact just a ball of muscle, and they seem to be able to bounce down a mountainside without injury.

Sometimes when bears act in a strange manner, there is a good reason for it if we can only figure it out. An example of this occurred the day Clarence, Bill and I glassed what we thought was a sub-adult (three-to-five-year-old) grizzly as it worked its way across a moun-

Rick Guenther with his hard won prize.

tain just below timberline. In late afternoon this bear began acting in a peculiar manner: it would run a short distance, then run back. Then it would climb the mountain a short distance, and then run down again. We had an excellent view of the mountainside but didn't see anything that could have upset the bear. After carrying on in this manner for about an hour, the bear took off downhill and disappeared into the alders thickets far below. A couple hours later the mystery was solved when a heavy snowstorm moved in which lasted for several days.

Years ago, I noticed that some of the older, smarter boar grizzlies seemed to be able to get sufficient sustenance during the long nights of late fall and therefore were very elusive and seldom seen during the day. This does not apply any more, because since they are not being hunted to any degree they have lost much of the fear—or perhaps I should say the necessary cunning—they once needed to survive. Now it is common to see boar grizzlies feeding during the day, especially during the months of September and October. As for mothers and cubs or yearlings, they never could afford the luxury of lying in seclusion all day, and have always needed to be up and about for the greater part of the day. I have often seen them out feeding from dawn to dusk with only a couple of hours rest around midday.

Something that has always puzzled me is why grizzlies have such a need to make a liar out of me. I'm thinking of an incident that occurred during the summer of 1985, when I was working a forest fire on the East Torpy River. One afternoon a radio call came from district office that an aircraft had reported another fire near Mt. Alexander, about 30 miles from our location. After we had lifted the crews back to camp for the evening, pilot Blair Wood and I flew a recce to find the fire. As we came around a mountain with the Jet Ranger helicopter, we spotted a huge grizzly climbing well above timberline. As soon as it sensed our presence, it began running up the mountain. When we reached the area where the fire was supposed to be, we quickly determined that the pilot had erred on his grid and reported the fire we were taking action on. On our return to camp we flew around the same mountain only to find that the grizzly was gone. At that point I said to Blair, "It will be down in the timber because bears always run down from the alpine when threatened." At the same instant Blair pointed up the mountain to where the bear was still running uphill. It was at least 2000 feet above timberline and still climbing. Blair summed it up exactly when he said, "It just did that to make a liar out of you."

"You've got that right." I responded, "this is the only time in my life that I've ever seen a grizzly go far up into the alpine when threatened."

What I didn't say was that this was just one of many times that bears had made a liar out of me. In fact, it seemed that every time I suggested that bears wouldn't do a certain thing, then they immediately proved me wrong. Could it be a conspiracy?

I have always done my best not to let bears make a liar out of me when it comes to the size of their tracks. And perhaps this is a good time to say that the biggest front pad I ever measured from a sow grizzly was 6-3/4 inches across. This bear walked with a lone cub across a mud flat and left very clear tracks. But the biggest grizzly tracks that I ever witnessed were high in the mountains during the month of June. I have had people show me these huge tracks on snowfields and have had them suggest that they were 20 inches long. I had to agree on the size, but I also had to point out that the tracks had melted out in the summer sun until they were many times their original size. I wouldn't be surprised if this is where many Bigfoot stories originate.

Many people confuse black and grizzly tracks, especially if the black has long claws. We have a rule of thumb that has served us well: if there is doubt, then you can bet it is a black; if it is a grizzly, you will not have any doubt.

I think that there is more 'bovine scatology' involved with the weights and sizes of bears than in any other aspect of wildlife. Their long fur coats make them appear far heavier than they really are— especially in spring. The times that we did weigh bears, almost all guesses were high—in some instances as much as double. There was the day that ranger Carl Rohn shot a good-sized black bear. It was taken to the CN station where it was weighed. Many guesses were made as to its weight, with some going over 400 pounds. The bear tipped the scales at exactly 240 pounds.

While Interior sow grizzlies can weigh at least 450 pounds, I am certain that I have seen some with cubs in early spring that weighed less than 200 pounds. They were quite literally skin and bones.

In an effort to be competitive with these tall-story tellers, Rand and Kirchner—two former Prince George taxidermists, resorted to the ridiculous: they found a set of horns that had been taken from a domestic cow and placed them over the horns of a mountain goat that was displayed in their shop. Even though these horns were so big that they were laughable, hunters still came in and said that they had seen bigger ones. Go figure!

I suppose the thing that impresses people most about bears is their great strength. And I sure go along with that. Clarence remembers the time a grizzly came to a horse carcass that he was hunting on. The horse was lying on its side, rigor mortis having locked its legs together. Along came a grizzly bear that grabbed one hind leg of the horse with each paw and then proceeded to lift one leg right up and over, bringing it to the ground on the other side amid the snapping and cracking of bones. When it let go, the horse stayed in that position. Clarence took this bear and it weighed out at exactly 415 pounds—imagine what a 700-pound grizzly could do.

We also have seen sign that showed where a grizzly has taken away a big moose without leaving a drag trail. An elderly guide told me that they grab the moose with their teeth, hold their head high, and then turn around, dragging the moose over their back. This allows most of the weight to be carried on their backs. I sure would like to watch that just once.

It is probably their great strength and ferocity that has given grizzlies their 'horrible bear' reputation. And this is really driven home when they decide to stalk us. Clarence and Olga walked into a situation like this back in the mountains in 1989. They were crossing an alpine area when they spotted a lone sub-adult grizzly coming in their direction. They climbed up onto a ridgetop and watched as the grizzly cut their trail. It stopped, checked it out, then began following them. When it got within a hundred yards, Clarence hollered at it and it took off and ran back to where it had first cut their trail. Here it stopped, turned around and started toward them again. It came to the top of the ridge and in spite of their hollering, was coming right up to them when Clarence fired a shot. The bullet hit the mountain beside it and this caused the bear to turn and leave. It ran back through the alpine and disappeared into the forest below. They believe this was a three- or four-year-old grizzly—the worst age as far as getting into trouble; It seems they're too young to be smart, but old enough to cause trouble.

I asked Clarence what he would have done if he hadn't had his rifle, and 'ever the comedian' he answered, "The only thing I could have done—hope like hell that I could outrun Olga." When I suggested that she might hold a grudge over a little thing like that, he added, "Yes, but not for long."

This story only had a happy ending because Clarence had a rifle along. Without it, they would have been completely at the mercy of the bear, because there is nowhere to hide above timberline.

Just after this happened, I asked a conservation officer what he thought the bear's motive was and he replied, "If I had to bet, I'd say it was predation."

My daughter Kim and sister Margaret at timberline, 1989.

I find it interesting to observe people on their first trip into the high country. Many seem so surprised at what they find there. During the summer of 1988, my sister Margaret and I took my daughter Kim into the mountains for the first time. She was 11-years-old at the time and it was a pleasure for me to notice the wonder in her eyes as she gazed at the incredible beauty around her. The wildflowers were in full bloom, adding a special touch to the already abundant color. As we sat on a mountain peak viewing the surrounding area, Kim asked, "How come it's so quiet?" It brought back memories of the wonder I felt when I first visited the high country. Wonder that has not ceased to this day.

While on these mountain trips, we are always hoping to see a grizzly chase, because this really is a highlight of any trip. Something I've noticed, though, is that these chases are not what I used to think they were. Of the times that I have seen grizzlies chasing other grizzlies, only the two-year-olds seem to leave the area. During September, 1998, Bill and I made several trips into the high country. On one trip, Bill had to return home, so I stayed another three days by myself. The day before I returned home, a large black boar grizzly spent the entire day digging up roots just half a mile from the cabin. The next morning, it was nowhere to be seen. As I left the cabin to return home, I glanced at the mountain just in time to see what I thought was a two-year-old grizzly come galloping along. Then, right behind it I saw the black grizzly which had been just out of sight around the ridge. It pursued the young bear for perhaps a quarter-mile before it stopped and resumed feeding. The other bear seemed to take the attack seriously for it continued running away into the distance. Twice I saw it stand up to look back; each time it got down and ran. There seemed to be no doubt, this bear had packed its suitcase and was leaving town.

This doesn't seem to apply as much to sub-adult bears as they may run away, but only for a short distance, then they may come back again. The following story by Paul Paulson of Prince George substantiates this:

"It was September 1994 when my son Grant flew me and my grandson, Dylan, into Ice Mountain Lake to hunt moose. Grant dropped us off with his Helio Courier and departed, intending to pick us up a couple days later. Just before dark that evening, we saw a moose across the lake from us so we crossed the lake and shot it. By the time we got finished cutting it up it was dark, so we loaded the moose into our Zodiac and went back across the lake by moonlight. That evening I studied the regulations and realized that I had forgotten to take evidence of sex off the moose, so the next morning we went back to get it. The lake was shallow near the kill, so I wore my hip-waders to approach it. Dylan stayed at the Zodiac with the rifle, so I was unarmed as I went to the kill."

"Why did you go to the kill without a gun?" I asked.

"I didn't expect there would be anything on it yet. But I realize now that I really put myself in danger. I walked to the remains to get the evidence and realized that a grizzly had been feeding there. This really gave me a jolt, so I quickly got the evidence and hurried back to the Zodiac. We moved out from the shore a ways and then a really big, black grizzly came out of the woods to the remains."

"You could easily have been mauled or killed." I suggested.

"I know, and I sure wouldn't do that again. But the interesting part of it all is that a few hours later a mid-sized blonde grizzly came out of the woods and tried to approach the carcass. When the big grizzly spotted it, he chased the blonde back into the woods again. The next day Grant was supposed to pick us up, but because he was fogged in, he couldn't get off with his airplane. This forced us to stay an extra two days at the lake. Several times during those days that big grizzly chased the smaller bear away, but every time it came back. Many times it stood up about 30 feet away and watched the big bear eat."

Paul's story fits in so well with observations we have made. Perhaps these bears believe that they will eventually be rewarded if they wait long enough. There's also a lesson to be learned from Paul's experience: if you ever have to return to a carcass or a kill, then act as though there is a bear on it until you prove otherwise. I would also like to point out that I'm prepared to bet that this blond grizzly was a sow, at least it has been my experience that most light-colored grizzlies are sows.

The aggressiveness now displayed by grizzlies was made evident to Bill Benedict and I in July, 1998, when we were watching two large grizzlies that were together for mating purposes. As they made their way across a mountain, we noticed two other mating grizzlies a short distance above them. Suddenly the two big grizzlies went tearing up the mountain and separated the other two bears. Then they proceeded to chase the sow, and continued until they were lost to view at least a mile further along the mountain. Luckily, we were able to catch some of their flight on camera.

Bears are not the only animals one can have problems with. Although we have never had problems with bears trying to break into our cabins, I can not say the same about porcupines, which I think are the most troublesome creatures in the mountains, especially if they manage to break into a cabin. Twice we have had this happen, and both times they got in by breaking windows in mid-winter. Bill Benedict and his son Wayne were the unlucky ones that discovered one of these break-ins, and they had an incredibly dirty, stinking mess

Bill and Wayne Benedict.

to clean up. We solved that problem and any worry about break-ins by wolverines or bears by putting heavy fencing material over the windows.

'Porkys' are also a nightmare when they find an unoccupied tent camp in the forest. Once we returned to our camp and found a porky hard at work, we knew we had trouble. It had chewed the tent to ribbons, chewed holes in all the tin cans—even the empty billy can had several holes chewed through it. At a time like that a person wishes there were a lot more fishers in the woods—the porcupines' natural enemy.

Right behind porcupines for causing trouble are mice. And when you find about 40 of them in a cabin at the same time, then you can relate to how Churchill must have felt when he stated, "You realize of course that this means war." When they start holding drag races across the floor at midnight, then it's time to take action.

In late fall, 1998, a weasel took up residence under our cabin. In summer 1999 she raised three young under the floor. On one of our trips to the cabin in July, she brought out her three young and showed them to us, then took them back under the floor and we never spotted them again. The bright side of this is that we have not noticed any sign of mice in the area of the cabin since they moved in.

Of all our forms of entertainment in the mountains, one of my favorites is watching and feeding Stellar jays and whiskey jacks, or camp robbers as they are commonly and appropriately called. Now and then we will clean all the food out of our cabin that is over a year old and feed it to the birds. When we first put some food out, these birds will come along, sing us a song, and then pack away a load. But after several trips, it becomes a job and then the singing ceases. It is just a scream to watch them try to pack away caramel corn. They try to pick up several kernels at one time, but because they are hard, each time they pick up another one, the first one drops out. They will cock their heads to the side and give it strange looks, then try again.

One fall Bill and I put out a bit of food and about an hour later a jay showed up. It sang us a song, took a load of food and flew away. After it had made several trips, Bill and I loaded the outdoor table with an incredible load of food. When the jay came back, it couldn't believe its eyes. It looked the table over for a minute and then flew away without a load. We assumed it had left for good, but not so. It had gone for help, which became apparent a short time later when it returned with three other jays. Then two camp robbers showed up, and they would feed when all the jays were off-loading. To make matters even more interesting, four ground squirrels discovered the food and the table became a blur of activity. At one point we were lucky enough to get pictures of a jay flying away with a full slice of bread. Several other jays tried it and failed.

As the day wore on, the birds took longer and longer between trips. Which either meant they were playing out, or else the trees were full and they were taking the food farther and farther away to cache it. Regardless, they never quit until the table was empty and I think it's a safe bet that no jays or squirrels starved to death within 20 miles of there that winter.

6

MOUNTAIN SAFETY

IN MY BOOK *CRAZY MAN'S CREEK*, I TOLD THE STORY OF A MAN named Frank Lehman who was mauled by a grizzly bear along the McGregor River. During the mauling, Caribou John, who was with Frank, was unable to shoot because he was afraid of hitting John. This situation should not arise because it is imperative that the bear be destroyed immediately or the mauling may be fatal.

I cannot imagine a situation where a person could not safely shoot, providing they realize that the best place to shoot the bear in this situation, is in the hips. The bear will immediately let go of whatever it has hold of and whirl around to attack whatever has attacked it from behind. Then it can easily be dispatched, because for them to move with broken hips causes extreme agony. I know of two cases where they were shot in this way and managed to make cover just at dark, yet the following morning both bears were still less than 100 feet from where they had been shot. This is not to say that the bear cannot attack with only its front legs, it simply means that it should not pose a problem to an armed person.

The notion that a rifle will afford protection against bears doesn't always hold water; not even in the hands of an experienced woodsman. I'm thinking of a story about a prospector's confrontation with three grizzlies that took place in the East Kootenays back in the '20s. This incident occurred to a man named Nessie Phillips, a resident of Grasmere, BC. Nessie was prospecting along Rabbit Creek when he ran right into a sow grizzly with two yearlings. The sow attacked, so he fired several shots and knocked her down; then went to reload his 30-30. While attempting to side load a couple cartridges, he dropped one on the ground, then picked it up and went to insert it into the magazine. In the process, he pushed a twig in with it, causing the rifle to jam. At that instant one of the yearlings attacked and Nessie swung the rifle with all his might. The blow struck the bear across the head knocking it senseless; but it also broke the stock off the rifle, leaving Nessie defenseless. Then the other yearling attacked and Nessie jumped to the side to avoid the rush. The bear turned and charged again, and Nessie threw himself to the side and avoided that rush as well. Puzzled, the bear stood up, and in desperation Nessie ran at it. This caused the bear to turn and run away. Only after the bear was gone did Nessie realize that he was injured. On one of its attacks, the bear had severely damaged his arm, although he was unaware of it at the time. Badly hurt, Nessie wandered back to where he had left his horse, then rode to a cabin on the Grasmere side of the mountains. Some much-needed luck came his way later that day when Colin Sinclair, also of Grasmere, came along with a pack train load of supplies, and rendered his assistance.

Nessie survived that battle, but his injured arm was nearly useless for the rest of his life. The men later checked the battle scene and found that only the sow was dead. The two yearlings were gone.

While hoping that the day never comes when the reader has to face a charging grizzly, I simply have to point out a fact that many people are unaware of. This is making sure that you aim low if a bear is charging up a steep hill or mountain toward you. If you fail to do so, you will shoot above the animal and may find yourself out of ammunition when the bear arrives. The normal pull of gravity that affects bullets on level ground does not apply when shooting down a steep incline. Those who may have to trail wounded bears would do well to practice shooting both up and down steep inclines so they become acquainted with this phenomenon.

Speaking from experience, I have to describe a fault or weakness that is inherent in all of us. That is, we tend to panic when confronted with a terrifying situation—such as a charging grizzly at close range. If there is one thing that I can impress upon people who may find themselves in this situation, it is to know the status of your rifle or shotgun. If you have a cartridge in the barrel, then drive that fact into your consciousness, so you do not try to put a shell into an already loaded gun. Alternately, so you do not try to fire the gun when there is no cartridge in the firing chamber. You do not have the extra seconds that you may need if you are at all confused, and a charging bear sure can create that confusion.

Some people may remember a case back in the '50s, where an Alaskan guide led his hunter toward the den of a grizzly. It was springtime when they spotted the bear's den from an aircraft, so they found a place to land and then walked on the snow toward the den. They moved to a point about 100 yards from the den and were trying to figure out a way to get the bear to come out, when it saved them the trouble and charged. The guide got away only one shot; the panic-stricken hunter emptied all his unfired cartridges out on the snow. The bear killed both of them.

There is one thing certain about bears: anyone that goes into the woods can be mauled and killed by one and to pretend that one is too experienced or knowledgeable to be mauled is just empty-headed egotism. My friend Marlin Priebe and I were out hunting when I walked into a situation where I could easily have been killed. This came about when we decided to hunt moose along a series of old logging roads. We agreed to meet where the roads rejoined which was about a half-hour walk from the spot where we split up. After an uneventful walk, I reached our meeting spot only to find that Marlin had not arrived. I hadn't heard any gunshots, so I sat down and waited for his arrival. After waiting about an hour, I noticed it was starting to get dark, so I headed back along the road he had been following, hoping to meet him. After I had walked only a short distance, I was suddenly startled out of my skin by a loud roar right beside me. Then a bear started slapping the brush around only a few feet off the road. As I was hunting alone, I had a cartridge in the firing chamber. I threw the safety off and then with my back against the thick willows on the opposite side of the narrow road, I walked by, talking to the bear all the while. I never got a glimpse of this bear, so thick was the undergrowth in that spot. After I got past the spot where the bear was, it finally quieted down, so I started calling to Marlin. I was terrified that he may have been attacked by this bear, although I didn't notice any sign to support my fear. After I called several times, Marlin finally answered, much to my relief. That same evening we found out that two people had ridden by that spot just the previous day on horseback, and they had been roared at as well.

It seems obvious that the bear had a kill it was protecting, and it is just as obvious that it could easily have mauled or killed me. I don't think it was more than 10 feet from me when it first roared.

There have been so many books written about safety around bears; so many things one should do or not do, that it has resulted in more confusion than assistance. Some people say that to throw many do's and don'ts at them only results in confusion, and then they are not sure what to do.

Some books tell the readers to watch for bear sign—like droppings, tracks, claw marks on trees, pieces of hair caught on limbs, rotten stumps or logs that have been torn open, or just the smell of bear which can be very pervasive. Readers are advised that if they find these indications, then they should immediately leave the area.

In my years with the Forest Service I often worked in areas where I saw bear sign every day. Imagine what would have happened if I had returned day after day and told my boss that I was unable to do my job because there was bear sign around. I'm sure that by the end of the first week I would have joined the ranks of the unemployed.

Some people wear bells so the bears can hear their approach. This prompted one caller to a radio talk show to tell the host that he knew how to tell the difference between grizzly and black bear scat. "It's easy," he offered, "you just stir around in the droppings and if they are grizzly droppings you will find bells."

Seriously though, I think making a great deal of noise is about the only preventive action one can take. And there is no guarantee that it will work. Also it must be remembered that the noise has to be loud enough to rise above any ambient noise—such as a high wind, streams, rainstorms, etc. To each his own, though, I know that I would not even consider hiking in the mountains with someone that was continually making noise; I'm out there to enjoy the wildlife, not scare it away.

Certainly, a high-powered rifle or a slug from a shotgun is the best defense against an irate or predacious bear, but for many field workers, carrying a rifle or shotgun is out of the question. Tree planters for example, have enough to carry without packing a gun. They are often the most exposed of all woods workers because they continually stop and go—the type of movement that can arouse a bear's curiosity. As well, they are so preoccupied with their work that they are unlikely to notice an approaching bear.

It has been my belief for many years that the worst thing a person can do is to yell or holler when confronted by a mother and cubs. This only tends to excite the mother who is obviously excited enough already. There is something I have tried a few times that seems to work well with mothers and cubs. That is to cough; the same sound they make. I have seen mothers take their cubs and leave when coughed at by another bear, and this is what gave me the idea in the first place. It seems a mother would be foolish to lead her cubs in an attack against another bear, as it may be a big bear that would kill them. I would like to see some studies done on the effects of coughing at mothers and cubs to prove whether or not it is a viable defense. I would not try this against lone adult bears as they may take it as a challenge and act accordingly.

I do want to make a suggestion that may be helpful: when hiking around timberline, especially during September and October when the grizzlies are there in great numbers, try to avoid walking through the islands of subalpine fir whenever possible. Weather permitting, grizzlies spend most of their time up near timberline at this time of year, and they make a habit out of resting in these islands. When startled, they may not choose to leave their cover if other cover is not close at hand. If one walks into an island that contains a mother and cub(s), they may run out of ideas, courage, and toilet paper all at the same time. Also, people must remember that even if they are making a fair amount of noise around these alpine islands, it can easily be swept away by the winds that are almost a constant in the high country. We also have to remember that cubs can make a considerable amount of noise that can prevent the mother from sensing approaching danger.

Other places where grizzlies like to hide on hot afternoons are under snow-slides by avalanche tracks where spring runoff or streams have cut out openings. I have seen mothers and cubs emerge from these spots. If hikers walked into theses openings when bears were in there, they would be at very close range indeed.

I know for a fact that grizzlies can pick up sound through the ground, but I don't know if they can tell what direction the sound comes from. This means that in attempting to escape, they may run right into the person(s) making the sound—the worst possible situation, as the bears may feel that they are surrounded or trapped. When they're in a thicket, there's no way to know if they're standing up or lying down, and that may explain why they don't seem to pick up the sound sometimes. It could be that they're lying down and can't pick up the sound through their bodies as well as they do through the pads of their feet when they're standing. They may also be prevented from picking up the sound through the ground by the constant movement of their cubs.

I suggest that people prove this effect for themselves—simply lie down on your back with your head touching the ground and get a friend to walk toward you at a normal fast walk. You will be amazed at how the sound travels through the ground—especially high in the mountain ridges. Anyone who has traveled the mountains can tell you that they often have a drum effect, and for some reason bears seem to have an extraordinary ability to pick up these sounds.

Stan Hale, who packed with horses for years, told of a grizzly that he tried to drive from his camp. When he fired his rifle, the bear ignored it; then the gun malfunctioned. He finally drove the bear away by mounting one of his horses and waving a large pack cover. In short, the bear was driven off by something that appeared much bigger than itself. This fits in well with what many experts advocate: take off your jacket and hold it as high and as wide as possible. There is a lot of bluffing in the bear world.

A word to the wise—if you run into a bear and it pays little or no attention—then watch out. Bears are not deaf, and the reason they pay no attention is because there are other animals around—namely—more bears. They think you are one of their own kind.

It's just basic common sense that many bear attacks could be avoided if hikers would stay together as opposed to spreading out. Otherwise a bear may attempt to run from one person only to run into another.

Watch for scavenger birds such as crows or ravens, especially if there are several in a group. This may indicate carrion that bears could be feeding on. It obviously makes sense to avoid these spots.

Note the growls or roars which are a fairly common sound in the mountains when the grizzlies are there in abundance. Often these are produced by cubs or yearlings play-fighting, a mother scolding her young, or a bear warning other bears that they are close enough.

Perhaps the most important thing of all is to keep people posted of your whereabouts. If your plans change and you must go somewhere else, leave a note in your vehicle or at the place people expect you to be.

Climbing a tree may seem like a good idea if you have time. I would just suggest that people who travel the forests a lot, try a practice run, and after you have climbed what you think is a safe distance, take note of the spot where your feet are. Then, when you come down the tree, measure the distance from the ground to where your feet were. You may well find that your feet were only six or seven feet above the ground—not nearly high enough.

Many people carry pepper spray, and the debate about its effectiveness rages on. It is worth remembering, though, that if you spray against the wind it will come back in your own face. Something that has been suggested, is that all the pepper sprays should contain a bright-colored dye. Then, in the event of a mauling, the guilty bear can be easily identified if it has been sprayed.

Quite often when there is a mauling, people will say that they don't want the bear destroyed. I can't help but wonder if anyone has the right to make such a decision. If that same bear should maul or kill someone else, should there not be some legal action taken against both that party and everyone else involved? If it was a member of our own family that was mauled or killed, perhaps we would say yes.

I was recently told by a person that spends a fair amount of time in the wilderness, "If I am ever mauled or killed by a bear, I don't want it to be harmed. I have told the authorities of my wishes and asked that they do not destroy the bear under any circumstances."

After I mulled this over in my mind for a few minutes, I replied, "If we're ever together in the woods and a bear attacks you, I sure hope I don't have a rifle with me."

"Why?" Came the response.

"Because contrary to everything I have ever believed in, I would have to ignore your screams and walk away, respecting your choice." I received a very strange look in response to my statement. Quite frankly, this attitude has me shaking my head. Perhaps people with this point of view should wear a brightly-colored armband, so that other people don't make the mistake of killing the bear when they come upon someone being mauled.

As dangerous as bears can be, I think there is something in the forests that is far more dangerous, and that is several hunters walking around together with shells in the firing chambers of their rifles. I have learned from experience that there is no such thing as a fool-proof safety catch. And bolt action rifles with the firing pin resting against a cartridge are an even greater time bomb; for to trip or fall and strike the back of the bolt against a solid object will surely discharge the rifle.

Of all the things people have to face in the forests, I doubt that there is anything that ruins more mountain trips than worry. And a major cause of worry in my experience comes from splitting up and agreeing to meet somewhere later on, then being unable to do so. Any number of things can arise that will delay a person, and this puts the other party in an awkward position. You don't know if they're injured, or if they have lost their directions. As the hours drag by, one can conjure up any number of horrid things that may have happened. This is a real trip-spoiler, and as long as people split up, there seems to be no way to avoid it.

One helpful hint that is worth remembering, is that a pair of binoculars when reversed and placed close against an object, make an excellent magnifying glass. Binoculars used in this way can be useful in the removal of splinters, devil clubs or foreign objects in the eye.

People who spend a lot of time in the backcountry should avail themselves of some knowledge of first aid. People have perished because they did not have the basic knowledge to deal with a minor artery cut. I also highly recommend an avalanche training course.

There are so many ways that people can get into trouble in the mountains. Even with the greatest care not all accidents or mistakes can be avoided. On the other hand, there are dangers that can be avoided if we are aware of them. A case in point occurred in early October 1964 to a man employed as a section foreman for CN Rail. Located at Erling, about 40 miles west of McBride BC, this fellow decided to go hunting for a mountain goat up the Goat River. When he failed to return, a search party was formed. Among the searchers were Everett Monroe and Steve Kolida, both residents of McBride. After a short search, the body of the hunter was found and the search party pieced together the events leading up to his death. This man had climbed up to the top of a mountain peak to view for game and had walked out on a cornice or snow overhang, then had broke through and fell several hundred feet to where he landed headfirst on a boulder.

These cornices occur on the lee side of ridges and peaks where snow drifts out and builds up during the winter months. As a young man I walked out on one and only later when I viewed it from a different position did I realize the danger I had been in. I have read that these cornices have claimed experienced mountaineers.

Another experience that showed the dangers inherent in mountain climbing occurred when Bill Benedict and I were wandering through the mountains in the early '60s. It started when we approached an area of slides and cliffs, and it got worse when I told Bill that we should skirt the area because it was too steep. Either Bill didn't hear me or else he didn't agree with me, because he kept right on climbing. I skirted the steepest portion and had some difficulty, but managed to make it up to the top because I had some arctic willows and stunted trees to hang on to.

I arrived on top and sat down for a needed rest, then waited for Bill. He didn't show up so I listened and could hear rocks rolling below me. I walked out to the edge of the cliff and saw Bill about 200 feet below me. I hollered to him and he called back, "I can't move, every time I take a step I start sliding."

I went down around the cliff until I was level with him, and then sized up the situation. I noticed a piece of solid rock right beside where he was standing, so I made a circular run for it, not putting much weight on the loose, broken rock. When I got to the rock, I took Bill's pack and rifle from him and said, "Follow me!" Again, I made a circular run across the loose rock and caught hold of the stunted trees at the slide's edge. Without looking back, I climbed up to the top and waited. After a few minutes of silence, I heard rocks rolling. A minute later Bill's head appeared on the ridge top.

This is the type of situation that people can and do get themselves into back in the high country. When this happened, there was no help readily available, and a serious injury would mean at least a day, or perhaps several days, alone while the other person went out for help.

Another situation that can at the very least lead to embarrassment in the mountains, is to set up your camp and then go hiking, hunting, or whatever, without taking great care to make sure you can find the camp on your return. This has happened to many people including yours truly. In my case, I camped in a row of timber about 500 feet below timberline with a friend, Eric Umstaetter. Early the next morning we arose to find a bit of fog hovering over the mountains. We took a good look around, then walked about eight miles through the McGregor mountains. Just before dark we returned and found the area socked in solid with an October snowstorm in progress. We searched for almost one hour, and it was only by the greatest luck that we stumbled right into our camp. We honestly didn't have a clue where our camp was, and we were just making circles through the endless rows of timber when we found it. We were drenched, exhausted, out of food and ideas. Since then I try to camp near a stream, or near (not under) cliffs or some other landmark that is easy to find.

I used to cruise timber with a young man named Dave Riley, who was a lot more careful in the woods than most. Yet he got into an odd situation when he was sent on a lightning-caused fire. Along with another man, they carried their packs until they were tired, then set their packs down and went looking for the fire. After several hours of futile searching, they gave up and decided to get their packs and camp for the night. They never found their packs and ended up spending the entire night sitting under a tree in a pouring rainstorm. The next evening after Dave had told me this story, he added, "Imagine, a timber cruiser getting lost and then not being able to find his pack, either; I've never been so embarrassed in my entire life."

The lesson? Never leave your pack in the forest unless you know for certain you can find it again. If for some reason you have to leave it, then hang it up in a tree by a stream or some spot that you know you can find—even if the weather socks in solid.

Another unpleasant experience is getting caught in a hail storm high above timberline. If you are just out on a day hike, you may not have a packsack to hide under. Even if you take off your coat and use it as a cover, your hands and arms can still take a terrible beating.

I think that the most important thing a person can take into the high country is very warm clothing. Equally important is head covering, where most body heat is lost. Many people combine the two by having a hood on their coat. In my opinion, the heavy raincoat/jacket combinations are the pits. They cause a person to sweat too much and they are too difficult to dry. Whoever suggested that layering clothing was the best idea sure got it right. Basic common

The endless Rockies.

sense tells us that having several layers of clothing allows us to be comfortable in all conditions.

It's no secret that weather in the mountains can change in minutes. These changes are often accompanied by strong winds that dissipate body heat so quickly that hypothermia is only a heartbeat away. And hypothermia, with its accompanying mental confusion, is not recommended when one is traveling in rugged mountains.

Probably the worst enemy a person can possibly confront in the mountains is panic, which may have been the leading factor in the following tragedies. In two different incidents, the bodies of hunters were found at the bottom of cliffs in the McBride area. Since many people have guessed why they fell, I would like to take a crack at it too. On two different occasions I got in trouble on cliffs, and both times I was after mountain goats. Both times I climbed up steep rock faces and had no problem on the ascent as I could see the hand holds as I went up. But when I tried to come down, I couldn't see where to put my feet and this was a frightening experience. When a person gets scared, then panic can set in. I believe this is what may have happened to these other hunters. Because to be caught high above cliffs with a heavy storm approaching, or perhaps night coming on, is a frightening experience that really puts pressure on a person, especially in the long, cold nights of October.

During the summer of 1954, I spent a few weeks working as a compass-man for Ian Scheetel, who taught forestry at the University of BC. We were cruising timber for the local logging company in Penny. While we were working the area between Tumuch and Pinkerton Lakes, I noticed something was wrong—if I didn't tighten the chain and shout "Chain" on a regular basis, Ian would start hollering and acting very nervous. Finally I asked what the problem was, and he confided, "A couple years ago I was cruising with a young lad as compass man and for some reason the chain didn't tighten. I started hollering, but I got no response. Then I followed the chain up to its end, but he was not there. He had vanished, and no trace of him was ever found. No sign of foul play; no sign of an animal attack; no blood drops, and no clothing." I was a heap more understanding after that; I made sure he knew where I was at all times.

When a person gets turned around in the forest, the first impulse is to run and get out of there. This impulse must be overrode or panic will prevail. I recall the time Lindy Chambers and I were returning from a fishing trip at Slim Lake in the '50s. As we walked along the 14 miles of grown-over trail in a pouring rain, we didn't pay close enough attention. This resulted in our wandering off on a game trail. There were no roads in the mountains in those days, so a person could wander for a long time without recognizing any landmarks if it was clouded in. We walked all day and finally, just before dark, hit the Fraser River. Then the rain stopped and the clouds lifted and we could see the mountains. As luck would have it, we had hit the river in a turn where it was running back up the valley. This meant that we were looking at the mountains downriver instead of upriver. We didn't recognize the mountains and this really blew us away. We were at the point where we believed we were on a different river. If that isn't lost, then it must be getting very close to it.

We kept right on walking, and refused to stop walking until it got dark. Luckily I had a flashlight and hand axe in my pack because we had to fall a dry snag in the dark in order to get a fire going. Once we got a fire going, I couldn't believe how much it changed our perspective. We got dried out and then sat down and started figuring out where we had gone wrong. Inside of one hour we knew where we had gone wrong, why we didn't recognize the mountains, and what we had to do the next day to get home. The next morning we set out as planned and four hours later we were home.

There is not as much chance of getting lost now that there are roads everywhere. If it should happen people should use every bit of will power they have to force themselves to sit and think, and if necessary make a campfire. Even if there is a forest closure because of high fire hazard, one could safely build a fire in a swampy area or on a gravel bar by a stream. The smoke from this fire will either bring searchers or fire attack personnel to the area, hopefully in short order. No question about it, a campfire is truly a home away from home.

Rolling ridge country is the easiest to get lost in, especially if the ridges keep turning. In this situation, if the sun is not visible and a person does not have a compass, the only sensible choice is to stay put. If one is determined to move, though, then the direction of the wind should be noted and used as a guide to prevent one from going in circles. Though it may change, it is better than no guide at all.

There are so many things that can happen in the forests and mountains that can cause injury. An example occurred the day our hunting and mountain climbing friend, Virgil Brandner, came upon a strange find while walking along near the Slim Lake Trail. He found a .303 rifle leaning against a tree. A quick check showed that the end of the barrel was split wide open halfway back to the firing chamber and the split ends of the barrel were at least 12 inches apart. We later found out that it had been owned by a Hungarian lad who had inadvertently plugged the barrel with mud. He had then fired it in an effort to clear the barrel.

Just how easy it is to get in trouble in the woods was clearly demonstrated to me when Vic Litnosky and I were on a goat hunt near Tweedmuir Park. We worked ourselves into position for a shot on some goats and I fired, only to get a wicked surprise. The gun gave a tremendous roar and kicked my shoulder a heavy blow. At the same time I got a blast of burning powder across my forehead. Vic, who was off to my right a couple feet, also got a load of powder across the side of his face. For a minute I thought my gun had blown up, but a quick check showed that it was intact. When I tried to eject the cartridge case, it wouldn't budge, and so I was unarmed for the remainder of the trip.

When I returned to Prince George, I took the rifle to a gunsmith who removed the cartridge case for me, and then it became apparent what had happened. Just a few weeks earlier, Bill had visited with me and we had gone into the mountains for a few days. Then when we returned home, he threw a box of 30-06 shells on top of mine without telling me. As I only had one rifle, there was no need for me to check the ammunition, and so I took the wrong cartridges with me. When I fired the rifle, the 30-06 cartridge case completely came apart in my .300 H&H magnum. And so the devil does his dirty work!

Another scary situation that can happen to anyone who fires a gun, is to experience a dud, or hangfire. According to a gunsmith I talked with, they are basically one and the same thing. In modern factory ammunition they are virtually unknown. But among hand-loaded ammunition such as I was using when I experienced a hangfire, they occasionally happen. They are a direct result of lack of cleanliness in the loading operation, in that dirt or grease is allowed to contaminate the primer.

A dud, which is a cartridge that won't fire, is not much of a problem unless one is facing a charging bear. The real danger is a hangfire—a cartridge that may fire a second or two after the firing pin hits the primer. If a person is in the process of ejecting the cartridge when it fires, then the results could be serious to fatal. This same gunsmith assures me that in the event of a perceived dud or hangfire, one should point the barrel skyward and wait about a minute before opening the action and ejecting the cartridge.

Since so many people now wander the wilderness with packs, there is a point I would like to make about them. This concerns waist straps that are a staple on all modern packs. There is no question that they can be a great help by taking some weight off the shoulders and adding stability, but they also have a downside: if a person is negotiating cliffs or very difficult terrain, then they should unhook this waist strap. Because if one gets in trouble and has to throw the pack in a hurry, they are unable to do so. I learned this lesson the hard way.

While on the subject of safety, there is a common danger that is faced by all mountain hikers, and this has to do with contaminated drinking water. In another story I mentioned the case of Dave getting violently ill after sucking on snow. Perhaps I should add the fact that he sucked on this snow right after we had been climbing very hard. This is just one of many cases I noted where people got ill from sucking snow or drinking water when they were overheated from climbing. I believe that many of these mountain illnesses are caused by the cold snow or water reacting to an overheated body. Obviously, many are caused by other factors, such as a fungi or some other toxic substance. In some cases it may be caused by the poisonous plant Indian hellebore *(veratrum veride),* which is so prevalent in the mountains I've traveled. Many people have reported getting stomach cramps and diarrhea after drinking water in which hellebore is growing.

Forest wanderers should use great care when approaching a small stream which they intend to drink out of. One had better not step on and crush the roots of plants such as water hemlock, which is extremely poisonous. If the poison gets into the water and a person drinks even a small amount, it could prove fatal. Bruce Johnson, who was a range specialist for the Ministry of Forests in Prince George, told me that there is evidence of cattle dying after drinking water that they have contaminated in this manner.

Another plant that can exude toxic levels of poison into the water if stepped on, is baneberry (actaea rubra). This plant commonly grows along streams, and its red or white berries are reported to be so toxic that the contents of as little as six berries can cause internal hemorrhaging. This problem can be easily avoided if a person makes a habit out of drinking upstream from the spot where they approach a small stream.

Because I and the people I have been with who experienced these problems always felt well later, they did not go to their doctor. This resulted in our not being able to find the culprit or culprits responsible for these sicknesses.

Some people put the blame on *giardiasis,* or beaver fever, which is caused by the parasitic protozoan *giardia lamblia.* This disorder is most prevalent in daycare centers, or in immuno-deficient patients, where it causes travelers' diarrhea. This is an intestinal disorder that usually infects and shows symptoms within two to three weeks of exposure. Children are the main source of infection as they excrete large numbers of cysts, although mammals such as dogs, muskrats, and beavers may also excrete cysts. These cysts can survive in water for up to three months.

Chlorination may not kill these cysts, therefore boiling all infected drinking water is a must. Water should be boiled a minimum of three minutes, with an extra minute added for each 1000 feet of altitude gain. Acute attacks may last three or four days, but many people are asymptomatic.

It appears obvious that this is quite different from the attacks I have witnessed, where people get violently ill within an hour, or a few hours at most, and in some cases feel no effects the following day.

Others have effects that last much longer, and I feel that this is a different condition. Prince George wildlife artist Wilf Schlitt describes his experience with beaver fever as follows:

"Contrary to what I had always thought, beaver fever is not something you get from seeing beautiful women after a prolonged stay in the bush. My bout with it began with the first day of our hunt in the northeastern portion of the Rocky Mountains. After we set up camp, we decided to go in four different directions to scout out the area. Although it was the last week of September, it was very hot in the mountains. I climbed with my rifle and pack for about three hours and when I got to the top of the ridge, I was very thirsty—not just for a drink—but a deep thirst for anything liquid.

"On top of the ridge was a pool of water-like substance beside a small snowpack. I noticed a number of tracks and other items that the sheep and caribou had left in the pool, but without a second thought, I drank my fill. I assume what I drank was water, but it tasted unlike any water I have ever drank or hope to drink again.

"Five days later, while we were still two days away from base camp, I got diarrhea for the first time. This was followed by attacks every four to six hours. The next morning, my partner and I decided to climb another ridge, even though the weather was turning bad. Again I got the runs and became so weak I ended up in my sleeping bag. Over the next four hours, it snowed six inches, with the result that I spent the entire night leaving footprints in the snow.

"The next morning we headed back to base camp, where two fellows in our party informed us that they had shot a caribou far from camp, and they asked us to help carry it out. As we hiked along to get the caribou, I started lagging behind and began to hallucinate. Two doctors in our party examined me and decided to take me back to camp. Along the way I stumbled and fell a lot, but I can't remember much else.

"Again, after a day's rest I felt fine, but I went to see my own doctor as soon as I got home. It was his opinion that I had contracted giardia, so I was treated accordingly with no return of symptoms."

It is worth noting that there was a five day lapse between the time that Wilf drank the water and the onset of symptoms. From everything I have read on the subject, which is everything I could find from many sources, this is not giardiasis, the symptoms of which take at least two weeks to appear.

It is my firm belief that poor old giardia gets blamed for a lot of things it doesn't do. It seems more likely that Wilf ingested some other toxic substance—possibly a fungi.

As for Wilf, he was lucky to have had people to help him. Had he been alone he may very well have perished. Certainly it is not a good idea to be stumbling and falling when one is in among cliffs and canyons.

I think we all know that any water that appears doubtful should be boiled for several minutes. But quite often when people are out on day trips, they don't have the container necessary to do this. Other times the forest is so dry that a fire ban is in place. I avoid the need for worrying about the water by always carrying canned fruit. I find the sweet juice to be the second best thirst quencher and energy booster of all with the exception of ice water. If a person is just leaving home on a day hike, a plastic bottle of water kept in the deep freeze is the answer. If it is wrapped in plastic and then wrapped with

Devil Mountain. The image of the devil stands out on this mountain north of Mount Robson.

several layers of newspaper, it will melt slowly and stay cold almost all day. I find the ice-cold water to be the best thirst-quencher of all if sipped slowly. But I think it is most important after climbing hard, that a person should always rest and let their body cool down before taking a drink. One of the first things our father taught us about horses was to never take them to water right after they have been working hard, as it will cause them to founder. Surely it is possible that it has a negative effect on people too.

Often, common swamp water or stagnant water will have an oily tinge, but this doesn't mean you've struck oil. This is caused by protozoans called *synura*, that discharge oil globules in the water—water that tastes like cucumbers.

Something forest wanderers should always be on the lookout for is ticks. A puncture wound caused by a tick is dangerous because they are vectors for such diseases as Rocky Mountain spotted fever, Q fever, Lyme disease, tularemia, and a host of other diseases as well. Hikers should always ask a friend to investigate any annoying itch or sore spot that they cannot see themselves. Ticks can be easily removed by the application of petroleum jelly, oil, or nail polish applied to their bodies. They should never be smashed and the body should not be pulled out leaving the head behind. If it has to be pulled out, then it should be by gentle traction only.

Winter is the time when a little additional planning should go into mountain travel. For instance, if one breaks through the ice when the temperature is below zero, then some method of getting a quick fire going is a must. And this fire-starting equipment is of no use if it is carried on a snowmobile that is lost under the ice somewhere. Lighters should be carried in waterproof containers right on your person, and chemical fire-starter is a must. Almost weightless, it is amazing how quickly a fire can be started with it. There are times when one can get caught in a pouring rainstorm or a snowstorm, when it can be difficult to light a fire. That's when fire-starter is worth its weight in gold.

The mountains in winter can be compared to Heaven and Hell. They can be a place of striking beauty, yet within minutes they can turn to a place unfit for man or beast. A strong wind can quickly arise that will set the surface of the snow in motion. In this situation all depth perception is lost and a person could walk off a cliff without seeing it. In this environment the choice is simple: dig in, find shelter, or perish.

Blue grouse certainly know what to do when the weather gets bad–they fly full-speed into a snowbank and instantly disappear from view. Then, when the cold weather or storm abates, they can explode up out of the snow and startle a person that happens to be close by. If it is a bright, sunny day, they sometimes have to fly around a bit before they can land. Coming out of the darkness under the snow, their eyes need some time to adjust to the brightness.

Baldy and Saddle Mountains, a windswept winter wonderland.

7

WILDERNESS HUMOR

THERE IS NO SUBSTITUTE FOR HUMOUR IN THE WILD, FOR IT keeps everyone's spirits up and prevents cabin fever from creeping in. On the other hand, a lack of humour can lead to problems such as the Sahara Syndrome. This is believed to have been caused by a race of super-intellectuals who once frequented the formerly lush and fertile Sahara area, causing the place to dry up. As we didn't want to be accused of any such thing, we always tried to keep jokes and humorous stories the order of the day.

Some of the best humour, I think, took place down on the flats at some of our weekend parties. I'm thinking of a Saturday night when we were whooping it up at a house party. One of the guests, a fellow named Carl Berg, had arrived by riverboat with two cases of beer in tow. At the party was an elderly woman who was very self-conscious about her appearance, and this led to an interesting confrontation. During the evening Carl opened a case of beer and started passing the drinks around. When he walked up behind this lady and asked, "Do you want a beer?" he got the surprise of his life. Instantly she whirled around and yelled, "A mirror? Piss on you! You don't look so hot yourself!" Poor Carl, he stood there with the most helpless 'what did I do' look imaginable.

A story that received more than its share of laughs at a party went like this: a husband was entertaining the guests by telling them how he had been having trouble getting it up. One night after another failure, he told his wife to go to the drugstore the next day and get some stifferene. Dutifully, she went and after studying all the shelves, approached the druggist. Unable to determine what she meant, he asked what it was for. When she told him, he answered, "Lady, I'm afraid someone has been pulling your leg."

When the laughter subsided, the good-natured woman responded, "Well, how was I supposed to know? They've got everything else."

Some of the best humour always seemed to be saved for the beer parlors. Maybe that's because they were such common meeting places for the boys during spring breakup. I know I sure got my come-uppance one afternoon in the Columbus Hotel beer parlor. I met a friend named Bill Michaylenko who had just arrived in town from Burns Lake, along with several of his friends. We pulled two tables together and soon there were 10 people sitting there. One of Bill's friends told a story and when he got finished, I wanted to ask him a question. I was unable to get his attention, though, because nine out of the ten people seemed to be talking at the same time. Finally I asked Bill, "What's that fellow's name?"

"Oh! Just call him Scotty." Bill replied.

I did what he said and shouted, "Hey, Scotty!"

Instantly this big man stood up, leaned over the table, put his finger right in front of my nose, then shouted, "Don't you ever call me Scotty again!"

It took a few minutes for Bill to stop laughing, but when he did, I asked, "What was that all about?"

"Oh! He's an Irishman." Bill replied.

I did like he said and didn't call him Scotty anymore.

The Columbus Hotel used to be the centre of activity in Prince George, especially as far as fisticuffs were concerned. Would-be tough guys came from far and wide to try out their knuckles on other people that considered themselves just as unbeatable. One unforgettable incident occurred when a rather miserable looking individual came and sat at a table I was sharing with a fellow named Sid Newman. Already seated, was another chap that was reputed to be very fast with his front feet, and he too appeared to be aching for a fight. One of them said to the other, "You don't look too good, what's your problem?"

Instantly the other guy jumped up and said, "C'mon, lets go outside.'

Within 30 seconds of meeting each other, these two fellows were heading out the back door to perform a few dental alterations on each other. About 10 minutes later they re-entered the room, wiped the blood off their faces, and sat down at our table again. It was interesting to note that they talked civilly to each other after that.

No matter what we think of these rowdies, one thing is certain: they were not quitters. Some of them had the supreme hell beaten out of them, yet a week or two later they were right back for more. As ridiculous as it seems, some of them felt that the weekend was a complete waste if they didn't get into a fight. It was at times, an unreal world in which one found it hard to believe that these things were really happening.

An example of this was when a person would get up and leave the Columbus Hotel with a glass of beer in each hand, then make his way across the street to the Europe Hotel to visit some buddies. When a patron pointed this out to one of the beer slingers, he calmly replied, "Oh! That's okay, some other guy will bring them back."

Then there was the evening that two chaps were mixing it up and one got the other by the throat. He choked him until the man's face was blue and his eyes were bulging out of his head. Then, in an act of kindness, he turned to the man's brother and asked, "Well, what do you say? Should I kill him or shouldn't I?"

Hardly fazed, the brother responded, "It's up to you; it's your fight."

In another gesture of goodwill, he let the poor fellow go.

There was also the evening when a certain young trouble-maker came into the bar and commenced making an ass of himself. On two different occasions he took glasses of beer off our table without asking. One gentleman that was seated at our table told him to shut up and bugger off. Then when that didn't work, he said, "I'm going to take that asshole outside and pound some sense into his head." Out the door they went, and when they came back it appeared obvious that he had worked on that fellow's head all right. But the fight was pointless because I talked to that same chap a week later and he didn't have a bit more sense that he had before the fight. It struck me that you can't get an education that way.

I think one of the incidents that best summed up the '50s occurred when two fellows were down on the floor trying to kill each other.

Present was a very comical chap named Bud Ganton. He watched for a minute, then jumped up on a table and shouted, "Ladies and gentlemen, step right up and see the last of the cavemen." It was said in jest, but it was, oh so, close to the truth.

Another incident that really summed up the '50s, took place upstairs in the Columbus Hotel. It would be pointless to say who the perpetrators were because through the years so many people have come forward to take the credit, or depending on your point of view, the blame for it. This started when a group of loggers were sharing two adjoining rooms in the hotel. During the course of the evening, one of the loggers lucked out and managed to get a woman up to one of the rooms where he immediately locked the door to keep the others out. After begging and pleading with this fellow to share the wealth, one of the loggers went into the adjoining room and fired up his chainsaw. He then proceeded to cut a doorway between the two rooms. It was rumored that the desk clerk put in his resignation the next day. Apparently he didn't like the sound of a chainsaw upstairs at midnight.

I doubt that there is a more shining example of the foolishness that went on in these beer parlors than the story of the pig. This took place back in the '50s, when a Prince George hockey player named Doug Sims decided to liven up the town. Along with a friend, he took a pig over to the Corning Hotel on a Saturday night. They opened the door to the beer parlor, pushed in the pig, then closed the door and left. Friends that were in the bar at the time later told him that the pig tore around the place upsetting tables and caused a great deal of chaos. After Doug related this story to me, I told him that it explained something that had puzzled me for over 40 years. When he asked what I meant, I said, "One Saturday night I took a date home from the Corning Hotel and I've always wondered why she never stood up."

And then there was the Saturday evening that two buddies and I were whooping it up in the beer parlor when I suggested we go to the dance at the CCF Hall a few blocks away. We went, and a short time later I asked a member of the female persuasion to dance. As we whirled about desperately trying to avoid being trampled by other dancers, I turned on all my alcoholic charm and shouted, "You're lucky that there are laws in this land."

She gave me a serious look and asked, "Why?"

Over the din of music and dancers, I shouted, "Because if there wasn't, I'd hit you over the head with my club and drag you off to my cave."

Well apparently she wasn't the romantic type because quick as a wink she stopped dancing and said, "I'll have you know that I don't do caves." Then she whirled around and left me standing alone on the dance floor. I changed my technique after that.

I'm sure that many would agree with me that many of our funniest times happened high in the mountains. There are so many great memories, but there are some sad ones too. I suppose it is inevitable that when things are going great that something has to spoil things, and in our case, that something was terrible. It started when Clarence found a huge frying pan and it got worse when he began making full-sized pancakes several inches thick. It was at this time that many strange stories and jokes made their way off the mountain. There was a story that the cabin had sunk about four inches after Clarence manufactured one of these giants; we also noticed that dad refused to come up into the mountains after that. At breakfast time, people were found hiding under bunks or out in the woods. We also noticed that the ground squirrels had moved away from the cabin, and that the two porcupines that had been eating plywood off the outhouse all summer were seen running through the alpine over a mile away.

So many cruel jokes were made about these monstrosities that Clarence finally decided we should put them to the absolute test and let the grizzlies decide if they were edible or not. For as Clarence used to say, "You just can't fool a grizzly."

That evening, four of us got together and rolled one of these mountain pancakes out the cabin door and placed it on a boulder some distance away, then we returned to the cabin and retired for the night. Sometime after midnight we were awakened by the roaring of a mad grizzly bear, which carried on for several hours before fading away in the distance.

Never have I seen Clarence in such a state. He paced forth and back in the cabin, muttered to himself about secret recipes, and refused to let the rest of us get any sleep.

At first light we headed out the cabin door with Clarence in the lead, and when we got to the boulder he let out a mighty yell, "Yahoo! It's gone. He ate it. See, there's your proof."

The rest of us weren't too sure, though, so we followed the bear's tracks in the skiff of snow that had fallen overnight. We found that the bear had fought it down the mountainside for about half a mile

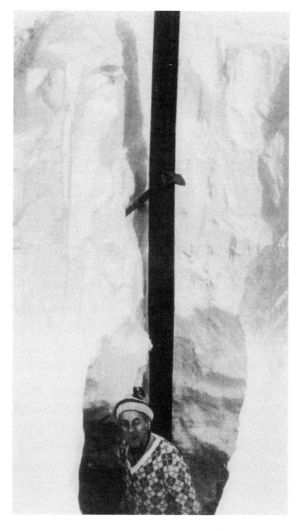

Standing on the cabin roof, Clarence needed seven lengths of stovepipe to get above the snow level.

and had jammed it into a large crack in the cliff. In the binoculars we could see its tracks heading over a distant mountain in what obviously was a search for a new range. We never saw that bear again.

The next morning I was sitting outside the cabin when Tommy Wilson came back from the outhouse. As he didn't look too swift, I asked, "Pancakes?"

"Yup!" he replied, "they don't digest, they just sort of die."

Some of the suggested uses for these pancakes were: sew 12 of them together to make a durable non-sag mattress; another was to place your boots in the batter and make instant snowshoes.

Not a quitter, though, Clarence carried on, and since that time has tried to find new uses for them. Tommy claimed that he used part of one to make a pair of insoles and they just never wore out. Clarence got his revenge against Tommy on a fishing trip—by loading up his pack. When Tommy wasn't looking, Clarence placed several rocks in his pack. After carrying the pack for several miles and reaching the point of exhaustion, Tommy made the discovery. Then there was a rumor floating around that he was going to put a contract out on Clarence.

Clarence and his son Larry were out together when the "rocks in the packsack trick" was used. Now when they travel together, they act nervous, and both keep a very close watch on their packs.

There was also the evening we were sitting around one of our cabins discussing how we should go about getting some boar grizzly bears, as they had been making fools of us. Suddenly Clarence came up with a once-in-a-lifetime, million-dollar idea, "I'm going to catch a sow grizzly in heat, take some scent off of her and put it in a bottle, then rub it all over myself in hunting season to attract a big boar grizzly."

There was silence in the cabin for a few minutes while everyone digested this bit of wisdom, and then Tommy asked, "What are you going to do if a horny boar grizzly sneaks right up on you, knocks your gun away, and demands a little loving? I mean if he gives you a couple slaps, you'll have to hold still, won't you?"

Clarence finally allowed that it wasn't such a good idea after all.

It was always great to get a joke on Clarence, because it was just self-defence. In order to appreciate what a weird sense of humour he has, I must tell the story of the earthquake. Clarence was standing in our home at Penny with several other people present when an earthquake struck. During the ensuing shaking, someone pointed to the gas lamp that was swinging wildly from the ceiling, and said, "Look at the gas lamp!"

Then someone else pointed at Clarence and said, "Look at Clarence!"

There was Clarence rocking back and forth, keeping time with the gas lamp, and now you get an idea what we had to put up with back in the mountains.

Another example of his off-beat sense of humour occurred when we were joy-riding in his Terraplane—part of a car he owned as a young man. As we sped by a neighbour's house, the lady of the house came running out screaming at Clarence to stop. Since his car didn't have brakes, he did his best to gear down until the lady caught up with us. "Clarence" She screamed. "you're going too fast for the children."

As Clarence sped away, he stuck his head out the window and shouted, "That's okay, I didn't expect them to keep up anyway."

Always the consummate comedian, Clarence has a little joke he likes to pull on people. Right near our cabin is a tiny spring that only flows in wet years or after spring breakup. Clarence takes great delight in taking guests out to this spring to get water for the cabin, making certain that he shows them our biffy, which is right close to the spring. After they have taken a drink of water or have had coffee or tea made from it, he will say, "There's sure something funny about that spring—it never started running until after we put the toilet there."

Another joke that made the rounds concerned an elderly trapper. He was sitting in his cabin in the middle of the wilderness when the door opened and a strapping young man entered.

"Who are you?" asked the trapper.

"I'm your new neighbor; I live about three mountain ranges over. I just came to invite you to a party."

"What kind of party, stranger?"

"Oh! There's going to be lots of sex, lots of booze, and even a bit of fighting." offered the stranger.

"That sounds good, what should I wear?"

"Oh! It doesn't really matter what you wear." The young man continued, "there's just going to be the two of us."

Probably my favorite joke is about the cowboy that was forever bragging about his roping ability. He was in a bar telling all who would listen that he had roped everything that moves. During a break in his speech, a voice was heard to say, "Have you ever roped a grizzly bear?"

Crushed, the cowboy replied, "No! I haven't, but I'm going to real soon."

With that, he immediately stocked up on supplies, mounted his horse and rode away. Two weeks later he came limping back into town, his clothes all tattered and his boots worn out. The men quickly ushered him back into the bar where they plied him with drinks and then asked him what happened.

A large black bear walks up to us.

"Well," He began, "I left town and rode hard for three days and got far back in the mountains. Then, early the next morning, I spotted a grizzly in the middle of a big meadow. I spurred my horse hard because I knew I had to catch it before it got into the trees. Then I threw my loop and roped it, but this was no ordinary grizzly. As soon as the rope hit it, it grabbed the rope and started pulling the horse in, paw over paw. When I saw that, I jumped out of the saddle and headed for the woods as fast as I could run. Well, I got to the trees and just as I was going into a heavy thicket I glanced back and couldn't believe my eyes—the grizzly was in the saddle and it was pulling the rifle out of its scabbard."

Another of my favorite jokes concerned a trapper that told a story about a close call he had with grizzlies. "It started when I was out picking berries one fall and noticed two grizzlies following me. I immediately climbed a tree about 30 feet above the ground and waited for them to go away. Instead of leaving, though, the bears began digging at the roots of the tree in an attempt to tip it over. After an hour of alternately digging and pushing, the bears quit and then stood with their heads together almost as though they were talking. Suddenly one of the bears left and the other stayed to guard the tree. About an hour later the first bear returned with a beaver under each arm. He put them down and they went to work falling the tree I was in. I figured that was the end of me, but when the tree started falling, I jumped to another tree, and the bears had to move the beavers over to that tree again. Once again, the beavers fell the tree and I jumped to a different tree. This kept up for several hours, and the only thing that saved me was the fact that beavers always fall trees toward water. Late that day, they finally fell one that reached a river and I managed to swim away to safety."

A strange conversation took place in the cabin one evening. Just as a joke, Clarence asked a fellow hunter, "What would you do if you came home and found another man in bed with your wife?"

There was only silence in the cabin for the next five minutes and we all assumed that he had not heard the question. Long after we had given up, he came back with his reply, "There's nothing else you could do." He then went into great detail about how he would do away with this fellow and where he would put the body and what the odds were of his getting caught. Amid the roars of laughter, his message was clear: "Don't mess around with my wife."

We also had a special mountain trip to remember in September, 1967, when we took an Australian reporter named Rob Barrett into the mountains with us. We had so much fun with Rob on that trip; fun that started when we told him that he must be very quiet if a grizzly was mauling him. He gave us a serious look and asked, "Why do I have to be quiet?"

"Because we just hate that damned screaming," we answered.

As many other people have responded when faced with their first grizzly bear, Rob was some impressed. In his newspaper article he wrote in part, "...even walking through alpine country, past fresh diggings and tracks, is guaranteed to give a greenhorn a stiff neck from glancing over his shoulder."

During our third day on the mountain, it poured rain, with the result that we were all soaked when we returned to the cabin. As Rob had not brought spare socks along, he asked if we had any spares. I pointed to a pair hanging on a drying line and said, "Use them."

He gave them a suspicious look and asked, "Whose socks are they, anyway?"

"They're mine, why?" One of the other hunters asked.

"Because I wouldn't want to get athlete's foot or anything." He responded.

Quick as a wink, the other hunter came back with, "You can't get athlete's foot from me because I've only got 10 inches."

After a hearty haw-haw, Rob offered, "There's no bloody stopping you, is there mates?"

We had a really great trip that I'm sure Rob will never forget. And I'll bet those stories grew a great deal by the time he returned to Australia.

Some of the incidents that took place up at the cabin were very frightening at the time, but seem humourous in retrospect. Such as the evening Bill and I arrived at the cabin in a pouring rainstorm. Once inside, we noticed that the roof was dripping badly and in desperate need of repair. We found a large piece of plastic tarpaulin which we draped over the roof, then we placed a great number of rocks on it to protect it from the wind. During the night an extremely strong wind came up. It lifted the tarpaulin off the roof, which resulted in about fifty rocks rolling down the roof at the same time. Sound asleep, I came up off my bunk with a great shout, thinking that a whole bunch of grizzlies were breaking down the door. As I settled back down, Bill went up on his side of the cabin with a mighty roar of his own. Then, after we realized what it was, we both settled down for a good, nervous laugh.

In August, 1972, my son Kelly, my brother Joe, and his son-in-law, Bob Gobbi, went into the mountains with me. We spent a few days around timberline watching grizzly bears and enjoying the scenery. After our second night in the cabin, we were lying in our bunks resting when Bob decided it was time to get up. As it was cold in the cabin, we suggested that he make a fire in the stove to warm up the cabin for the rest of us. Bob poured what he thought was

My son Kelly and my sister Margaret in alpine heaven.

some kerosene into a can and went to throw it on the fire which was refusing to burn. On his way to the stove, he had spilled a trail of this liquid behind him. When he threw this liquid into the fire there was a tremendous explosion, as well as a trail of fire that backed across the floor. At this time, Bob and the rest of us realized that it was gasoline he had used. What a commotion! Before you could count to three, all of us were out of our warm beds and heading for the exit. Bob swears it was an accident, but I'm not so sure. If his aim was to check our reaction time, then I'm sure we passed with flying colors.

Something people may find hard to believe is that we have never had to clean out our outdoor biffy up in the mountains. As long as there is a small hole for access, the ground squirrels will constantly keep it cleaned out and will even eat the toilet paper. For a time, we thought it was the porcupines, but by quietly sneaking out there, I have on several occasions caught the squirrels right in the act.

Do I eat ground squirrels, you ask? Not around the area of the cabin, I don't.

Humour is an elusive thing. Snoring for instance, may seem humorous, but there are times. I'm thinking of the time Bill and I were sharing a cabin with a sometimes hunting buddy named Virgil Brandner. Virgil was a fellow that didn't just snore, it sounded more like things were tearing and breaking. After climbing around the mountains all day, we were in dire need of a good night's sleep, but it was not to be. All night Virgil kept us awake as the cabin shook from the vibrations of his breathing.

The next day we again traveled the ridges and when bedtime came Bill and I were past the point of exhaustion. No sooner had our heads hit the pillow, than Virgil started up his motor. Unable to take anymore, Bill screamed at him to wake up. Instantly Virgil rose to a sitting position, gave us a dirty look, then laid back down and said, "goddammit, I can see that I'm not going to get any sleep again tonight!"

The moral of the story? We returned home the next day.

Something that kind of tickled my laugh buds was the time high in the mountains when my hunting buddy ran out of our camp yelling, 'Helloooo, Helloooo' in answer to what he thought was someone calling for help. I called him back and asked, "How long have you been carrying on conversations with coyotes?"

He sat down with a rather embarrassed look on his face and was relieved somewhat when I told him that I too had been fooled by their calls. The reason I haven't mentioned this fellow's name is because I promised Bill I wouldn't tell.

One individual that I had many great trips with was Prince George businessman Vic Litnosky. On one trip back into the mountains, we rode our Honda motorbikes part way in and then spent a few days around timberline. On our way back down, we ran into fresh black bear tracks just a short distance from our bikes. Just in fun I suggested to Vic that it sure would be funny if the bear had torn the seat off his bike as they are known to do. Sure enough, when we arrived at the bikes we found the seat had indeed been stripped off the bike and the foam was scattered all over the area. Trouble was, it was my bike. Vic sure got some enjoyment out of that.

Vic Litnoski with his 185 Cessna at Penny. Grizzly Bear (Red) Mountain in background.

Well, when we got down off the mountain, we stopped at my folks house for lunch and a cup of tea, where I decided to tease Vic a bit. I said to my dad, "We certainly established something up there on this trip."

"What's that?" he wanted to know.

"Well, we found out that if a bear has a choice between a frog and a Polack that they'll take the frog every time. I guess they figure if they've got to eat, then they might as well eat good."

Vic sat there for a minute and then a big smile crossed his face as he asked, "Do you know why bears prefer frogs over Polacks?"

"No!" I said, "but I think I'm going to find out."

"It's no secret," he continued, "everyone knows that bears prefer rotten meat."

Truly, that was Vic's finest hour.

Just a short time later, Vic flew out to Penny in his Cessna 185 for a visit. He landed on the river, and then made his way to our home. As soon as he got in the door, he bragged, "Guess what? I've lost 20 pounds in just over a month."

In an effort to get even with him for past transgressions, I responded with, "That's nothing."

"What the hell do you mean, that's nothing?" He demanded.

Unable to contain my joy, I answered, "I just read in a scientific magazine that it's common for a Polack's weight to fluctuate up to 100 pounds between bowel movements."

Guess what? He called me one of those things that dispense scat.

It's a good thing that I got a lot of enjoyment out of that, because I was about to pay a terrible price for it. This occurred just a few weeks later when I received a phone call from Vic, "Jack, how would you like to go trout fishing?"

"Sounds good" I enthused, "what should I bring?"

"Just bring what's left of your body" he added, "I've got sleeping bags, food, tackle, rods and everything else you can imagine."

That evening as we moved into an old tarpaper shack by the lake, the cold September downdrafts were coming off the mountains. As we entered the shack, I noticed that there was no stove in this old cabin, just two wooden bunks. Vic pulled out the gear, then handed me a tiny see-through sleeping bag that weighed about one pound. I looked at it and said, "Man! It's going to be cold tonight."

Vic then pulled a huge sleeping bag out for himself and answered, "Oh, no, I think it will be quite warm tonight."

Well, it turned out that we were both right—I was cold and Vic was warm. All through that long night I shivered and listened to him snore. I had noticed that the swing-type bunks we were on had only an upright board to support the outside edge, and heaven only knows how many times through that long night that I wanted to stick my foot out and kick away that support. Only the thought of the long walk out restrained me. Sometimes during the night Vic muttered in his sleep, and I'm almost certain that he said something about a Polack's weight fluctuating. I took my own sleeping bag on trips after that.

Just as we were about to head into the mountains on one of our trips, I noticed that Vic was wearing a pair of oxfords. I told him he needed ankle protection and that his shoes simply wouldn't cut it. I found a spare pair of hiking boots, so l gave Vic my new hiking

Vic Litnoski with his grizzly at timberline, 1969.

boots to try on. With a bit of effort he managed to get them on, although he did complain that they were too tight. On our way into the ridges it poured rain, with the result that we got our boots sopping wet. The following day Vic let me know that the boots were quite comfortable. Well, about a week after that trip, I went to put on the boots he had worn and found that they no longer fit me. In fact, I had to use a pair of insoles and two pairs of socks just to take up some of the slack. The next time I talked with Vic, I told him that he had stretched my best hiking boots and ruined them. I also let him know in no uncertain terms that he had better stay away from my woman.

Vic had a real penchant for adventure, so with his 185 Cessna aircraft we traveled a good portion of the province. Among my favorite places was Tweedsmuir Park, and Sustat Lake. It was on a trip to Sustat that I asked him if he had any emergency equipment on the plane and he answered, "Sure, I have lots of emergency equipment: a first-aid kit; rations; an axe, and a sleeping bag."

I digested that for a minute and then asked, "Is that a double bag?"

"Nope, just a single bag."

Remembering the long night in the see-through bag, I insisted, "In the event of an accident or forced landing, who gets the bag?"

He wouldn't answer; he just sat there and grinned. I never had full faith after that.

When people run around the mountains for years, they get pretty ingenious at preventing others from sharing the earth's bounty. Such as the guide and his hunter that were heading into the mountains to hunt grizzly bears. These men knew that two hunters were coming up the same trail the following day and this really bothered them. As they moved along near timberline, they came upon an abundance of grizzly sign with a large pile of scat right on the trail. A quick check showed that this bear had dug up a huge area and had left several large piles of scat behind. Suddenly inspiration struck. They carefully gathered up four piles of scat and placed them on the pile that lay on the trail, then they stood back to admire their work. It wasn't long before one of them said, "If I was a first-time hunter, there's no way that I would walk by a pile of droppings that big."

After spending several days on the mountain, these two men returned home without getting a glimpse of the two would-be hunters, and no mention was ever made about the world-record sized pile of bear droppings.

A similar ploy was used in this manner. A stream that ran through a culvert under the railway grade used to be a fantastic fishing hole when the trout ran upstream in May. The problem was that too many people were aware of it and the competition got out of hand. Then some miscreant spread the word that three grizzlies were feeding on a moose carcass just a stone's throw from the stream. Best darned undisturbed fishing we ever had. And since we never checked, we never knew for certain whether those bears were there or not.

There is something about bears that many people refuse to believe—that they have an ivory bone running the length of their penis. When one considers that bears mate for a week or two straight, the advantages become apparent. I've often suspected that this is where the saying 'bone tired' originated.

One smart-aleck forest ranger used to call them 'whistles'. When I asked why, he answered, "Because if you blow on them you'll hear some musical sounds, especially if the bear is still alive." I had to ask.

In adult bears, these bones measure from five to six inches, with just under seven inches being the largest I ever noted. This bear

Glacier on Eutsuk Lake, 1970. Incredible fishing

might have made the cover of *Playboar,* the leading sex magazine for sow grizzlies.

Enough humour about bears.

Some of my best jokes were saved for my co-workers in the forest service, where they became known as Jack-jokes. There was the day when several men were sitting at a coffee table, and several women were at another table. One of the women made the statement, "Do you know what that stupid husband of mine did?" When she finished her story, another woman came out with a similar story. It was like we were not in the room. Suddenly I slapped the table with my hand, jumped up, waved my hand over my head, and shouted, "I've had it up to here with you women running down us men." As they all looked at me with shocked faces, I added, "You women started all of this by taking one rib from us men, and ever since that time, you've just taken one bone after another." After a few seconds of silence, the entire room echoed to the sound of laughter.

This prompted one of the men present to say, "I don't know how you get away with that, Jack, if I said that I'd probably spend two years in jail."

There was also the day in the coffee room when I suggested, "I think I'm going to go down to Mexico in a few weeks"

This prompted one of the blondes present to reply, "Oh! Goodie! Take me along in your suitcase."

Instantly I came back with, "No way! If they check and find a blonde in my suitcase, they'll charge me with smuggling dope into Mexico."

Another day several of us were discussing killers and how some of them had killed so many people. At one point I suggested that people such as Clifford Olson should be thrown in jail and fed nothing but corn flakes for the rest of their lives.

There was just silence in the coffee room for several minutes as the ladies present had already been stung by me so they refused to ask. Finally one of the men present asked, "Why corn flakes?"

My obvious answer, "Because they're serial killers."

Back came his response—"I had to ask; I knew better but I had to ask."

And there was also the day that several women were discussing men and how they like to think that they are such great lovers. Finally one of the women stated, "As far as I'm concerned men are all the same—all smoke and no fire."

I couldn't put up with that, so I responded with, "Hold on! I'll have you know that one woman told me that I gave her the best 30 seconds of her life."

Instantly she came back with, "Oh sure, you probably just made that up." Then a few seconds later she added, "Oh sure—30 seconds."

I couldn't leave it at that so I added, "Actually I exaggerated, she only said 15 seconds."

This caused me to be nicknamed 'The Fifteen Second Kid'.

The jokes were not always on others though, sometimes they backfired. An example occurred the day I was joking with operations superintendent. Del Blackstock. At one point during our conversation I said, "This may surprise you, Del, but my father told me that when I was born, a real bright star came and shone down on the farm for about one week."

Del's response was quick and to the point, "C'mon, Jack, that wasn't a star, that was a pole light out behind the Columbus Hotel."

You win some and you lose some.

Perhaps the best 'gotcha' of them all was the story of two fellows named Joe and Jerry that worked together in a logging camp. These two men got in the habit of pulling jokes on each other and it finally came to a head one day when Jerry got a good one on Joe. In response, Joe started telling the men gathered around about some trouble he had with the police. Immediately he had everyone's attention, so he carried on, "I got in this fight in the beer parlor and things got out of hand. The next thing you know, chairs started flying and several people got hurt. I knew I was in trouble so I ran back to my hotel room and locked the door, which was stupid of me because they knew me back at the bar. Well, I had only been in my room for about five minutes when I heard a car screech to a stop, so I looked out the window. There were two policemen coming straight to the hotel, and just then one of them looked up, shook his fist and yelled, 'We'll get you, Joe!'"

"Well, I knew they had me, so I thought I would show them what I thought of them. I pulled down my pants and stuck my bare bum out the open window at them. Then I was surprised to see the other policeman shake his fist and say, 'Yes! And we'll get you too, Jerry.'" Amid the roars of laughter, everyone agreed that Joe was the decided winner.

An example of a story that was both humourous and sad began the day I received a visit from the local woods foreman, Buster Van De Reit. He told me to get some clothes and personal things together because we were going to drive logs down Slim Creek. Then, just as he was about to leave, he added, "Don't forget to bring a cookbook."

Immediately suspicious, I asked, "What do I need a cookbook for?"

"Because you're going to be the cook!"

"You've got to be kidding, Buster. I've never cooked anything in my life."

"There's nothing to it," he continued, "the cookbook will tell you what to do; besides, if you need any help, just holler, I'll give you a hand."

Several hours later I found myself in an old cookhouse on the bank of Slim Creek with a cookbook in one hand and my rifle in the other, not sure which to use first. The most helpless feeling imaginable overcame me as I looked about, not knowing what to do. My first impulse was to get the crew before they could get me. Buster, who had promised his help if I needed it to get started, had disappeared into the surrounding forest and could not be found.

Well I did my best and had something resembling a meal on the table when the ravenous horde descended. Although they tried to be polite, I noticed plenty of grins being passed around the table. Among the crew was a likable young fellow named Eric Klaubauf, who had a habit of saying what he thought before he thought it. At one point during the meal, instead of saying that the meat was too rare, he said,

"Hey Jack! A piece of roast just jumped off my plate and ran halfway across the table before I caught it."

A few minutes later I was walking around the table pouring coffee when Eric said, "That's coffee? That's not coffee, that's water."

Late that evening as I retired, I knew two things for certain: I had to cook the meat a little more, and I had to deal with Eric.

The next morning I arose before five and went into the cookhouse, where, after a short search, I found a smaller coffee pot. I filled it half full of coffee, put it on to boil, and then added a bit of water now and then as needed. When the crew arrived I began pouring their coffee, making it a point to bypass Eric. When he gave me a quizzical look, I said, "I've got some stronger coffee for you, Eric." I then brought the other pot over and tried to pour it, but it didn't really pour, it just kind of oozed out like lava. After taking a sip, Eric offered, "That's coffee."

With the crew staring in amazement, Eric drank that cup of coffee, but he passed when I offered a refill. During the course of that day I think that some strange vibrations must have gone on in his digestive tract, because when I passed the regular coffee the next morning he held out his cup and said, "That's coffee."

Shortly after breakfast that morning I felt adventurous so I decided I would try to make some cream pies. I followed the cookbook to the letter, and when the pies were baked I put them out to cool. Perhaps an hour later the door opened and in came Buster with the manager, Bill Batten, who had arrived to look over the operation. Buster asked, "Do you have anything to eat?"

"Sure do," I said, wanting to make a good impression, "there's some fresh pies on the table; help yourselves."

I returned to making lunch for the crew, and was surprised when the two men finished eating and left quickly. I went to check and found that only a sliver of pie was missing. Suspicious, I took a bite and then quickly spit it out; the rest went into the garbage.

After the manager left, Buster came in and asked, "What the hell happened to the pies?"

"I don't know," I answered, "I followed the cookbook exactly."

After I explained in detail everything that I had done, Buster exploded, "For God's sake, man, you forgot to bake the crusts!"

"What do you mean, forgot? I followed the cookbook exactly; it didn't say I should do that."

"Well you're supposed to know that." He continued.

"Buster, if I knew how to cook, what would I need the cookbook for?"

We finally both sat down and had a knee-slapping laugh, and then Buster closed the issue by saying, "Maybe it's a good thing that we tried the pies, because if the crew had got to them first, that could have been the end of you."

I heartily concurred.

In the days that followed I kept a close watch on the crew, remembering only too well how Captain Bligh had misread the mutinous intentions of his crew on the *Bounty*.

I have so many funny memories of my years in the forests, among them, this story about a young timber cruiser I worked with for a few years. As he was very religious, he used to go on day after day about God and the Devil in an effort to convert me to his faith. One winter day while we were eating lunch in the forest, he went on and on about what a mess the world was in and how he didn't worry because he was ready to go anytime. Well as luck would have it, the very next day we were going out to cruise timber and as we came around a curve in the logging road, we came face to face with a moose; a moose that had been chased back and forth along these roads until it reached the point where it refused to run any more. As soon as it noticed us, it lowered its head and its hair came up as it started walking toward us. We quickly put on our snowshoes and went into the deep snow around the moose and then came back on the road where we were going to take off our snowshoes again. It was then that impulse struck, so with a glance over my shoulder and without a word of warning, I tore up over the bank on my side of the road where I pretended I was trying to climb a tree. Then I looked over at my partner who had beaten me over the snowbank and was climbing a tree with his snowshoes on. I called to him and pointed up the road where the moose was still standing in its original spot. As my ex-friend came back onto the road, I said, "Now I know what you meant when you said you were ready to go anytime. Wow! You weren't fooling, were you?"

His ashen-faced response was, "I'll bet you laugh at funerals."

The jokes were not always on the other person, though, as the following story will prove. Because I was a licensed log scaler, I prided myself on the ability to distinguish between the different species of trees and also felt that I had a passing knowledge of shrubs in the area. This was put to the test one fall when two friends dropped in for a visit. During our conversation, Roy, who had lived in Penny as a young man, asked if there were any hazelnut bushes still around because they were absent where he lived in the East Kootenays. I assured him that some of them grew on the hill right behind our house. He then informed me that he wanted to take one back with him to see if it would grow there.

Together, we took a shovel and went out to the hillside. The leaves had dropped, but I saw several hazelnut bushes and chose a small one so that we could get the complete root system. Roy and Betty took the bush back to Grasmere with them and that was the last I heard until several years later when a Christmas card arrived. In among the greetings was a brief note that read: "That hazelnut bush you gave us finally matured; we got our first crop of saskatoons off it this fall."

Another story that I found quite humorous took place during an interview with an elderly guide for my book *Crazy Man's Creek*. I asked this gentleman, "You were married years ago, isn't that true?"

"Yes, I was married, but I had to divorce her because she was too dirty."

"What do you mean?" I asked.

"Well, every second time I went to piss in the sink it was full of dirty dishes, and a man can't put up with that."

If he was looking for sympathy, he sure didn't get any from me.

One thing I've noticed about humour is that it depends which side your on whether it's funny or not. To know what I mean, a person should have spent a couple days in Brian Latham's shoes, or perhaps I should say snowshoes. An engineer by trade, Brian spent some time in Penny in the early '50s, and it was then that he decided to try for a moose. He did his level best to get one, but couldn't even get a look at one. Finally, after a heavy snowfall, he decided to find a fresh set of tracks and follow them until he caught up with the moose. With this in mind, he set off on a Saturday dawn on his snowshoes and in a short while had found fresh tracks, and so the race was on. All day long he followed those tracks, many times getting so close that he could hear the moose breaking brush as it ran away. As darkness set in, he broke off the hunt and returned home, convinced that he would connect the next day.

At daylight Sunday morning he was back on the moose's trail and followed it until late afternoon when he finally caught up with it. There was a problem, however, Clarence and a hunting partner were dressing it out. He had driven it right into them.

Understandably, they saw the humour in it—Brian did not.

There's one story about incredible courage on a hunting trip that I simply must tell. This took place at a remote lake when my hunting buddy, John Currie and I were hunting moose. One night we were lying in our tent with John fast asleep, when I heard a bear sniffing at the door of the tent, right beside my head. At once I let out a tremendous yell. Then I was surprised to find John about a foot off the ground in his sleeping bag. As he came back to earth, I told him about the bear. We listened, but could hear nothing. Then I took my rifle and went outside where there was only silence. Finally I came back into the tent and got into my sleeping bag. Only a few minutes passed and I heard the bear sniffing again. This time I turned on the light before I hollered, and the bear turned out to be a mouse that was dragging a piece of tissue paper across the floor of the tent. Man! Did John give me a ribbing over that.

I got quite a few miles out of that story in later years, because anytime John started giving me a bad time about anything, I would respond with, "You should be grateful to me, John, for risking my life to save you from that bear."

Another of my favorite stories concerned my brother Joe. This took place because he bought a whoopie cushion with which he intended to play a few jokes. A couple days later I was at his home when he glanced out the window to see an old-timer coming to visit. Then Joe remembered the cushion, so he placed it on a chair. When the old man entered, Joe asked him to sit in that chair. No sooner did he touch down, though, than the most horrible sounds imaginable emanated from the area of his behind. Instantly he exploded off the chair, and before anyone could explain that it was a joke, he bolted out the door without even stopping to pick up his jacket. From all the noise, this poor fellow probably thought he had lost the bottom half of his colon.

There is one story that I intended on omitting, but I have been informed that the word is out so I may as well include it. This story started in September, 1999, when I decided to be adventurous and take a new type of tea into the mountains. Called nature tea, there was no further elaboration, but since it appeared to be a health tea, I bought it. The next day back in the mountains, Bill drank one cup while I drank four. That evening the show got on the road when Bill and I began passing each other on our way to the outhouse. This kept up until the wee hours, when we finally managed to get a bit of sleep. The next day we walked the ridges, and when we returned to the cabin we dumped out the water, as that is what we blamed for our misfortune. Once we boiled up the new water, I had four more cups of tea, while Bill drank coffee. That evening I was on the road again, but Bill didn't have a problem. While I was in the outhouse doing my business, Bill came out and let me know that he had found the culprit responsible for my diarrhea. He had pulled the tea container out of its box and read, "Do not drink more than one cup per day, and no one under the age of 15 or over the age of 60 should drink it at all." There was no warning on the outside of the package, only the words *Nature Tea S M*; I think I've figured out what the S M stands for.

Finally, I would like to say farewell to this chapter with a story about a rather unusual fishing trip. This story was told to me by a fellow named Bill Fitzsimmons, who was present when it took place. He and three friends had traveled for two days to get to a remote lake famous for its huge trout. When they arrived at the lake, they found an old shack that had been abandoned when a mine closed. They moved in, and after two days of fishing they returned to the shack to find they had a visitor. It was the local guide who informed them that he owned the shack and charged $50 per day in rental.

Bill told me that he was flabbergasted. He couldn't believe that the guide would try to charge that much for an old tarpaper shack that he didn't own in the first place. He also added that they didn't have that much money with them anyway. Things were at a standstill for about one minute and then one of his buddies stepped forward to address the guide, "That sounds reasonable. I'll tell you what—I'll pay you as soon as my brother straightens up."

"Your brother owes you some money?" Queried the guide.

"No." came the reply, "he's a hunchback."

The rent money was not mentioned again.

8

FORESTRY

DURING THE YEARS THAT I SPENT WITH THE PROTECTION Branch of the BC Forest Service, I had many interesting adventures. I loved to fly along in helicopters to and from fires or other chores. Often I would see grizzly bears along the beautiful mountains and along the salmon streams, or perhaps see caribou standing on snowfields where they would attempt to escape the flies and heat of the day. It seemed hard to believe that I could get paid for doing something so exciting and interesting.

In the many hundreds of fires that I fought in my life, I had some very unusual experiences. Some of which I will share here.

I suppose one could say that my firefighting days started when I was 14. My brother Joe and I, along with four friends, were mountain climbing when a thunderstorm passed by. Just a short time later we smelled smoke and then walked right into a fire. The only tool we had was a hand axe, but we went to work and managed to put the fire out.

The following week I was in school when the forest ranger walked in, gave a short speech to the class, and then handed me a check. It seems someone had seen the lightning strike and reported it to the ranger station. The ranger made the decision that we should be paid, and while the monetary gain was minimal, the thought seemed very important. It also made me look good in the eyes of my peers.

The next year, I volunteered to go on a fire in large cedar trees where I learned just how hard some fires are to put out. The year after that, I was 16 and of legal firefighting age, and the Forest Service took good advantage of it. Along with my two brothers, we were regularly nailed for fires. They didn't ask if we wanted to go, they just told us what time to be at the ranger station. We didn't really mind, though, because we were always out running around the forests anyway, so why not get paid for it?

The first many years, the only fires we fought were along the main valleys and adjacent mountains. Remote areas were left to nature unless access could be gained by riverboat or float plane.

It was often hard and frustrating work trying to find small fires in the huge wilderness that existed then. Usually all we had to go on was a compass bearing from a lookout tower, with all our food, camp supplies and firefighting equipment being carried on our backs. We got pretty cagey at finding the fires after a while. We would pay close attention to the wind, and if we didn't find it on our first pass, we would assume that we were upwind of it. Then we would circle downwind on our return pass, and so on until we smelled smoke. Once we got a whiff of smoke, we would home right in on it, having kept track of the wind. Sometimes we would miss a fire burning high in a dry snag because it gave off no visible smoke, but by looking just over the tops of broken snags, we would eventually find it by seeing heat waves dancing against the sky. Other fires we found by stopping to listen now and then for the snapping and crackling always associated with wood fires. Another trick we used was to put our ears against trees adjacent to the fires; in this manner we were often able to determine if they were burning inside.

It was during this time that I found out how fires jump down a mountainside. I often wondered how fires could jump downhill when there were tremendous updrafts. It didn't make sense. Then one day it happened right before my eyes. A snag that had burned off in several places was the culprit. Devoid of limbs which would have prevented it from rolling, a three-foot piece took off down the steep mountain spreading coals and ashes in its wake; a few minutes later we had a fire below us—a dangerous situation in high or extreme hazard. The message? Get those burning snags down on the steep slopes as soon as possible.

Ranger Carl Rohn sent eight of us to a fire he had spotted from a Beaver float plane. He gave us a compass bearing from a sharp bend in the Fraser River, then had us dropped off by a riverboat at that point. We combed the area for several days and walked a lot of miles but were unable to locate the fire. Back at the Ranger Station, Carl was starting to bad-mouth us as a group of incompetents. Then in desperation, he called for the Beaver to return and went up for another look. A short time later we heard the plane set down on the river near us so we straggled out to the river bank to meet them. Upon seeing us, Carl came up the riverbank and asked, "Is my face red?"

"Why?" someone queried.

"Because it should be; I gave you guys the wrong turn on the river; the one you should have started from is about five miles from here."

Thank God for the aircraft or we may still be out there looking for that fire.

These Beaver aircraft were true workhorses, and it may be hard for people to imagine just how much hard work they saved with their food and supply drops in isolated areas. I remember the first time I witnessed an airdrop. It occurred on a fire near Kenneth Creek in 1958, when a Beaver piloted by Bill Harvey, with Ernie Marynovitch as drop man, was slated to deliver fire equipment. Several of us gathered around a small meadow just a short distance from the fire, and then the plane arrived. Bill circled the area once, then on his second approach, cut the engine and Ernie made the drop which landed smack in the middle of the small meadow. On every ensuing pass, he made another drop, and when they finished, all the chutes were touching each other in the center of the meadow. It was impressive to say the least, and it certainly saved us many hours of packing.

Bill, along with fellow pilot Bernie Bergeron, were two of the top-notch bush pilots who flew the Interior at that time. Along with their drop men Ernie and Steve Marynovitch, they earned the reputation that they could 'make a drop and clean your chimney' at the same time.

There was a story back in the '50s about an errant food drop that was made at Longworth Lookout. Apparently the pilot badly misjudged the wind with the result that the drop went far over the mountain into the abyss below. A few days later, Bill Harvey made the drop and the lookout man, John Flotten, had a hard time getting out of the lookout building. It seems that the drop was jammed against the door.

I asked Steve Marynovitch how he could stand being in the back of that Beaver on a hot day as it circled repeatedly and bounced up and down in the turbulent air. In the understatement of the decade, he replied, "You had to have a good stomach."

Steve was also involved in 1960 when they dropped bentonite or 'driller's mud' on fires from Avenger aircraft. Husky, Beaver and single-engine Otter were also used to drop water on fires during this same period.

The Forest Service had a strange method of acquiring the services of firefighters back then. They would sometimes resort to cleaning out the beer parlors and ordering every man that could breathe, walk, or crawl, to report for fire duty. Some men would try to make a break for it out the back door, but surprise, surprise, more rangers were waiting out back. I hope it is not too difficult to realize that some of these draftees were not exactly the cream of the crop. In fact, some of them were more nuisance than help. Such as the load of conscripted barflies that came on the Beaver to a fire near the Grand Canyon in 1958. As they got out of the plane, they had to walk along the float in order to gain the riverbank. One gentleman had a large object under his jacket and when asked what it was, answered, "Just some clothes." At that minute he lost his balance and toppled into the river.

Now this fellow must have been some kind of a magician, because he went into the river with some extra clothes, yet came up a few seconds later with just over half a gallon of wine. The wine was seized and dumped into the river, which prompted the man to state, "How in hell do they expect a man to work with nothing to drink!"

Some of these conscripts could not do a day's work and would often sleep behind trees. This caused endless worry that they might be ran over by equipment or trapped by a spreading fire. The end result was that the practice of raiding the bars for firefighters was given up, and rightfully so.

Great as these fixed-wing aircraft were, it was the helicopter that allowed fires to be fought in even the remotest parts of the province. Truly, they completely transformed firefighting. Suddenly every swamp, meadow, gravel bar, or alpine opening was an available base for a fire camp or fire attack crew dispatch. A fire that had previously been out of reach was now only minutes or hours away, depending on the distance from a landing spot.

When the first choppers became available in the Interior, there were vast tracts of forest with no road access. In the steep heavily-forested mountain areas this often meant that we had only two options: being let off along the rivers, or else in the alpine. Sometimes we had to climb for several miles or else descend for several miles through heavy timber where we ran into cliffs and alder thickets that were near impassable. This meant that we often arrived at the fire so exhausted that we were unable to fight it.

Some of my chopper work in the '60s was with Jack Millburn, who opened the Okanagan Helicopter base in Prince George in '61, and with Dick Beggs, who joined Jack in '62. Flying Hiller 12E or Bell G2 choppers, there was never an abundance of power. In fact, I still joke about the telescopic pole I used to carry to help lift the chopper up above the trees.

Jack Milburn in the Royal Air Force.

By 1961, Bill Harvey, an ace fixed-wing pilot, had switched from flying fixed-wing to helicopters. Early that summer, he got involved in a terrible accident at the Grand Canyon on the Fraser River. Two timber-cruisers—Sterla 'Slim' Roe, who had fractured an ankle, and his partner Ernie Pement—had called for a helicopter and Bill had answered their call. After he picked up the two men, Bill decided to show them the canyon. While doing so, they flew right into an unmarked cable that spanned the river. The helicopter crashed into the river, and all three men managed to get out. Slim was doing his best swimming toward shore with a broken ankle, while Ernie swam along near him. Suddenly Ernie cried out, slipped beneath the water and drowned. At the same time, Bill, who could not swim, was in deep trouble. Then a miracle happened—a ten-gallon empty gas drum that had been tied on the helicopter broke free and popped up right beside him. He clung to the barrel and eventually managed to get to shore. Slim had already made it to safety.

Bill survived his river ordeal just in time for one of the worst fire seasons I was ever involved with. There were so many fires burning and so much smoke in the air that we never caught a glimpse of the sun for many days on end, and when we did see it, it hung as a dull red ball in the sky.

I had been on many lightning strikes that year but that ended when a lightning-caused fire roared up a steep mountainside only five miles from Penny. I was flown in to this fire in a helicopter by Bill Harvey, and how he managed to find it is beyond me. Visibility was reduced to almost zero. This meant that he was forced to follow the treetops until we reached the mountain. Then he followed the mountain up, flying right at treetop level until he finally found the fire camp which was being constructed on the ridgetop. As we came in to land, Bill spotted an antenna wire for the camp radio stretched out across the opening we were to land in. As he had just finished an encounter with a cable in the river, he was not amused. When he sat the chopper down, he got out and tore that wire down, rolled it up and threw it into the woods. Believe me, everyone in camp got the message.

After we set up the camp, we scouted around and found a small lake about half a mile from our camp. We set a fire-pump on the lake, then ran a hose lay down the slope to the fire. The fire boss, the same Slim Roe who had escaped the river, knew that I was an experienced pump operator so I was elected to run the pump.

The next morning we rose early and gathered around the camp-fire to watch our Chinese cook prepare breakfast for the twenty-man crew. Word quickly spread throughout the camp that this gentleman was worth watching, and that is what we did. He would take an egg in each hand, crack them, flip the shells open with his thumbs, and then throw the eggshells into the campfire all with one motion. In one minute he had enough eggs frying for the 20-man crew. This fellow had previously owned his own café and had become rather adept at his trade. I don't mind saying that he held our undivided attention for a few days.

About the fourth day on this fire, we woke to find we had a vis-itor. A black bear was feeding on the garbage pile we had left unburied right beside our camp. One firefighter gave chase and the bear went scurrying back into the forest. A few minutes later it returned and the lad chased it away again. It was interesting to note that the bear didn't run quite as fast the second time. Within an hour the bear would not run anymore; it would just growl if any-one came near.

I would have given plenty for a camera that evening when the bear took a roll of toilet paper from our makeshift biffy and began playing with it. It rolled over and over, wrapping the paper around itself until it resembled a mummy. There was a sad ending to this affair, though, for a few days later a gun had to be flown in to dispatch the bear who had taken over as camp boss; a situation that could have been avoided by burying or burning the garbage.

At this same time, Clarence was punching a fireguard around the mountain below us with his D6 tractor. He was following along Slim Creek with the guard as a preventive measure in case the fire backed down the mountain. One evening they were camped on the bank of Slim Creek where they watched the salmon going up to spawn. A large tree had fallen across the creek and the salmon were unable to pass. As the men watched, salmon would go up to the tree, look it over and then go back into the pool below. Suddenly a big salmon went up to the tree and began digging. With rocks moving in the spray of water, it bulled its way through under the tree and then the other salmon followed. The men noticed, though, that the big salmon had torn itself to pieces in its effort to get through. It had sacrificed itself, but the others got through.

The fifth day on the fire was to be a very entertaining day. Just at noon, I filled the pump with gas and then walked back into camp to have lunch. Just a short time later, we heard a strange sound, something like, whooo, whooo, woooooo, and within seconds the fire came up over the ridgetop and right into our camp. Then everything seemed to happen at once. Brother Joe, who had taken over as fire boss from Slim Roe, grabbed a chainsaw and asked me to assist. He started falling the trees closest to the camp in an effort to save it. He just cut the trees off and I pushed them away from the tents with a pole. The trees were afire all around us, but were well spaced at that elevation, so we were easily able to stand the heat. We were putting the trees down in record style, when I felt a hot spark on my temple. Then several more sparks joined in and I realized that I was being attacked by hornets. I grabbed a bit of dirt off the ground, spit on it to make it moist, and applied it directly to the stings and within seconds the intense burning stopped.

Although this method of treating insect stings works remarkably well, I must repeat what a doctor told me, "That one had better be certain that they have had their tetanus shot, because good old *clastridium tetani,* a soil-borne bacterium, can cause lockjaw and death."

After I finished fighting the hornets, I rejoined Joe, but our effort was for naught, as all our tents were burned to some degree. To make matters even worse, someone had called out on the radio that the camp was burning up. Unknown to us, back at the ranger station Carl Rohn was in a frantic state. Because of all the smoke from the many fires, he didn't know if the big fires were joining up or if people had been lost in the flames. It was about that time that he is reported to have said, "If I get through this fire season I'll probably live to be a hundred."

One picture that stuck in my mind was of our Chinese cook. Right in the midst of the flames he came out of a tent with a suitcase in each hand and headed over the ridge. After everything calmed down we went looking for him and found him in the middle of a meadow, a suitcase in each hand, standing there as calm as could be, as if he was waiting for a taxi.

Twenty-miles west of us, the Tsus fire had made an 18-mile run in one burning period and ended up to be about a 40,000 acre fire. Burnt needles from that fire showered down on us day and night. 30 miles west of the Tsus, was the Grove fire which also totalled about 40,000 acres.

To the south of us about 50 miles, a huge fire burned in the Wells area. These, along with many smaller fires that remained undetected, simply overwhelmed the firefighting potential of the district. Added to the endless smoke, was a heavy ground fog that sometimes made flying impossible.

One morning while we were eating breakfast, I heard one of the firefighters say, "It sure pays to be related to the boss, because you get all the soft jobs."

Hiller 12E with the original monsoon bucket.

Instantly I came back with, "I agree it's not fair, so I'm willing to switch jobs with you if you like."

I took him to the pump site, and showed him how to run it, and then I went down on the fire. Late that night this same man stuck his head into what was left of our tent and said, "You had better go back on that pump tomorrow because I refuse to." I did go back, but this was the worst job I ever had on a fire. It got dark real early around the first of September and I spent many hours alone there in the dark. I had no idea where the fires were, no contact with anyone, and at times clouds of burnt needles would fall on me.

The recovery at night was such that one could not walk more than 20 paces through the vegetation in the mornings without getting sopping wet, yet shortly after noon the fires were on the run again. Finally the long nights and a weather change brought a welcome respite to weary firefighters.

I never did understand how song writers came up with the idea that rainy days are blue days. It seems obvious to me that they never spent a month on a big fire. Trust me when I say that if they had, they would change their tune in a hurry. After weeks of eating dust, smoke, and ashes, one wonders if there is any rain left on earth. I remember one such fire that was terrible. Finally the day came when we gladly noticed dark rain clouds approaching, but when they got to where we were it was just virga—streamers of precipitation from clouds which dissipate and evaporate before they reach the ground. When the rain finally did come, I just tipped my head back and let it fall on my face. It was sweeter than honey.

In 1962, Arne Jensen and I spent part of a summer building heliports in the mountains, and it got pretty dicey when the choppers tried to lift off on hot days. We would get up near the tops of the trees only to find that we would just hover there. By turning the chopper one way and then the other, the pilots were often able to get a little breeze that would let them lift out. Other times they would set down and let one of us off, then try again. Some of the heliports we made were laughable by today's standards, including the one on a ridge near Kenneth Creek that is plainly visible today. It looks more like an airport than a heliport.

These heliports were a new concept at that time. It was felt that strategically located heliports would facilitate rapid initial attack on fires, as helicopters were unable to land in the endless forests and steep mountainsides. Some of these heliports were constructed of wood, but this came to an abrupt stop when a wooden heliport collapsed. The chopper went sliding backwards down the mountain and was destroyed. This was quickly followed by an order that prohibited the use of any wood in pad construction. A short time later, the funds ran out and the proactive concept of heliports was abandoned.

During the summer of 1962, I was called to the ranger station to go on a lightning-caused fire. When I got there, I met Dick Beggs who was piloting a Hiller 12E. Also on hand was a firefighter who was conscripted from the local mill; a lad I remember only as Andy. We flew along the Torpy River until we saw a snag burning in the forest below us, then Dick circled a few times so I could get a good look at the fire. After a minute he asked me if that was enough. More

This S58 Sikorsky lifts a Bell 47 out of a lake after it lost power and got dunked.

than just a little airsick, I answered, "That's more than enough, my stomach is up touching my tonsils."

Dick whirred up and dropped us off in the alpine somewhere behind Baldy Mountain, then flew away. Minutes later a storm cell moved through and dropped a heavy amount of rain on us. It was at this point that I realized we were in trouble. Andy had worn a pair of shoes with smooth soles, which, on the wet vegetation of the steep slope, acted much like skis. I was carrying a chainsaw, tools and our food, while Andy was carrying a shovel and polaski (hand tool). Every few steps his feet would slip out from under him and he would go sliding downhill with the tools flying in all directions.

After going just a short distance, we ran into a cliff. We followed it and got around it, only to find another, and then another. What with fighting the cliffs and Andy's tools hitting the mountain every time his feet went out from under him, our progress was almost non-existent. Caught in an endless tangle of cliffs and alder swales, we found a spot with enough earth covering the rock that we were able to chop out a place to sit on the steep 50° slope. In this position we spent the night.

As we sat there in the darkness eating some sandwiches, a tremendous thunderstorm rolled up the valley. What a show we witnessed that night—with lightning flashing between the valley bottom and the clouds around and above us, we got the Doppler effect of the thunder from above and below at the same time. It sure gives one a different perspective to see and hear lightning and thunder from that angle.

We spent the entire night sitting up sopping wet, unable to move for fear of sliding down the mountain. Believe me, it was a very long night. But we survived it, and when daylight arrived, we gathered up some firewood and took it back up to timberline. Then, when we heard the helicopter coming, we lit the fire and threw a lot of green limbs on it to produce smoke. Dick had no trouble finding us.

Once we got airborne, we just headed for home. That snag may have gone out on its own but we were too exhausted to care. Without a radio, and with Andy taking those terrible falls, I was exceedingly thankful that he didn't get injured in among those endless cliffs.

Jack Millburn, the other pilot we quite often flew with, started flying helicopters in 1956, and continued until his retirement in 1984. Throughout those years he had many interesting adventures and some frightening ones as well. Shortly after he started with choppers, he was flying a Bell G2 with two geologists aboard when he got into an accident. He had just lifted off a ridge at the 5500-foot level when he noticed that the controls didn't feel right. The new helicopter started banking hard to the left and refused to respond to the controls. Instead, it carried right on into an island of subalpine fir trees just a short distance from Kakwa Falls. The main rotor, tail rotor, and boom were history, but the men got out without a scratch. The G2 was later flown out and rebuilt.

Jack then spent many years flying all over the globe. In 1964—East Pakistan; in 1968—New Zealand; In 1970, he was on the Mackenzie Delta with oil explorations, flying equipment from barges to the oil rigs.

After slinging in a load one day with a S58 twin-jet Sikorsky, he signaled that he needed fuel, then came around to land on the platform. As he touched down, the right wheel went through the pad, which in turn caused the chopper to flip over and land upside down. It thrashed about for a while, then finally settled in on its left side

Jack Milburn in S58 Sikorsky.

amid a horrendous cloud of dust. Jack's first concern was that the machine may catch fire, so he attempted to get out. Then he found he was being held tight. It was a new type of harness that held him securely in place and may well have saved his life. Once again he managed to walk away from an accident unscathed.

1974 found Jack flying in Greenland, and then in 1978 he was shipped to the Philippines where he flew until his retirement. I was at his retirement party in Prince George in 1984, and it was nice to see many of his peers there as well. Don Watson, who had flown the Interior for many years. Also Dick Beggs, who had gone on to start his own company, Vernon Helicopters. So many people were there, all with the same objective; to wish a happy retirement to one of the original mountain chopper pilots of the Interior. Jack's accumulated time in the air was 2000 hours fixed wing—much of that during the war—and 14,000 hours in choppers.

Down through the years I flew with a great number of different chopper pilots, and some excellent ones as well—men like Ken Knight and Don Buchanan. But there was one that stood out above the rest. Dan Wiebe was his name, and great flying was his game. He saved us more miles of walking, and saved the forestry more money than anyone can imagine. With his Hughes 500, he could land in very tight spots—such as between large cedar trees where his rotor tips would sometimes lightly tick the needles on the ends of limbs. Many times I told him, "Don't take any chances, Dan."

His answer was always the same, "I never take any chances, Jack."

Sometimes we would circle a fire and he would say, "I can get you in right there." I would look and see nothing but a solid stand of timber, but with his eagle eyes he had measured the distance between trees and knew he could do it.

Sometimes when he let us off, we watched in amazement as he rose vertically out of a very tight spot with only a foot or two on each side of the rotor. He went up as if guided by a laser beam. There were times when Dan dropped us off on fires and then had to leave the area. This meant that we had the choice of walking out or building a much bigger landing pad, as other pilots wouldn't even consider landing there. If the distance wasn't too far, we sometimes walked out.

In all fairness to other chopper pilots, I must point out that these Hughes helicopters rendered other choppers obsolete for initial attack on fires. With their shorter rotor, higher tail rotor and body, they can get closer to a fire by landing in very small openings. Their greater speed is also an asset in quick fire response. Only the fact that they are noisier and less comfortable prevents their greater use on fires.

The only time I ever felt that Dan came close to getting in an accident happened when he took four of us into a tight spot. After we had sized it up from the air, I told the others that when Dan hovered the chopper near the ground that we would get out one at a time. Then we would step off of the skid without pushing the aircraft sideways. As we were settling down through the trees, I told them again and all nodded in agreement. Three of us got out as agreed, then the last chap opened the door and jumped, pushing the Hughes to one side as he did so. Somehow Dan managed to recov-

Deputy Ranger Bob Richards, left with ace pilot Dan Weibe on Longworth lookout, 1979.

er in that tight spot and thank God he did, or else we all would have been chopped to pieces.

From that time on, I either went in alone or took only one trusted person with me. Then a heliport was constructed and the crew was brought in when they could be safely landed.

It is my opinion that many accidents are just the result of laziness or stupidity or both. Such as the accident that occurred when fellow officer Ken Llewellyn and I were in charge of a fire-camp on Dome Creek. We were servicing a large number of lightning-caused fires in that area, and we had an excellent young pilot named Paul Smith moving our fire crews with a Hughes 500. One evening he was moving crews back into camp when it became obvious that he was overdue. We called repeatedly on the radio but we were unable to reach him or the crew he was to pick up because they were behind a mountain from us, and in a blind spot from our radio repeaters. Finally the McBride Forestry Office called to say that a helicopter had gone down in the Torpy.

I just felt sick. I knew exactly where it was and that Paul had gone down vertically into a tight spot between tall cedar trees. Another Hughes was sent to the rescue, and after an agonizing silence we finally received another message that no one was injured.

When Paul was flown back into camp, we found out what had happened: he had gone vertically down through the trees for pick up, only to find that the crew had not leveled a pad for him. This forced him to toe in for pick up. No sooner had the front of his skids touched the sidehill, than firefighters jumped on the back of each skid at the same time. This forced the back end of the chopper down and caused a tail-rotor strike. Somehow Paul was able to keep the aircraft upright, which may well have prevented fatalities, but about $70,000 damage was done to the machine. As they waited for the rescue helicopter, Paul took a polasky and in 10 minutes made a level landing pad for the incoming chopper. Ten minutes work would have prevented that accident.

I can't understand why people would fight a fire without having a decent level landing pad to use in case of an emergency medivac. After all, the life they save may be their own. I used to tell the pilots that ultimately they were the ones in control, and all they had to do was leave a fire crew on a mountain overnight just once, and they would be guaranteed level landing pads for ever after.

When Dan left the Interior, and Paul gave up flying, it was back to the real world, which meant hours of packing through the forest to get to fires. One day I asked a chopper pilot if he would let me off in an alder thicket on a steep mountainside. By putting me right beside the fire, this would save me from having to spend hours climbing up the mountain. He agreed, so we went in and he hovered right on the alders. I threw out my tools, lowered the chainsaw with a short rope, and then climbed out on the skid. The rotor-wash made the alders dance about and allowed me to see the ground. I stepped off and the chopper departed. An hour later I had constructed a heliport and was fighting the fire.

I just couldn't believe the difference, as now I could use all my energy to fight the fire instead of the mountain. I used this technique for a few years in secret, then decided to feel out the ranger. I suggested to him that we give it a try, not telling him that I already had. His immediate response was, "No bloody way; that's too dangerous."

Jack Boudreau discussing fire tactics with forest officer Larry Badowski, 1979.

I bit my lip and didn't say that I thought climbing around cliffs with heavy packs was also dangerous. I didn't stop, though; I just kept on doing it as long as the pilots felt good about it.

One incident that took place on a fire will always stay in my memory. That was the day I was walking the fire boundary when a fire-fighter rushed up to me and said, "I'm getting hard." Just as I was getting ready to make a run for it, he made some motions around his abdomen and got the point across that he was constipated. In very broken English, he said, "Go radio; get rye crisp; rye crisp make it slip."

I assured him that I would, and an order was sent to the district office for rye crisp to be included in the next order. Next day a chopper came in and had no sooner touched down, then this man appeared out of the trees. We went through the supplies, but found no rye crisp. Instead, we found a box of rice krispies. More than just a little upset, this fellow went to great lengths to make me understand that he needed rye crisp, because 'rye crisp make it slip'.

Once again I assured him that we would take care of it and I heard the time-keeper order, "Make sure you send rye crisp, check, we don't want any rice krispies, check." Back came the answer, "Roger, Roger."

There was a lot of traffic on the radio from lookouts, aircraft, and other fire camps, but this time we felt confident. The next time the chopper came in, this same man seemed to materialize out of the trees. Again we went through the order but could not find any rye crisp. Instead we found two boxes of rice krispies.

I just couldn't believe the improvement in that man's English, because I had no problem understanding him when he told me what he thought of the forest service. He went out with the chopper.

Humour aside, the forces involved in raging forest fires are something to behold. To be close to them when they decide to run is truly a humbling experience no matter how many fires a person has been on.

The forces involved with a raging fire were well demonstrated to me during the Pink Fire in 1985. A fellow forest officer named Norm Canuel and I stayed up all night in an attempt to stop the fire from burning out a reserve of timber near a large stream. We set backfires and when daylight came we found that we had been successful in stopping the blaze. Our efforts were all in vain, though, for a week later the fire came back from a different direction and burnt the area out. Among the trees that were destroyed were a great many cottonwood trees which were two to three feet in diameter. These large trees were broken up into cordwood by the tremendous winds associated with the fire.

Don Redden of Prince George, who now flies Learjet for Canfor, told me of a fire that impressed him no end. The year was 1972 and he was flying a Cessna 337 Skymaster as bird dog pilot for the BC Forest Service—'bird dog' being forestry parlance for the aircraft that lays out the plan of attack for the air tankers on fires. He was based in Fort Nelson at the time when he was ordered to check out the Tee Fire just off the Liard River. On board was Don Thompson, acting as bird dog officer. This fire was between two and three acres

Pink fire, July 1985.

when spotted; in one half hour it was 500 acres, and in two hours it was 2000 acres. As they approached the fire, they beheld an incredible scene: spot fires were erupting as much as five miles ahead of the main fire. Trees would explode in a ball of flame, then the entire area would light up. Then trees would explode well ahead of the fire and the process would be repeated.

As they came over a ridge about 100 feet above the trees, they saw a solid wall of fire coming out of a valley and over the ridge. Suddenly a complete tree, roots and all, came up over the ridge and it was higher than they were. Just as Don turned the 337 to get the hell out of there, a strip of bark slammed into the windshield. This was where they drew the line, so they returned to Fort Nelson where a considerable amount of time was required to clean the fire debris off the aircraft.

As I had spent a lot of time working for the forest service, I guess it made sense that I should go to work for them full time. In 1976, I did just that. I went to work in the Protection Branch, where I certainly did get more than my share of firefighting. Many times I was on three different fires in one day.

But of all the fires, it was the prescribed burns, or slash burns, that were the most dangerous. Sometimes we jokingly referred to them as controlled burns just before they escaped and ran over the mountain. They were so dangerous because we used hand light-up, which involved several people carrying drip-torches and lighting-up at the same time.

I'm sure that my worst scare occurred when several of us went to light-up a large area of windrows. We spent a lot of time going over the procedure until everyone affirmed that they knew what to do. Then we began lighting-up, moving against the wind. Each person was responsible for watching the person on either side of them to be sure that no one was left behind. When we got through to the far end and the light-up was complete, the man in the next row from me turned and went back into the fire. I screamed at him to come back, but he could not hear me over the tremendous roar of the fire. Just then the crew boss on the other side of him realized what had happened so he ran down along one of the windrows and found a break in the otherwise solid lines of windrows. He ran through and found the man trapped inside the rapidly spreading fire which was already broadcasting between the rows. When he brought him out to safety, we asked what possessed him to go back, and he replied, "I saw one place that wasn't burning too good, so I went back to put more fuel on it."

Only the fact that there was a break in the windrow saved his life, and this was just one of several close calls that we had with hand light-ups. A short time later several young people were burned to death in Ontario during a hand light-up, and I believe that this is what prompted the move to helicopter light-up which is a much safer and more effective method.

Slash burns are every bit as impressive as forest fires. Especially when we consider that a 100-hectare slash burn gives off the same amount of energy as a Hiroshima-sized atomic bomb; it just takes longer to do it. The column of rising air can cause a strong wind a couple miles away, as air is sucked into the raging inferno. On one occasion I saw a passing bird become overpowered by the tremendous wind and drawn into the inferno. It was a fairly common occurrence to see full-sized waste trees picked off the ground and sent flying through the air, then slammed back to earth where they were broken up like so much cordwood. Truly, the forces involved in fires are beyond comprehension.

Of all the factors involved in firefighting, it was the helicopters that made life so much easier for us, and they were used with more and more frequency. Sometimes it wasn't always fun such as in the early '80s, when there was an abundance of chopper pilots, many of whom were ex-military types. Some of these pilots were so used to flying low that they gave us the creeps. One individual that I flew with had to be repeatedly told to fly higher, as he would barely clear tall trees and snags. A fellow forest officer named John Currie had the misfortune to fly with one of these hot-dog pilots when he clipped the top of a tree. John gave him a talking to, and just a few minutes later, as he was mapping a fire, he noticed the pilot was studying his map, too. John looked up to see that they were flying right into a rock cliff, so he yelled, "Look out!"

The pilot just managed to avoid a collision with the mountain, and that did it for John. He demanded to be let off on the adjacent highway, where he dismissed the pilot. A couple weeks later this same pilot died in the wreckage of his helicopter.

On a July morning in 1980, I awoke with a splitting headache. I didn't feel like going to work but I did. That morning a report came in to the ranger station at Aleza Lake that there was a fire burning on Purden Mountain. Along with two firefighters, I was lifted into the area of the fire and put off in a small opening by Dan Wiebe with his Hughes 500. We walked around the ridge until we came to a steep spot with heavy brush. The other two men tried to climb above it, but I noticed a downtree lying on the sidehill so I went to cross on it. As I walked along, my feet slipped and I crashed down on a broken limb, driving it up into my armpit. I realized at once that I was hurt bad, so I yelled to the others to come to my aid. They rushed to my side and examined the injury and like myself,

Kelly Boudreau at Pinkerton Lake, 1979.

were surprised that it was scarcely bleeding. The two men took the chainsaw and fell a few trees, then Dan flew the chopper in and hovered while I climbed aboard. A couple hours later I was in the emergency room at the Prince George Hospital where the doctor examined me and then said, "Someone must be taking care of you because that limb went in and brushed along the artery and main nerve. If it had severed the nerve, you would have lost the use of your arm. If it had severed the artery, you most certainly would have bled to death."

This accident was not caused by my walking that downtree, as I have walked thousands of downtrees in my life. Rather, it was a result of going to work sick, and because of that being less than alert.

My closest brush with disaster occurred a few years later when I was on a fire with Forest Officer Brent Anderson. We were dropped off by a Jet Ranger near Stony Lake and we walked a short distance to where a lightning strike had set a snag afire. It was obvious that the snag had almost burned off in two spots, so I was reluctant to fall it for fear that the top would break off and fall on me. Finally I asked Brent to stand beside me and give me a slap if the top portion broke free, then I moved in and began making the undercut. Just as I was finishing, the top portion crashed down and drove into the ground so close to me that it scraped the saw. Brent said he hollered, but I heard nothing.

Then we had a stalemate, as the other portion of the snag was still standing and burning, and I was not about to take another chance. I realized that this snag could slowly burn for days, so I looked for an alternate solution. Suddenly I came up with an idea: I called Ivor, the pilot, and asked if he had brought along a long-line. When he said he hadn't, I asked if he had noticed any cable lying on that landing. A minute later he called to say that he had found a 20-foot piece of cable left over from logging. I asked him to pick up a piece of log and bring it over, which he did. Then, as he flew slowly up to the snag, the piece of log he carried bumped the snag and broke off the burning piece, making it safe to fall. This technique was used several times by me at later dates and it is simply perfect; if the snag doesn't break from the impact, then it is safe to fall.

One of the side benefits of my work was the many strange sights we saw. One example of this occurred when Blair Wood was flying me to a fire. As we moved along behind a storm cell, we spotted a beautiful rainbow. At that point Blair asked, "Have you ever seen a perfect rainbow?"

"I don't know what you mean." I responded.

"Well, I'll show you." He answered, as he turned the Jet Ranger around and approached the rainbow from the side. Several times he moved back and forth until we had a rainbow that formed a complete circle; the only one I've ever seen.

Many other times we saw wildlife, often spotting grizzlies along salmon streams or in the alpine heights. Perhaps the most memorable event took place on a July day in 1987, after a fellow worker and I had just finished setting up a lookout tower with provisions. We lifted off Wendle Mountain with pilot Ken Knight, in a 206 Jet Ranger, and had just started down when we immediately spotted what we thought were two moose entering Wendle Lake far below us. What seemed strange, though, was the way one moose seemed to be outracing the other. Then it was suggested that the one animal didn't look like a moose. Sure enough, we took another look and all agreed that it was a grizzly, and a pretty good-sized one at that. As they raced across the lake, we dropped several thousand feet, and by the time we reached lake level the cow moose had reached the other side of the lake. We hovered right in front of the grizzly to see if it would turn, but instead it just curled its lips in a snarl and kept going after the moose. It was most interesting to note that the moose with its four-leg drive easily outdistanced the grizzly which swam only with its front legs. We took several pictures and then watched the grizzly climb out on the bank not too far from where the moose did. For a minute I felt bad, thinking that it may have continued on and got the moose; then I gave my head a shake and realized that if it caught the moose then that's exactly what nature intended.

When you spend your life in the mountains, you are certain to run into odd things. One very strange thing occurred in the '80s when we had a rash of lightning-caused fires in the Torpy Valley. Several two-man and three-man crews were put out on the different fires, and all were doing great except for one crew. This crew was on a small fire burning at ground level, and when they didn't have the fire out by nightfall, I wanted to know why. They informed me that there was a big squirrel's nest that was burning and that they were having trouble putting it out. Convinced that they were slack-assing, I got the pilot to let me off at the fire the following morning. As I walked to where these two men were working, I couldn't believe what I was seeing. There was a huge pile of cones spread out on the mountain and smoke was still emerging from a large hole in the slope. We worked for another two hours and finally got all the burning cones dragged out of the hole. However there was still a great amount of cones left inside of what I figured must have been an old grizzly den. Just how many squirrels it took over how many years to fill that den with cones is anyone's guess. I know for certain that if I hadn't seen it, I would never have believed it.

Then there was the day that I really felt sorry for a pilot. This was in the 1980s during a fire-flap after he had dropped off eight crews on lightning strikes. As we had more fires than radios, one crew went without one. When it came time to pick up the crews, the pilot found all but one crew, and let it be known over the radio. Someone came on the radio and said, "Why don't you call them."

His reply was, "You're not going to believe this; it's the crew without a radio."

Roger kept looking, though, and after a few hours eventually found them, but he sure looked stressed out that evening. He really had a rough day.

Unlike some people that seem to go though life without making mistakes, I was a party to a fiasco on a fire in this same Torpy area. Lightning struck just below timberline one evening and during the night a strong downdraft took the fire downhill about half a mile. The next day it ran back up the mountain in the form of a huge V, and we had a big fire to deal with. We noticed that there were two small runoff lakes in the alpine, one just above each side of the fire. This inspired me and another fire-boss—Scott Almond (yes, you're taking some of the blame)–to place a pump in each lake, then run a hose lay down each side of the fire. When morning came we were going to hit both flanks of the fire to get it under control. As it was evening by the time we finished setting up the pumps, the choppers came to take us back to fire-camp, so we quickly started the pumps to make certain everything was ready for morning. It worked fine, so we all got aboard the choppers and left.

The next morning I was moving a crew to another fire, and as we flew along the valley, we passed by the big fire and saw a most ridiculous sight: two pumps, complete with hose lays lying in the alpine, and not a drop of water to be seen anywhere. It seems that the pumps had been shut off the previous evening, but the water had continued to siphon through and had drained both of these small lakes dry. Believe me when I say that red faces were the norm around that fire-camp for a few days thereafter.

Perhaps some explanation of lightning should be made, at least what is generally accepted at this time. Also known as Thor's hammer, a cloud to ground bolt, or a ground to cloud bolt—depending on the source of the information—can carry up to 1,000,000 volts and up to 100,000 amps. A pathway for the bolt is created by ion-

Jack Boudreau at timberline, 1980.

ized molecules in the form of a stepped leader that comes down from cloud level and makes contact with leaders from the ground, then the main burst follows these leaders. If a person sees where lightning strikes in sand, it is a worthwhile endeavor to dig up a fulgurite, where it will be noticed that the fused walls come together like the roots of a tree, then join into one fused tube at ground level.

A great amount of water inside of dead trees (snags) or in porous rocks can literally explode from the 30,000°C temperature of the lightning bolt. This, in turn, can send pieces of wood or rock flying hundreds of feet from the strike area. The sound of thunder is caused by the explosive expansion of air along the ionized path, which may be only a couple centimeters in diameter.

Another point of interest is astraphobia—a morbid fear of thunder and lightning. I once had a dog that would tremble in terror during thunder storms. Even indoors it could not be consoled. I can't help but feel that any animal that has ever been wounded by gunfire must go through hell during thunderstorms, because the sound of both are inseparable. Surprisingly, to me at least, I have watched grizzlies feeding high in the mountains during thunderstorms and they paid no attention whatsoever. Obviously they get used to it.

9

MOUNTAIN MEMORIES

ARCTAL PINE: DEFINED AS ABOVE OR BEYOND TREE GROWTH; A different world; often a place of striking beauty and eternal silence.

Is there anyone that has stood among the peaks where mountain goats and sheep dwell, who has not been overwhelmed by the sheer drops into oblivion? Anyone who has not stared in wonder as a mountain goat crosses a cliff that any reasonable person knows is impassable? Truly, it is a breathtaking world that they inhabit. Just to sit on mountain peaks and contemplate their orogenic history; then add to that the processes of glacial activity, wind and water erosion, and it is small wonder that they exude such majestic elegance. It is another world—this land above timberline, where some mornings you arise to find the valleys below completely filled with fog and so perfectly level on top that it seems you could walk across to the distant mountains that now seem so near in the clear morning air.

Mount Alexander (Sitzi) with Mount Ida to it's right, tower above a sea of mountains in the headwaters of the McGregor River.

It is a place where glacier–or snowfield-fed waters–emerge from the mountainside so cold that they make your teeth ache, even in the heat of August; where one may come upon some spaerella or pink snow. As a lad I didn't know it was an alga, I thought it was some mysterious substance that fell from the sky.

It's a place where a person can be lulled into the most peaceful of sleeps by the endless murmur of the wind in the forests below, where fields of varied wildflowers dance eternally in the restless mountain air, their species and colors changing with the season until we have the striking red and pink vacciniums and epilobiums of late fall.

Here, the dippers sit on rocks at stream's edge and continuously bob up and down. I like to think that their endless bobbing is their way of keeping time to the music of these mountain streams.

It is here where the early morning silence may be broken by the shrill whistle of a marmot as it spreads the warning that potential danger has entered its domain. The Columbian and beautiful golden-mantled ground squirrels head for the safety of their burrows.

It's where the incredible camouflage ability of a ptarmigan is demonstrated as it alights on a scree terrace and disappears instantly from view, where a flash of white feathers may betray the presence of a bald eagle as it drops at high speed onto a ground squirrel that

A golden-mantled ground squirrel high above the timberline.

has wandered too far from its burrow. During 54 years in the mountains, I must say that I have only seen these high-altitude dives a handful of times.

A person may here watch a multi-colored sunset, silhouetted by rugged peaks, as it fades away into darkness and where in the subalpine one may find a tree squirrel hard at work as it gathers mushrooms and places them on branches to dry. There is a shortage of cones at this elevation, and the creature must improvise. Many kinds of mushrooms are stored by it for winter use, among them several kinds that are poisonous to man.

Here, gnarled and twisted trees cling tenaciously to the slopes taking everything nature can hurl at them—perhaps burial under 30 feet of snow-pack; snow that may last up to 10 months of the year—followed by summer winds of up to 80 miles-per-hour. These trees can become so pliant, so resilient, that they may be tied in knots without breaking.

Here's where a person can see alpine cushion plants, such as moss campion, that have the unique ability to increase their root temperature as much as 10°C. above the ambient temperature.

There are so many things to see and do in the high country that every day is a new adventure. Every peak that is climbed affords a different view, and every sunset is a unique experience.

Any person that has spent much time in the McGregor Mountains has surely been tangled up in alder thickets and devil's club at one time or another. In some places these thickets blanket the slopes for miles. Snow-press lays the alders side by side pointing downhill, and this can make them virtually impenetrable. In frustration, some people will grab them and try to force them out of their way, only to find that they are forked, and that their twin strikes back viciously in return. I have first-hand knowledge that many highly creative vulgarities and obscenities were born in these thickets, and so I will try to say something in their defence.

Recent scientific discovery shows that devil's club has great anti-viral and anti-bacterial properties, while alders are just one of many plants that fix nitrogen in the soil. When we consider that the earth's atmosphere contains almost 80 percent nitrogen and that nitrogen deficiency is the most limiting factor in plant growth, then their importance becomes apparent. Nitrogen-fixing soil bacteria convert atmospheric nitrogen into a form that plants can utilize. By forming symbiotic nodules on the roots of leguminous plants, they become, in effect, fertilizer factories.

Another way that alders contribute is by providing cover for wildlife. Many times we have seen grizzlies and other animals head into these thickets when danger threatened, and they could never have found a safer place to hide. As well, alders are a great soil stabilizer—often being the only plant tenacious enough to cling to avalanche tracks.

There was one lesson I learned about alders that I will never forget: don't cut a trail through them unless you have no other choice. In 1954, a young immigrant from France, Robert Brandy, helped me cut a trail through several miles of alders. It was an enormous undertaking, but it allowed us access to some beautiful alpine so we considered the effort worthwhile. Three years later I went back into the same area only to find that the trail was gone. Several weeks of hard

Doctors Carolyn and Jack McGhee with me in the alpine, 1991.

work had gone for nothing. Now I will go to almost any length to avoid alders, and if I have to go through them, I prefer to go straight up or down the hill. The snow-press in winter lays them down the slopes, the new growth quickly hiding any trail.

When this same Robert Brandy came from France in 1952, he joined two friends who had arrived the previous year—Jean Andre and Georges Odier. For a couple of years they lived and worked in Penny, where we became great friends and traveled the mountains together. During this same time, Prince George radio and television talk show host and newsman Bob Harkins climbed the ridges with us. Then each went his own way: Bob to Prince George, where he became involved with radio and television, Jean to Victoria where he became a world-renowned museum consultant, specializing in design and interpretation. George went to Aspen, Colorado, and Robert back to France.

Bob Harkins at Slim Lake, 1950.

Just before Robert left Victoria for France in 1954, he bought a bottle of wine which he gave to Jean on the condition that he would keep it until they met again; only then would it be opened. Thirty-eight years later that promise was fulfilled when Robert returned from France with his wife Danielle, George from Aspen, Jean and his wife Joan from Victoria. Together with Bob and Barbara Harkins, Clarence and his wife Olga, and myself, we all got together and hired a Jet Ranger helicopter to fly us back into those same mountains. It was September 1992 when we flew in, and although the weather left something to be desired, what with a light snow steadily falling, our consolation was a thousand memories revisited. Late that first day, we opened the wine that had been purchased so many years earlier and it was truly a special moment. As Bob so eloquently put it, "Both the wine and the friendships had aged perfectly."

We spent three days up near timberline, and the icing on the cake was produced during our last evening on the mountain when two grizzlies spent several minutes bellowing in the valley below us. Perhaps over a territorial dispute. Or perhaps the strong downdraft had taken our scent down to them, and they may have been expressing their hatred of man. Their roars echoed through the mountains, and left each of us with another special memory.

As I look back through the years at the mountains I have traveled, I reflect on many changes that I have noticed there. One change that occurred in my youth was the disappearance of huge weasels from the Interior mountains that I have traveled. Called mountain giants, they were almost as big as martens. My father said they were quite plentiful in the 1920s.

Another change that is very obvious is the great number of snowfields that have disappeared. Many of the snowfields that I played on as a lad were up to half-a-mile long, yet there is not a sign left to show that they were ever there.

One of the most obvious changes to me is that the sense of wilderness is gone. When we ran around the mountains as young men, there were no trails and help was not readily available. We really had the sense of separation from society, and we knew we were in deep trouble if we got injured. Many modern bushwhackers carry radios and they know that help is as close as the nearest helicopter.

Another change I have noticed is the improvement in clothing that mountain types now have at their disposal. When we first traveled the ridges, we carried woolen blankets that were heavy and offered little protection from the cold. Our boots were often heavy and uncomfortable, leaving us with many a blister by the time we returned home. For protection from the rain, we wore bone-dry pants and jackets that were little more than sweat boxes, and offered no protection from the cold. Now people have gortex clothing that allows them to stay both warm and dry; lightweight and durable hiking boots that offer the ultimate in ankle protection, and lightweight sleeping bags that we would have given an arm and a leg for. With dehydrated food supplements, modern-day hikers can head into the forests for days with as little as 20 pounds on their backs. In our case, we often carried 50 to 70 pounds.

Another change I have noticed in the mountains concerns ravens. When I was a lad they were extremely wild and hard to sneak up on. If they were feeding on a carcass, they always had guards posted that would warn of approaching danger. Now it seems they spend half their time in the cities. Another comment I would like to make about ravens is that I firmly believe they have one of the best telecommunication systems in the world. I was near a moose carcass once when a raven flew over and spotted it. It didn't even land, instead it flew off toward a distant mountain, croaking steadily as it went. Within 20 minutes there were a dozen ravens feeding on that carcass.

One of the changes most troubling to me is the disappearance of marmots from some of the areas I travel. Where their shrill whistles used to echo through the high country, now there is only the sound of ground squirrels. In areas around cliffs where colonies used to live there is not a sign left to show that they were ever there. The guards that were always on duty to prevent a surprise attack by eagles, wolverines, coyotes, or bears, no longer grace the highest boulders in their area.

I personally believe that pesticides are the leading cause of their decline. During this past winter, studies showed alarming increases in pesticide residues in the Rocky Mountains, with the levels increasing with elevation. Certainly in the areas I frequent most there has been a continuous spraying program for many years, especially along the Torpy River in an area that used to be a wonderland of game. It should now have a name change and appropriately be called Death Valley.

The large bush toads that were seemingly everywhere are now almost absent from those mountains. How many times I remember being entertained for hours by these unique creatures. In the long, dark evenings of late fall when we were cutting trails for the Forest Service, we used to light our gas lamp and hang it over a cardboard box which contained a large toad. The lamp would attract moths and other creatures of the night, which in turn would simply disappear when they flew near the toad. The toad's tongue would flick out and capture them with such speed that we seldom saw more than a blur. In one instance Herb Metzmeier and I kept a toad named Sam in a box for about one week and I'm sure he must have been sorry to see us leave. I doubt that he ever had it so good.

Ptarmigans and blue grouse have also declined in numbers during the last 20 years, in fact, I seldom see them anymore.

Another animal that appears to be absent from those mountains is skunks, and to be quite frank I don't miss them at all. Many people used to have a problem with them digging in under their houses, and this led to confrontations at times. Our neighbor set a trap under his house and succeeded in catching one, to his sorrow: the skunk sprayed and stunk the place up for the next six months. It is common knowledge that their spray is among the most pervasive and enduring scents in nature, and anyone that has had the misfortune to be sprayed can attest to that.

There used to be a saying that tomato juice would remove the scent from soiled clothing, but it doesn't do the job. There is a sure-fire scientific method though, and it requires washing soiled clothing in a solution which contains one litre of three percent hydrogen peroxide, one-half cup baking soda, and two tablespoons detergent soap. This is guaranteed to remove the smell.

Not all is doom and gloom in the mountains though, as there is one species of animal that is on the increase, and that is grizzly bears.

I believe there are three main reasons for this, with limited hunting being one of them. But I believe the most important cause of their increase in numbers is the short, mild winters that have virtually eliminated den deaths—their greatest enemy in my opinion. Certainly they appear to be much fatter just prior to den time now than they were many years ago.

The third reason, I feel, is the abundance of feed available because of logging. I have seen five lone bears in a small cut-block at the same time and surely we can all agree that bears are where their food is.

Another change that really stands out in my memory, is the change in colour that grizzlies have undergone throughout the years in the areas I frequent most. In the late '40s and through the '50s, most of the bears were shades of brown with the odd blonde one thrown in. Black-colored grizzlies were not as common as they are now. In the late '50s, a huge black boar either entered the area or else suddenly matured there and through the next 20 years his genes became evident as more and more black grizzlies appeared. By 1995, at least half the adults were dark to black. Then a new big brown boar grizzly appeared in the area and I will be very surprised if the trend does not swing back the other way again in the future. Nature ultimately finds a way to keep the gene pool moving.

Grizzly following salmon stream.

In all the years that I have watched grizzlies, I am certain that I have never seen a mother grizzly with two year-old cubs, although I have had many people tell me that they have seen them. Whether they have seen two-year olds or just large yearlings is debatable. Also, I have never seen a grizzly with more than three cubs, although I did see an unusual family of grizzlies once.

This happened when Bill and I were glassing for bears in September 1986. It did not take us long to realize that this was not a normal family because there was a mother, two cubs, and what was at least a yearling, and may well have been a two-year-old, as this bear was well over half the size of the mother. The reason I feel it was hers is because at one point it walked right between her and the cubs—something she would never have allowed any other bear to do. As it was late evening we had no chance to get closer, and although we returned to the area again the following day, we did not see them again.

In the area of Grizzly Bear Mountain, where I have spent so many years glassing bears, there was a brown sow grizzly with a large dark cross on her back—a very easy grizzly to recognize. In 1966 she was alone. In 1967 she had three cubs. In 1968 she still had the three as

A marmot stands guard, ready to alert other marmots with a shrill whistle if danger threatens.

yearlings. In 1969 she was alone and obviously mated, because in 1970 I saw her several times with three cubs. In 1971 she was with them as yearlings. In 1972 she mated again because I saw her with three cubs in 1973. I last saw her in 1974 with her three yearlings. A road had been punched into that general area and she may have been shot the following spring when she was alone.

The only other bear that I positively kept track of was a blond grizzly. It had one cub in 1967, and I saw her with another lone cub in 1970. Several times I was fooled by bears that I thought I recognized, then when they would change position their color changed. This is especially true when they emerge from shadow into sunlight.

If I had kept track throughout the years of the number of cubs that grizzlies have, I'm sure it would have averaged over two. I say this because I am certain that I have seen many more mothers with three cubs than I have seen with just one cub.

Now I want to look far back in an effort to show why grizzlies ceased the phneomenon of staying out during the winter in the McGregor area. In order to do this, I have to point out why I believe they started staying out during the winter months in the first place. During my interviews with old-time woodsmen for *Crazy Man's Creek,* I noticed time and again that there were only a few wolves in the McGregor/Torpy River areas until after 1915. Ole Hansen, who trapped and then guided the McGregor area from 1911 until into the '60s, seldom heard wolves for the first several years. When he did hear them, they were up near timberline. And just why were the wolves up that high? I'm sure they were hunting caribou which were in abundance at that time.

Next, I would like to deal with the arrival of moose in this area. Most sources say that moose did not arrive in this area until somewhere between 1900 and 1930. The first record I could find of moose in the Prince George area was in 1912 when two men first saw their tracks and had no idea what they were following.

But along the Big Salmon (McGregor) River, the December 18, 1909 edition of the *Fort George Herald* tells of "…three to five moose on every bar in spring". The same edition shows an advertisement for a wife by guide and trapper Frank Kibbee of Barkerville. In this ad he describes "…grizzly bears, moose and some deer." As well, Dome Creek trapper Ernest Jensen told me that he shot several moose for the railroad construction camp at Dome Creek in 1912 and 1913.

In his book — *Three Years Hunting and Trapping in America and the Great Northwest,* author J. Turner Turner tells how he spent the winter of 1887/88 trapping 25 miles upriver from the Grand Canyon on the Fraser River. This was right in the area of Penny, my hometown. During the entire winter, the most wolves he found together in one pack was three. They shot a few lone wolves that may have been part of this pack. As well, he saw one set of moose tracks, and found one moose skull. The Indians, who brought food and mail to him on occasion, told him that there were more moose about 100 miles upriver. It is also worth noting that he never mentioned finding grizzly tracks in the snow during the winter. As well, when Mr. Turner went south along the Fraser the following spring, they found where someone had shot a moose below Fort George canyon.

At this point, I want to mention that this is contrary to everything I have ever read or heard about moose in this area. The going story has always been that moose were absent from this area until after 1900

Leaving behind a plainly visible trail in which 100-year-old trees are growing, and moving downhill at only millimeters a year. An erratic boulder (deposited by glaciers) is victim to the forces of freezing and thawing, snow press and gravity. Sometime in the distant future it will reach the bottom of the ridge.

when a huge migration took place from out of the northeast. Mr. Turner makes it plain that moose were here in small numbers, and I believe that the reason the numbers were so small was because of their limited food supply.

Next, I want to bring in the diary of Ida Sykes, who along with her husband Ben Sykes, came down the Fraser River in 1912. They settled in the Penny area, where Ben trapped and later guided until 1924. Beginning on August 19, 1912, Ida kept a diary which ended on May 11, 1915. Every animal or bird they saw or shot for food is mentioned in that diary. I find it most interesting to note that there is not one mention of seeing wolves, their tracks, or of hearing them howl. The reason, of course, is the moose populations were just starting to explode at that time and deer were extremely scarce. Though she mentioned all the different tracks they noticed, there is not a mention of seeing grizzly bear tracks in the snow.

I have already pointed out that moose were on the increase by this time, and her diary tells of shooting many moose and caribou for food and sale to the railway construction camps. Several years later, three things happened: moose became very abundant, wolf packs appeared in large numbers, and boar grizzlies started staying up and about during the winter months. The obvious connection I make is that the great number of moose, deer, and caribou carcasses left by the packs, prompted some of the boar grizzlies to stay out during the winter. This was attested to by my father who trapped the Slim Lake area during the '30s. He told us that he saw grizzly tracks in the snow many times—once in very deep snow conditions in mid–February.

But what prompted the great increase in moose populations and the rapid decline in caribou populations? I think the answer is so obvious that we overlooked it. Again in his book, Mr. Turner tells of his journey up the Fraser from Fort George, and the many enormous forest fires that were burning. On his return trip the next year, he again mentions the many forest fires that were burning. During the next 25 years, other travelers tell similar stories of monster fires burning, including many fires during the surveying and construction of the Grand Trunk Pacific Railway—1908 to 1913. All these fires destroyed much of the old growth forest so necessary to caribou, and so their numbers diminished. And what did many people blame for the demise of the caribou? Why, the wolf packs, of course. But it wasn't the wolves, or the caribou would have made a recovery after the wolf packs were poisoned off, which they did not.

All these fires did succeed in bringing a bonanza of feed for the moose and deer. They quickly multiplied and the wolf packs multiplied with them. The great amount of carrion left from their kills, in turn, kept some of the large boar grizzlies out during the winter.

The great increase in the number of these wolf packs, as well as the increase in the number per pack, caused a lot of pressure to be brought to bear on the game department from ranchers, homesteaders, trappers, as well as the general public. This pressure resulted in a massive wolf poisoning program during the winter of 1952/53. Though it is not my intent to find fault with the wolf poisoning program, I do believe that it had a profound effect on the ecosystem. First off, I believe that it really decimated the bald and golden eagles in this area of the province, where many eagles were poisoned outright. As well, with the demise of the wolf packs the endless supply of carcasses disappeared and this had a profound effect on the food supply of the eagles and boar grizzlies that had been staying out during mild spells in the winters. This effect was noted by McGregor River trapper Arne Jensen, who said, "...before the poisoning took place it was common for me to see 40 to 50 eagles feeding on dead moose in one trip along my McGregor River trapline in spring. Later, I traveled my entire line and noticed only one."

With the demise of the wolf packs the generous supply of carcasses that had been available to these eagles and to the grizzly bears disappeared. I feel strongly that the boar grizzly bears quit staying out during the winter for this reason, and this is confirmed by the fact that within a few years of the wolf poisoning program, things changed to where a bear was considered sick if it was found out of its den during the winter. Obviously any bear that attempted to stay out would have starved to death.

I also believe that boar grizzlies that stayed out most of the winter were much bigger than our present-day grizzlies. This, I think, was for the same reason that the bears on Kodiak Island were so big: these bears were feeding at least 10 months of the year. Many of the old photos testify to the fact that boar grizzly bears were much bigger then. The police report on the grizzly that killed Tom Meaney in March, 1926, showed that this bear was taken in what was near midwinter in the upper Herrick River area, where the snow stays until July. It also told how this bear's hind foot measured 8 by 14 inches long—much bigger than any tracks I've measured in my lifetime.

As for the endless slaughter that was the reason for the poisoning—some people argue that it was a perfectly balanced ecosystem. With the exception of the caribou herds which obviously went to perilously low numbers, mainly because of their loss of mature tim-

Helen Hansen, wife of McGregor River guide Ole Hansen with huge grizzly.

ber, the wolves, moose, and deer found a balance. This means that the only reason there was such an abundance of moose, caribou, and deer kills for so many years was because there was such an abundance of these ungulates.

Throughout the late '40s and early '50s, about the same time that the wolf poisoning program was being implemented, deer populations began to wane throughout the Penny area, and continued to do so until it was an event to see one. And what was blamed for this? Why, many people blamed the wolf packs, of course. But the wolf packs were not the cause of their decline. If they were, then the deer would have rebounded after the poisoning program, which they did not. The obvious answer for their decline was the fact that their feed was being choked out by the deciduous forests and the incredibly thick coniferous forests that were replacing them.

This is not to say that wolves don't take a great many ungulates; I know they do. I'm only making the point that they were blamed for nearly wiping out the wildlife in certain areas when many other factors were involved.

Perhaps it was looked at all wrong; maybe there is no such thing as waste in nature. The half moose carcass that was left by the wolves and later found by a starving wolverine should not be considered wasted—certainly the wolverine doesn't think so. Nor would it be considered wasted by a hungry grizzly bear. A person may visit a carcass and find it being consumed by maggots and consider it wasted. Yet if they were to come back a day later, they may find these maggots being consumed by a hungry bear. The eagles and a host of other birds and small animals that found these remains would all testify that little if anything was ever really wasted.

In November 1999, The University of Northern BC in Prince George sponsored a symposium by its Natural Resources Society. Among the speakers was Dale Seip, a habitat specialist with the Ministry of Forests. He told how the ministry had attached radio collars to moose, caribou, and wolves to study their interactions in the Quesnel Lake—Wells Gray Park area. "We have a large number of adult caribou being killed by wolves," he said. "During the late 1980s, almost a third of the adult female caribou were being killed every summer." Seip also showed that the caribou calf population suffered heavily when wolves were in the area. In fact, less than 10 per cent survive. He also supplied statistics shoing that the calf population went from 220 in 1986, to 90 in 1993.

Doug Herd, a speaker for the environment branch, agreed that wolves affect moose populations as well, stating, "Other predators tend not to have as much influence on moose dynamics as wolves do."

The observations of these two men remind me of something from the distant past. It is almost as if the clock has been turned back 50 years. These are exactly the same conclusions that were drawn prior to the wolf poisoning programs of the early '50s. Isn't it amazing how history repeats itself?

Once again, some method of controlling wolf populations may become necessary, and once again the authorities will have to deal with public emotions rather than common sense. No one should be surprised that wolves take a great number of ungulates; I mean they can't live on carrots. I also feel that the food supply controls everything. If there is an abundance of feed for these ungulates, then it is amazing how they can withstand predator pressure. If there is a shortage of feed, the results are disastrous, and then any number of scenarios can be postulated.

The conflict that arises is caused by the number of ungulates taken by the wolves, and therefore the restrictions that are placed on hunters to compensate for this. Perhaps some day there will be certain areas that are left for the wolves to find a natural balance in along with the vast majority of areas where they will be strictly controlled. In that way hunters and guides will be able to take the overflow and the forests will truly be for multiple use.

At this point, I must state that I shudder at the goals of conservation groups that push to force hunters to pack out the carcasses of trophy animals they take. As one hunter so aptly put it after packing out an animal that wasn't fit for human consumption in the first place, "They can force me to pack it out, but they can't force me to eat it. I just hauled it to the dump." Some people suggest that to leave it in the forest is to waste it. What a strange view of nature they possess! The closest these carcasses can come to being wasted is when someone is forced to remove them from the forest, then take them to a dump where wildlife cannot get access to them. If they were left in the forest, they would not—in fact could not—be wasted.

Some of my most special memories of the mountains concern the wolverine, an animal that never ceases to amaze me. Where they get their seemingly endless supply of energy is beyond my comprehension. Many times throughout the years we watched them running about the mountains; something I never tired of. I recall the September morning near the McGregor River when Bill Benedict and I were hiking, and some rolling rocks drew our attention to a talus slope. We glassed the area and spotted a wolverine dog-trotting its way across the mountain. After running steadily for a couple of miles, it disappeared behind a ridge, only to reappear on the opposite side about an hour later and at least four miles further along. A few minutes later, it gave a short, sharp burst of speed and obviously caught something, probably a ground squirrel, which kept it occupied for about 10 minutes. Then it was on the run again. We finally lost track of it in late afternoon, and aside from its lunch break, it had been on the run the full time.

I was quite surprised when I first found wolverines up around timberline in the winter, as I didn't think there was anything up there for them to eat. I now know that some blue grouse stay up near timberline all winter, as well as ptarmigan. Most important of all, though, are the communal dens of porcupines, several of which we have found between the 4,000 and 5,500-foot level. Wolverines will attack and kill these creatures and don't seem to give a damn how many quills they absorb while doing it.

I did some trapping one winter and found that it wasn't for me. But during my short stint, I had a running battle with a wolverine that started when I set three traps on the carcass of a horse. I went back a few days later and noticed fresh wolverine tracks in the snow. It had walked right up to the horse to investigate, and had turned around and left, probably having sensed the traps. Several times in the weeks that followed I noticed its tracks where they criss-crossed behind the horse, and even though I moved the traps a few times it came no closer. On one trip, I was checking the traps when I noticed that the snow had caved in on top of the horse carcass. I took a closer look and realized that there was just an empty hole where the inside of the horse used to be. Then I realized that the wolverine had tunneled under the snow for about 12 feet, and had been feeding on the horse the whole time.

This made me more determined than ever to get the beggar, so I set two traps right on its trail and carefully dusted a light covering of snow over them in an effort to hide them. That wolverine never came back, and in retrospect, I'll bet it was sitting on the hillside watching me when I moved the traps. My final thought on wolverines is the age-old belief that they leave a scent on a carcass and then no other animal will touch it. I've had trappers tell me that this is a fact.

During February, 1971, one of my most beautiful memories occurred. We experienced what some people call a silver thaw, others—an ice-storm. For two days and nights a steady rain fell that froze as it touched the trees and snow. Soon there was a one-inch layer of ice around all the limbs and trees as well as on the surface of the snow. It was an unreal world where there was not one second of silence. Limbs and treetops heavily coated with ice were continuously breaking and falling to the ice-covered snow, creating a tinkling sound that was a symphony of tonal variations. When the moon shone down upon this scene on the third night, it presented an endless array of unique shapes and shadows, along with a glitter unmatched by any ballroom on earth. For at least an hour my wife Ann and I stood outside and soaked in this tinkling, glittering wonderland, and I consider myself truly privileged to have witnessed it.

Just this past September, Bill Benedict and I made several trips to Grizzly Bear Mountain. On one trip we saw 21 grizzlies in just over one day. At one point we had thirteen grizzlies in view at the same time. Once again we were treated to a grizzly bear chase, when an adult bear put the run on a two-year-old. It chased the smaller bear over a ridge into the next valley. A few minutes later a couple of roars erupted from that area. Perhaps the chase was successful and the young bear was moved out of the area. Possibly this is nature's way of moving wildlife to prevent in-breeding.

During our second evening on the mountain, a sow with a lone cub came across the mountain where we had walked just hours earlier. When she got our scent, she let out 12 loud roars. The next morning we glassed the entire area in vain, for the grizzlies were all gone. Can anyone doubt that the sow let the other bears know of our presence? It has been my experience that a great number of roars high in the mountains often means that grizzlies have detected the presence of man.

On our last trip to timberline before the snows forced us out of the mountains, we had an interesting encounter with a mother grizzly and her lone cub. As Bill and I were walking to a ridgetop where we intended to glass for bears, we were joined by two hikers—Jon Previant and his son Wilf. We watched the bears from a distance of less than two hundred yards, and then I decided to try coughing at them, in an attempt to get them to move out of our path. The sow had just lain down when we began coughing at her. She didn't hear us, so we had to bark and whistle to get her attention. Finally she stood up and tried to discern what was coughing at them. Unable to do so, she took her cub and slowly walked away, several times throwing her head to the side to show her displeasure. I couldn't help but notice, though, that she didn't seem alarmed, and she didn't run. I'm convinced she thought we were other bears.

I feel quite strongly that this coughing is the best defense against mothers and cubs, or mothers and yearlings. They would be foolish to attack another bear that might be a large boar that would kill or cripple them. Again I say that to holler at them is to get them excited, and an excited bear is a dangerous bear. This doesn't mean a person should stay and gloat, for if the bears have a food source such as carrion, one would be well advised to get away as soon as possible. Again I stress the point that I would not use this coughing against dominant or lone adult bears.

My final thought regarding Grizzly Bear Mountain, is that when I recall the many bears I have seen there and the thrilling experiences I have known, I have no problem feeling a great and lasting respect for the area. In fact, if for any reason grizzly bears were ever wiped out, I doubt that I would ever want to go back into those mountains again. For me, the grizzly bear represents the largest part of the magic and mystery of the mountains.

It is my sincere wish that these great bears will always wander the face of Grizzly Bear Mountain. May they forever dig for the bulbs of their beloved glacier lily, proud, mighty, and free. And may the silhouettes of these great beasts forever grace the skylines of mountain ridges as they wander into the setting sun on their eternal search for food.

Index

Air Force 190

Airplanes, Avenger 189; Beaver 187-189; Cessna 172 (photo)-173, 175, 204-205; Husky 189; Jet Ranger 208; Learjet 204; Otter 189; see also Helicopters

Alaska 58, 141

Alberta 69, 71, 92

Albino bear 126-127

Alexander, Mount 130, 213

Aleza Lake 207

Almond, Scott 210

Americans 1, 125

Anderson, Brent 208

Andre, Jean 217-218

Animals, see Bears, Beaver, Buffalo, Caribou, Cats, Chickens, Cougars, Cows, Coyotes, Deer, Dogs, Frogs, Goats, Gophers, Grizzly, Horses, Lynx, Marmots, Martens, Mice, Mink, Moose, Mountain goats, Mountain sheep, Muskrats, Pigs, Porcupines, Rabbits, Skunks, Squirrels, Toads, Weasels, Wolverines, Wolves

Anzac 128

Arnett, Dorothy 69

Arnett, Ray 69

Aspen (Colorado) 217-218

Australian 169

Avalanches 147

Badowski, Larry 202 (photo)

Baker, Fred 75

Baker, G.R. (Dr.) 57

Baldy Mountain 49 (photo)-50, 158 (photo), 197

Baneberry 154

Barkerville 92, 223

Barrett, Rob 169

Batten, Bill 180

Beard, Bob 90-91

Bears, black bears 10-11, 19-20, 24-26 (photo), 39-41, 53, 56, 60-63, 65-66, 68-73, 78, 86, 89, 95-100, 103-104, 107, 123, 131, 167 (photo), 172-173, 192, 219; see also Grizzly bears

Beaver 14, 29-30, 60-61, 110, 127-128, 154, 168

Beaver fever 154-156

Beggs, Dick 190, 196-197, 199

Benedict, Bill vii, 49-50 (photo)-53, 55-56, 66, 72-76, 79-80, 98, 102, 104, 111, 115, 119, 122, 129, 134, 136 (photo)-137, 147-148, 152, 169-172, 184, 222, 230-232

Benedict, Wayne 136 (photo)

Berg, Carl 159

Bergeron, Bernie 188

Berries 101, 154 (baneberry), 168, 182 (saskatoons)

Big Smoky River 91-92

Big Salmon River, see McGregor River

Bigfoot 131

Birds, see Crows, Eagles, Fisher, Geese, Grouse, Hawks, Jays, Loons, Ospreys, Ptarmigan, Ravens, Whiskey jacks

Blackstock, Del 178

Bligh, Captain 181

Boone, Daniel 35

Boudreau, Ann 68, 231

Boudreau, Clarence vii, 7-16, 20-21, 24, 34, 39-40, 42-44, 46-48, 54-55, 60, 63, 66-75, 78-80, 83, 87, 93-95, 97, 102-103, 105-106, 111-114, 118, 127, 129, 132-133, 163-166, 168, 183, 186, 192, 218; photos 21, 44, 94, 113, 127, 164

Boudreau, 'Dad' 8, 13-14, 16-17, 20, 44-45, 86-87, 95-96, 163, 173, 178, 218, 225

Boudreau, Dan 54, 69-70

Boudreau, Evie (McKinley) 22, 31; photo 21

Boudreau, Isabelle (Isie) 12-13; photos 21, 127

Boudreau, Jack (author) see references throughout; photos 21, 26, 44, 113, 127, 202, 211, 216

Boudreau, Joe vii, 7, 9-10, 12-13, 19-20, 22, 31, 33, 35-38 (photo)-39, 170, 184, 186, 193

Boudreau, Joie 21 (photo)

Boudreau, Josie (Proctor) 22-23, 34-35; photos 21, 64

Boudreau, June (Vandermark) 7; photos 21, 81

Boudreau, Kelly vii, 84-85; photos 85, 170, 207

Boudreau, Kim vii, 133 (photo)-134

Boudreau, Larry 54, 71, 108 (photo)-109, 165

Boudreau, Margaret 10-12, 134; photos 21, 64, 133, 170

Boudreau, 'Mom' 8-16, 19, 22, 39, 95, 97

Boudreau, Olga 63, 68, 70, 83, 94 (photo)-95, 132-133, 218

Boudreau, Rhoda 82 (photo)

Bouvette, Trudy 69-71

Bowron clear-cut 83

Bradley, Jim 91-92

Brandner, Virgil vii, 53-54, 83, 93-94, 120, 152, 171

Brandy, Danielle 218

Brandy, Robert 216-218

Buchanan, Don 199

Buffalo 92

Burns, Beverly 69-71

Burns Lake 160

Campbell, Jeremy 83

Canfor 204

Canuel, Norm 203

Cariboo Gold Rush 92

Caribou (animal) 2-3, 90, 93, 116, 155, 186, 223, 225-229

Caribou John 139

Caribou River 1

Cats 13-14, 17, 37, 97

CCF Hall 162

Chambers, Lindy vii, 24-25, 36, 112, 151

Chickens 7-8, 13-14, 97

Chilcotin 87-88, 90

Chinese cook 19, 192, 194

Churchill 137

Citizen see Prince George Citizen

Clark, Stan 92

Clear-cut see Forestry

Clements, Jack 89

CN Rail 147

CN station 131

Colorado 217-218

Columbian squirrels 214

Columbus Hotel 160-162, 178

Conservation Officer 85, 133

Corning Hotel 162

Cougars 9, 32-33, 89

Cows, cattle 11, 14, 16, 19, 90, 132

Coyotes 31, 90, 172, 219

Crazy Man's Creek (book) 29, 86, 139, 182, 223

Crows 145

Cummins, Melanie vii

Currie, John 183, 206-207

David and Goliath 12

Davies, Frank 77

Deer 32, 35, 88, 90, 92, 116-118, 224-226, 228

Devil Mountain 156 (photo)

Devil's club 215

Dogs 17, 23, 69-70, 84, 90, 95-96, 154, 212

Dolly Varden 18; see also Trout

Dome Creek 68, 89, 201, 224

Eagles 25-26, 31-32, 57-58, 61 (photo), 100, 110, 214-215, 219, 226, 228

Earthquake 166

Edmonton 92

Edmonton Journal 91

England 1

Epilobiums 214

Erling (BC) 147

Europe Hotel 161

Eutsuk Lake 176 (photo)

Evans, Jack 33

Evasin, Elarry vii

Fires see Forest fires

Fish, see Trout; Salmon; Squawfish

Fisher (bird) 29

Fitzsimmons, Bill 184-185

Flotten, John 188

Flowers, wild 32, 134, 214

Foreman Flats 100

Forest fires 4, 38, 83-84, 130, 148, 156, 186-196, 199-205, 208-211, 225-226; Grove Fire 194; Pink Fire 83-84 (photo), 203-204 (photo); Tee Fire 204-205; Tsus Fire 194

Forest rangers, officers 22, 85, 87, 131, 176, 186-187, 189, 193, 196, 200, 202, 206-208

Forest Service (Ministry of Forests) 4, 35-36, 69,71, 104, 142, 177, 186, 189,204-207, 220, 228

Forestry, logging 85-86, 104, 162, 178, 186-212, 221; Bowron clear-cut 83; Canfor 204; log driving,, timber cruising 110, 148-150, 179, 181-182, 191; logging companies 65, 150; logging roads 24, 41, 75, 441, 474; sawmills 19, 87; slash burns 205-206; tree planters 142-143; UBC forestry instructor 150

Fort George 1 3, 224-225

Fort George Herald 91, 223

Fort Nelson 204-205

Fort St. James 59

France 216-218

Frank, Sid 110

Fraser River 1, 24, 36, 47, 74, 87, 151, 187, 191, 224-225

Fretter, Bob 96

Frogs 67; see also Toads

Game Commissioner 92; see also Wildlife

Ganton, Bud 162

Geese 31, 80

Germany 26

Giardiasis, see Beaver fever

Gibbs, W.S. 58

Glacier lillies 72, 101, 118, 233

Goat River 147

Goats, domestic 84-85; mountain 112, 132, 147, 150, 152, 213

Gobbi, Bob vii, 170-171

Gold Rush 92

Goliath 12

Goose River 1

Gophers 12

Grand Canyon 1, 189, 191, 224

Grand Trunk Pacific Railway 225

Grasmere (BC) 139-140, 182

Green Mountain 77

Greenland 199

Grizzly Bear Mountain (Red Mountain) 1-3, 6, 94, 109, 172, 222, 231-233; photos 2, 94, 172

Grizzly bears 1, 3-6, 20, 22-23, 31-68, 72-77, 79-80, 86, 89, 93-98, 100-136, 139-146, 163-165, 167-170, 174-176, 186, 209-210, 212, 216, 218, 220-228, 231-233,; albino 126-127; largest 110-116, 122-126, 131-132; photos 44, 62, 74, 77, 93, 111, 113, 115, 123, 127, 129, 174, 221, 227

Grouse 3, 22, 67, 122, 158, 220, 230

Grove Fire 194

Guilford Creek 19

Guenther, Rick 127-129 (photo)

Hale, Ed 69

Hale, Stan 92, 144

Hansen, Helen 227 (photo)

Hansen, Ole 86, 223, 227

Harkins, Bob vii, 42, 217 (photo), 218

Harvey, Bill 188, 191

Hawks 97

Hazelnut bush 182

Helicopters 189-191, 194-202, 206-208, 210-211, 219; photos 194, 196, 199, 200, 202, 207; see also Airplanes

Hellebore, Indian 42, 153

Hemlock, water 154

Herd, Doug 229

Herrick River 227

Hockey 162

Hogs; see Pigs

Hornets 193

Horses 75, 78-79, 90-92, 112, 132, 141, 144, 157, 167-168, 230-231; wild horses 91-93

Hospitals 58-59, 208

Hreczka, Heller 69

Humphreys, John 38 (photo), 85-86, 88

Hungarian 152

Hydrant Creek 152

Hydro, BC 121

Hypothermia 150

Ice Mountain Lake 134

Ida, Mount 213 (photo)

Indian hellebore 42, 153

Indians 1-3, 59, 87, 92, 224

Insects; see Hornets, Mosquitos, Ticks

Irishman 160

Jays, Stellar 137-138

Jensen, Arne 86, 195, 224, 226

Kakwa Falls 198

Kenneth Creek 188, 195

Kermode, F. 30

Kibbee, Frank 223

Kirchner (taxidermist) 132

Klaubauf, Eric 179-180

Knight, Ken 199, 209

Kodiak Island 226

Kolida, Steve 147

Kootenays 139, 182

Koppe, Maxine vii

Koppe, Peter vii

Kovacic, Betty 108 (photo), 109

Lammle, Edith (Penny) 38 (photo)

Lammle, Roy 42

Lanehan, Slim 104

Latham, Brian 183

Leader (newspaper) 57-58

Lehman, Frank 139

Liard River 204

Library, Prince George Public vii

Lillies; see Glacier lillies

Litnosky, Alvin 33-34

Litnosky, Vic vii, 6, 65, 152, 172, (photo), 173-174 (photo), 175

Little Smokey River 91-92

Logging; see Forestry

Longworth 123, 188, 200 (photo)

Loons 25, 27

Lyme disease 157

Lynx 2-3, 61, 92

Lyon, Dr. E.J. 59

Mackenzie River delta 198

Mann, A.G. 29-30

Marmots 30, 214, 219, 222 (photo)

Martens 27, 29, 218

Marynovitch, Ernie 188

Marynovitch, Steve vii, 188-189

McBride 147, 150, 201

McGhee, Drs. Carolyn and Jack 216 (photo)

McGregor River area 56, 86, 115, 139, 148-149, 213, 215, 223 (Big Salmon River), 226-227, 230

McKinley, Barry 54, 117

McKinley, Evie; see Boudreau

McKinley, Jack 31

Meaney, Tom 227

Meisner, Ben 115 (photo)

Mellos, Anna 72

Mellos, Halvor 18

Mellows, Victor 89-90 (photo), 114

Metzmeier, Herb vii, 26-28 (photo), 45-46, 74-75, 111 (photo), 220

Mexico 177

Mice 5, 13, 105-106, 137

Michaylenko, Bill 160

Michaylenko, Joe 18

Michaylenko, Nettie 87

Mile 125 91

Millburn, Jack 190 (photo), 198 (photo)-199

Mink 18, 27, 29

Monroe, Everett 147

Mosquitos 68, 76

Moose 19-20, 22-23, 25-27, 32, 36, 40-41, 45, 47, 56, 58-62, 65-67, 74-76, 79, 83-89, 103, 111, 114, 122-123, 132, 134-135, 141, 176, 181, 183, 209, 219, 223-226, 228-229; photos 85, 88

Moss 215

Mount Alexander 130, 213 (photo)

Mount Ida 213 (photo)

Mount Robson 156

Mountain goats 112, 132, 147, 150, 152, 213

Mountain Sheep 155, 213

Mule deer; see Deer

Mulvahill, Roy vii

Museum (Victoria) 30, 217

Mushrooms 215

Muskrats 154

New Zealand 198

Newman, Sid 160

Norwegian elkhound 96

Novotny, Frank86

Odier, Georges 217-218

Oil explorations 198

Okanagan Helicopter base 190

Olson, Clifford 177

Olson, Corinne 69-71

Olson, Harold 125 (photo)-126

Ontario 206

Ospreys 25

Pakistan 198

Parsnip River 127

Pastor Joe 46, 104

Paulson, Dylan 134-135

Paulson, Grant 134-135

Paulson, Paul 134-135

Peemoeller, Guenther vii, 47-49 (photo), 95

Pement, Ernie 191

Penny (BC) 1, 3, 22, 25-26, 36,39, 65, 69, 72, 84, 86-87, 89-90, 104, 150, 166, 172-173, 182-183, 191, 217, 224-225, 228

Pepper spray 145

Pesticides 219-220

Philippines 199

Phillips, Nessie 139-140

Pierreway, Frank 57

Pierreway, M. 57

Pigs 11, 162

Pineview area 29-30

Pink Fire; see Forest fires

Pink snow 214

Pinkerton Lake 150, 207 (photo)

Pius, Portage 59

Plants; see Baneberry, Berries, Devil's Club, Ephilobiums, Flowers, Glacier lillies, Indian hellebore, Moss, Mushrooms, Saskatoon, Solomon's seal, Vacciniums, Water hemlock

Poisoning of wolf packs 226-229

Poisonous plants 42, 153-154, 215

Police 178-179, 227

Polish 173-174

Porcupines 29, 57, 136-137, 163, 171, 230

Prather, Oliver 24 (photo)-25

Previant, Jon 232

Previant, Wilf 232

Preibe, Ed 77

Priebe, Marlin vii, 101, 141

Prince George 1, 29, 57, 59, 85, 90, 99-100, 109, 132, 134, 152, 155, 160, 162, 172, 190, 199, 204, 208, 217, 223, 228

Prince George Citizen vii, 29, 57-59

Prince George Leader; see Leader

Prince George Public Library vii

Proctor, Bud 23, 34, 54, 88-89

Proctor, Dwayne 112

Proctor, Josie; see Boudreau

Ptarmigan 214, 220, 230

Public Library vii

Purden Lake 96, 127

Purden Mountain 207

Q fever 157

Quesnel 57

Quesnel Lake 228

Quinn, Abe 65-66

Rabbit Creek 139

Rabbits 3, 18

Rahotsky, Jim 79

Railroad tracks, railway 18, 20, 60-109, 122, 131, 147, 224-225

Rand, Al 125, 132

Rangers; see Forest rangers

Ravens 103, 145, 219

Red Mountain; see Grizzly Bear Mountain

Red Mountain Creek 71

Redden, Don vii, 204

Redden, Lana vii

Richards, Bob 200 (photo)

Riemland, Gus 91

Riley, Dave 98-100, 148-149

Robson, Mount 156 (photo)

Rocky Mountain spotted fever 157

Rocky Mountains 149 (photo), 155, 220

Roe, Sterla "Slim" 191-193

Rohn, Carl 85-86, 131, 187-188, 193

Ross, Gordon 121-123 (photo)-125

Rugg, Lorne 58

Russell, Andy 119-120

Saddle Mountain 158 (photo)

Safety 139-158

'Sahara syndrome' 159

Salmon 21-22, 74 (photo), 80, 105, 108, 122, 186, 192-193, 209, 221

Salmon River (Goose River) 1

Salmon River, Big; see McGregor River

Saskatchewan 15

Saskatoon bush 182

Saugstad, Greg vii, 61 (photo)

Sawitsky, Mr. & Mrs. 100

Sawmills 19, 87

Scheetel, Ian 150

Shlitt, Wilf 155-156

Schultz, Maurice vii, 68-69, 89

Seip, Dale 228-229

Semple, Matthew 58

Sheep 155, 213

Sherlock Holmes 10

Siguenza, Lou vii, 108

Siguenza, Luis vii

Sims, Doug 162

Sinclair, Colin 140

Sinclair Mills 88

Sinclair, Roy 33-34

Sitzi; see Mount Alexander

Skunks 220

Slim Creek 68, 110, 179, 192

Slim Lake 23-27, 151-152, 217 (photo), 225

Smith, Paul 201-202

Smokey River 91-92

Snow, pink 214

Spaerella (pink snow) 214

Squawfish 22

Squirrels 27-29, 32, 102, 105-106, 126, 138, 163, 171, 210, 214 (photo)-215, 219, 230

Stellars Jay 137-138

Stone, Dr. R.W. 59

Stoney Lake 208

Stuart Lake 59

Sumanik, Ken 99

Sustat Lake 175

Sykes, Ben 225

Sykes, Ida 225

Taylor, F.D. 30

Tee Fire 204-205

Tete Jaune Cache 91

Thompson, Don 204

Three Years Hunting...(book) 1, 224

Ticks 157

Toads 220; see also Frogs

Torpy River 14, 85, 130, 196, 201, 220

Torpy Valley area 209-210, 223

Tree planters; see Forestry

Trout 3, 18, 27, 173, 176, 185

Tsus Fire 194

Tularemia 157

Tumuch Lake 26, 28, 150

Turner, Ernest 24 (photo)

Turner J. Turner 1-3, 224-225

Tweedsmuir Park 152, 175

Umstaetter, Eric 148

United States; see Alaska; Americans; Colorado

University of Alaska 58

University of British Columbia 150

University of northern British Columbia 228

Vacciniums 214

Van de Reit, Buster 39, 42-43, 179-181

Vancouver 50

Vanderhoof 59

Vandermark, June; see Boudreau

Vandermark, Lloyd 71

Vernon Helicopters 199

Victoria 30, 217-218

Vincent, George 85

Ward, Gary 22

Water hemlock 154

Watson, Don 199

Weasels 97, 137, 218

Weaver, Harry 29

Wells (BC) 194

Wells Gray Park 228

Wendle Mountain 209

Whiskey Jacks 137

Wiebe, Dan 199-200 (photo), 202, 207-208

Wildlife biologist 99-100; officers 85, 127, 133; see also Bears, Beaver, Buffalo, Caribou, Cougars, Coyotes, Deer, Frogs, Gophers, Grizzly, Lynx, Marmots, Martens, Mice, Mink, Moose, Mountain Goats, Mountain Sheep, Muskrats, Porcupines, Rabbits, Skunks, Squirrels, Toads, Weasels, Wolverines, Wolves

Williams, Ted 29

Willmore Wilderness Provincial Park 92

Willow River 1

Wilson, Tommy 55, 90, 165

Windle, Dave 116-118, 153

Wolverines 89-90, 137, 219, 228, 230-231

Wolves 42, 57-58, 81-82, 86, 88-91, 223-226, 228-229

Wood, Blair 130-131, 209

Yacoutchee Indian 59

Yellowknife 57